THE SOCIOLOGICAL IMAGINATION

THE SOCIOLOGICAL IMAGINATION

C. WRIGHT MILLS

GROVE PRESS, INC.   NEW YORK

For Harvey and Bette

BOOKS BY C. WRIGHT MILLS

LISTEN, YANKEE *(1960)*

THE SOCIOLOGICAL IMAGINATION *(1959)*

THE CAUSES OF WORLD WAR THREE *(1958)*

THE POWER ELITE *(1956)*

CHARACTER AND SOCIAL STRUCTURE *(1953)*
    (with H. H. Gerth)

WHITE COLLAR: The American Middle Classes *(1951)*

THE PUERTO RICAN JOURNEY *(1950)*
    (with Clarence Senior and Rose Goldsen)

THE NEW MEN OF POWER *(1948)*

FROM MAX WEBER: Essays in Sociology *(1946)*
    (Edited and Trans. with H. H. Gerth)

Contents

THE SOCIOLOGICAL IMAGINATION

1

The Promise

NOWADAYS men often feel that their private lives are a series of traps. They sense that within their everyday worlds, they cannot overcome their troubles, and in this feeling, they are often quite correct: What ordinary men are directly aware of and what they try to do are bounded by the private orbits in which they live; their visions and their powers are limited to the close-up scenes of job, family, neighborhood; in other milieux, they move vicariously and remain spectators. And the more aware they become, however vaguely, of ambitions and of threats which transcend their immediate locales, the more trapped they seem to feel.

Underlying this sense of being trapped are seemingly impersonal changes in the very structure of continent-wide societies. The facts of contemporary history are also facts about the success and the failure of individual men and women. When a society is industrialized, a peasant becomes a worker; a feudal lord is liquidated or becomes a businessman. When classes rise or fall, a man is employed or unemployed; when the rate of investment goes up or down, a man takes new heart or goes broke. When wars happen, an insurance salesman becomes a rocket launcher; a store clerk, a radar man; a wife lives alone; a child grows up without a father. Neither the life of an individual nor the history of a society can be understood without understanding both.

Yet men do not usually define the troubles they endure in terms of historical change and institutional contradiction. The well-being they enjoy, they do not usually impute to the big ups and downs of the societies in which they live. Seldom aware of the intricate connection between the patterns of their own lives and the course of world history, ordinary men do not usually know what this connection means for the kinds of men they are becoming and for the kinds of history-making in which they might take part. They do not possess the quality of mind essential to grasp the interplay of man and society, of biography and history, of self and world. They cannot cope with their personal troubles in such ways as to control the structural transformations that usually lie behind them.

Surely it is no wonder. In what period have so many men been so totally exposed at so fast a pace to such earthquakes of change? That Americans have not known such catastrophic changes as have the men and women of other societies is due to historical facts that are now quickly becoming 'merely history.' The history that now affects every man is world history. Within this scene and this period, in the course of a single generation, one sixth of mankind is transformed from all that is feudal and backward into all that is modern, advanced, and fearful. Political colonies are freed; new and less visible forms of imperialism installed. Revolutions occur; men feel the intimate grip of new kinds of authority. Totalitarian societies rise, and are smashed to bits—or succeed fabulously. After two centuries of ascendancy, capitalism is shown up as only one way to make society into an industrial apparatus. After two centuries of hope, even formal democracy is restricted to a quite small portion of mankind. Everywhere in the underdeveloped world, ancient ways of life are broken up and vague expectations become urgent demands. Everywhere in the overdeveloped world, the means of authority and of violence become total in scope and bureaucratic in form. Humanity itself now lies before us, the super-nation at either pole concentrating its most co-ordinated and massive efforts upon the preparation of World War Three.

The very shaping of history now outpaces the ability of men to orient themselves in accordance with cherished values. And which values? Even when they do not panic, men often sense that older ways of feeling and thinking have collapsed and that newer beginnings are ambiguous to the point of moral stasis. Is it any wonder that ordinary men feel they cannot cope with the larger worlds with which they are so suddenly confronted? That they cannot understand the meaning of their epoch for their own lives? That—in defense of selfhood—they become morally insensible, trying to remain altogether private men? Is it any wonder that they come to be possessed by a sense of the trap?

It is not only information that they need—in this Age of Fact, information often dominates their attention and overwhelms their capacities to assimilate it. It is not only the skills of reason that they need—although their struggles to acquire these often exhaust their limited moral energy.

What they need, and what they feel they need, is a quality of mind that will help them to use information and to develop reason in order to achieve lucid summations of what is going on in the world and of what may be happening within themselves. It is this quality, I am going to contend, that journalists and scholars, artists and publics, scientists and editors are coming to expect of what may be called the sociological imagination.

1

The sociological imagination enables its possessor to understand the larger historical scene in terms of its meaning for the inner life and the external career of a variety of individuals. It enables him to take into account how individuals, in the welter of their daily experience, often become falsely conscious of their social positions. Within that welter, the framework of modern society is sought, and within that framework the psychologies of a variety of men and women are formulated. By such means the personal uneasiness of individuals is focused upon explicit troubles and the indifference of publics is transformed into involvement with public issues.

The first fruit of this imagination—and the first lesson of the social science that embodies it—is the idea that the individual can understand his own experience and gauge his own fate only by locating himself within his period, that he can know his own chances in life only by becoming aware of those of all individuals in his circumstances. In many ways it is a terrible lesson; in many ways a magnificent one. We do not know the limits of man's capacities for supreme effort or willing degradation, for agony or glee, for pleasurable brutality or the sweetness of reason. But in our time we have come to know that the limits of 'human nature' are frighteningly broad. We have come to know that every individual lives, from one generation to the next, in some society; that he lives out a biography, and that he lives it out within some historical sequence. By the fact of his living he contributes, however minutely, to the shaping of this society and to the course of its history, even as he is made by society and by its historical push and shove.

The sociological imagination enables us to grasp history and biography and the relations between the two within society. That is its task and its promise. To recognize this task and this promise is the mark of the classic social analyst. It is characteristic of Herbert Spencer—turgid, polysyllabic, comprehensive; of E. A. Ross—graceful, muckraking, upright; of Auguste Comte and Emile Durkheim; of the intricate and subtle Karl Mannheim. It is the quality of all that is intellectually excellent in Karl Marx; it is the clue to Thorstein Veblen's brilliant and ironic insight, to Joseph Schumpeter's many-sided constructions of reality; it is the basis of the psychological sweep of W. E. H. Lecky no less than of the profundity and clarity of Max Weber. And it is the signal of what is best in contemporary studies of man and society.

No social study that does not come back to the problems of biography, of history and of their intersections within a society has completed its intellectual journey. Whatever the specific problems of the classic social analysts, however limited or however broad the features of social reality they have examined, those who have been imaginatively aware of the promise of their work have consistently asked three sorts of questions:

(1) What is the structure of this particular society as a whole? What are its essential components, and how are they related to one another? How does it differ from other varieties of social order? Within it, what is the meaning of any particular feature for its continuance and for its change?

(2) Where does this society stand in human history? What are the mechanics by which it is changing? What is its place within and its meaning for the development of humanity as a whole?

How does any particular feature we are examining affect, and how is it affected by, the historical period in which it moves? And this period—what are its essential features? How does it differ from other periods? What are its characteristic ways of history-making?

(3) What varieties of men and women now prevail in this society and in this period? And what varieties are coming to prevail? In what ways are they selected and formed, liberated and repressed, made sensitive and blunted? What kinds of 'human nature' are revealed in the conduct and character we observe in this society in this period? And what is the meaning for 'human nature' of each and every feature of the society we are examining?

Whether the point of interest is a great power state or a minor literary mood, a family, a prison, a creed—these are the kinds of questions the best social analysts have asked. They are the intellectual pivots of classic studies of man in society—and they are the questions inevitably raised by any mind possessing the sociological imagination. For that imagination is the capacity to shift from one perspective to another—from the political to the psychological; from examination of a single family to comparative assessment of the national budgets of the world, from the theological school to the military establishment; from considerations of an oil industry to studies of contemporary poetry. It is the capacity to range from the most impersonal and remote transformations to the most intimate features of the human self—and to see the relations between the two. Back of its use there is always the urge to know the social and historical meaning of the individual in the society and in the period in which he has his quality and his being.

That, in brief, is why it is by means of the sociological imagination that men now hope to grasp what is going on in the world, and to understand what is happening in themselves as minute points of the intersections of biography and history within society. In large part, contemporary man's self-conscious view of himself as at least an outsider, if not a permanent stranger, rests upon an absorbed realization of social relativity and of the transformative power of history. The sociological imagination is the most fruitful form of this self-consciousness. By its use men whose

ᴉnentalities have swept only a series of limited orbits often come
to feel as if suddenly awakened in a house with which they had
only supposed themselves to be familiar. Correctly or incorrectly,
they often come to feel that they can now provide themselves
with adequate summations, cohesive assessments, comprehensive
orientations. Older decisions that once appeared sound now seem
to them products of a mind unaccountably dense. Their capacity
for astonishment is made lively again. They acquire a new way of
thinking, they experience a transvaluation of values: in a word,
by their reflection and by their sensibility, they realize the cultural meaning of the social sciences.

2

Perhaps the most fruitful distinction with which the sociological
imagination works is between 'the personal troubles of milieu'
and 'the public issues of social structure.' This distinction is an
essential tool of the sociological imagination and a feature of all
classic work in social science.

Troubles occur within the character of the individual and
within the range of his immediate relations with others; they
have to do with his self and with those limited areas of social life
of which he is directly and personally aware. Accordingly, the
statement and the resolution of troubles properly lie within the
individual as a biographical entity and within the scope of his
immediate milieu—the social setting that is directly open to his
personal experience and to some extent his willful activity. A
trouble is a private matter: values cherished by an individual are
felt by him to be threatened.

Issues have to do with matters that transcend these local environments of the individual and the range of his inner life. They
have to do with the organization of many such milieux into the
institutions of an historical society as a whole, with the ways in
which various milieux overlap and interpenetrate to form the
larger structure of social and historical life. An issue is a public
matter: some value cherished by publics is felt to be threatened.
Often there is a debate about what that value really is and about
what it is that really threatens it. This debate is often without
focus if only because it is the very nature of an issue, unlike

even widespread trouble, that it cannot very well be defined in terms of the immediate and everyday environments of ordinary men. An issue, in fact, often involves a crisis in institutional arrangements, and often too it involves what Marxists call 'contradictions' or 'antagonisms.'

In these terms, consider unemployment. When, in a city of 100,000, only one man is unemployed, that is his personal trouble, and for its relief we properly look to the character of the man, his skills, and his immediate opportunities. But when in a nation of 50 million employees, 15 million men are unemployed, that is an issue, and we may not hope to find its solution within the range of opportunities open to any one individual. The very structure of opportunities has collapsed. Both the correct statement of the problem and the range of possible solutions require us to consider the economic and political institutions of the society, and not merely the personal situation and character of a scatter of individuals.

Consider war. The personal problem of war, when it occurs, may be how to survive it or how to die in it with honor; how to make money out of it; how to climb into the higher safety of the military apparatus; or how to contribute to the war's termination. In short, according to one's values, to find a set of milieux and within it to survive the war or make one's death in it meaningful. But the structural issues of war have to do with its causes; with what types of men it throws up into command; with its effects upon economic and political, family and religious institutions, with the unorganized irresponsibility of a world of nation-states.

Consider marriage. Inside a marriage a man and a woman may experience personal troubles, but when the divorce rate during the first four years of marriage is 250 out of every 1,000 attempts, this is an indication of a structural issue having to do with the institutions of marriage and the family and other institutions that bear upon them.

Or consider the metropolis—the horrible, beautiful, ugly, magnificent sprawl of the great city. For many upper-class people, the personal solution to 'the problem of the city' is to have an apartment with private garage under it in the heart of the city, and forty miles out, a house by Henry Hill, garden by Garrett Eckbo, on a hundred acres of private land. In these two controlled environments—with a small staff at each end and a private helicopter connection—most people could solve many of the problems of personal milieux caused by the facts of the city. But all this, however splendid, does not solve the public issues that the structural fact of the city poses. What should be done with this wonderful monstrosity? Break it all up into scattered units, combining residence and work? Refurbish it as it stands? Or, after evacuation, dynamite it and build new cities according to new plans in new places? What should those plans be? And who is to decide and to accomplish whatever choice is made? These are structural issues; to confront them and to solve them requires us to consider political and economic issues that affect innumerable milieux.

In so far as an economy is so arranged that slumps occur, the problem of unemployment becomes incapable of personal solution. In so far as war is inherent in the nation-state system and in the uneven industrialization of the world, the ordinary individual in his restricted milieu will be powerless—with or without psychiatric aid—to solve the troubles this system or lack of system imposes upon him. In so far as the family as an institution turns women into darling little slaves and men into their chief providers and unweaned dependents, the problem of a satisfactory marriage remains incapable of purely private solution. In so far as the overdeveloped megalopolis and the overdeveloped automobile are built-in features of the overdeveloped society, the issues of urban living will not be solved by personal ingenuity and private wealth.

What we experience in various and specific milieux, I have noted, is often caused by structural changes. Accordingly, to understand the changes of many personal milieux we are required to look beyond them. And the number and variety of such structural changes increase as the institutions within which we live become more embracing and more intricately connected with one another. To be aware of the idea of social structure and to use it with sensibility is to be capable of tracing such linkages among a great variety of milieux. To be able to do that is to possess the sociological imagination.

3

What are the major issues for publics and the key troubles of private individuals in our time? To formulate issues and troubles, we must ask what values are cherished yet threatened, and what values are cherished and supported, by the characterizing trends of our period. In the case both of threat and of support we must ask what salient contradictions of structure may be involved.

When people cherish some set of values and do not feel any threat to them, they experience *well-being*. When they cherish values but *do* feel them to be threatened, they experience a crisis —either as a personal trouble or as a public issue. And if all their values seem involved, they feel the total threat of panic.

But suppose people are neither aware of any cherished values nor experience any threat? That is the experience of *indifference*, which, if it seems to involve all their values, becomes apathy. Suppose, finally, they are unaware of any cherished values, but still are very much aware of a threat? That is the experience of *uneasiness*, of anxiety, which, if it is total enough, becomes a deadly unspecified malaise.

Ours is a time of uneasiness and indifference—not yet formulated in such ways as to permit the work of reason and the play of sensibility. Instead of troubles—defined in terms of values and threats—there is often the misery of vague uneasiness; instead of explicit issues there is often merely the beat feeling that all is somehow not right. Neither the values threatened nor whatever threatens them has been stated; in short, they have not been carried to the point of decision. Much less have they been formulated as problems of social science.

In the 'thirties there was little doubt—except among certain deluded business circles that there was an economic issue which was also a pack of personal troubles. In these arguments about 'the crisis of capitalism,' the formulations of Marx and the many unacknowledged re-formulations of his work probably set the leading terms of the issue, and some men came to understand their personal troubles in these terms. The values threatened were plain to see and cherished by all; the structural contradictions that threatened them also seemed plain. Both were widely and deeply experienced. It was a political age.

But the values threatened in the era after World War Two are often neither widely acknowledged as values nor widely felt to be threatened. Much private uneasiness goes unformulated; much public malaise and many decisions of enormous structural relevance never become public issues. For those who accept such inherited values as reason and freedom, it is the uneasiness itself that is the trouble; it is the indifference itself that is the issue. And it is this condition, of uneasiness and indifference, that is the signal feature of our period.

All this is so striking that it is often interpreted by observers as a shift in the very kinds of problems that need now to be formulated. We are frequently told that the problems of our decade, or even the crises of our period, have shifted from the external realm of economics and now have to do with the quality of individual life—in fact with the question of whether there is soon going to be anything that can properly be called individual life. Not child labor but comic books, not poverty but mass leisure, are at the center of concern. Many great public issues as well as many private troubles are described in terms of 'the psychiatric'—often, it seems, in a pathetic attempt to avoid the large issues and problems of modern society. Often this statement seems to rest upon a provincial narrowing of interest to the Western societies, or even to the United States—thus ignoring two-thirds of mankind; often, too, it arbitrarily divorces the individual life from the larger institutions within which that life is enacted, and which on occasion bear upon it more grievously than do the intimate environments of childhood.

Problems of leisure, for example, cannot even be stated without considering problems of work. Family troubles over comic books cannot be formulated as problems without considering the plight of the contemporary family in its new relations with the newer institutions of the social structure. Neither leisure nor its debilitating uses can be understood as problems without recognition of the extent to which malaise and indifference now form the social and personal climate of contemporary American society. In this climate, no problems of 'the private life' can be stated and solved without recognition of the crisis of ambition that is part of the very career of men at work in the incorporated economy.

It is true, as psychoanalysts continually point out, that people do often have 'the increasing sense of being moved by obscure forces within themselves which they are unable to define.' But it is *not* true, as Ernest Jones asserted, that 'man's chief enemy and danger is his own unruly nature and the dark forces pent up within him.' On the contrary: 'Man's chief danger' today lies in the unruly forces of contemporary society itself, with its alienating methods of production, its enveloping techniques of political domination, its international anarchy—in a word, its pervasive transformations of the very 'nature' of man and the conditions and aims of his life.

It is now the social scientist's foremost political and intellectual task—for here the two coincide—to make clear the elements of contemporary uneasiness and indifference. It is the central demand made upon him by other cultural workmen—by physical scientists and artists, by the intellectual community in general. It is because of this task and these demands, I believe, that the social sciences are becoming the common denominator of our cultural period, and the sociological imagination our most needed quality of mind.

4

In every intellectual age some one style of reflection tends to become a common denominator of cultural life. Nowadays, it is true, many intellectual fads are widely taken up before they are dropped for new ones in the course of a year or two. Such enthusiasms may add spice to cultural play, but leave little or no intellectual trace. That is not true of such ways of thinking as 'Newtonian physics' or 'Darwinian biology.' Each of these intellectual universes became an influence that reached far beyond any special sphere of idea and imagery. In terms of them, or in terms derived from them, unknown scholars as well as fashionable commentators came to re-focus their observations and re-formulate their concerns.

During the modern era, physical and biological science has been the major common denominator of serious reflection and popular metaphysics in Western societies. 'The technique of the laboratory' has been the accepted mode of procedure and the source of intellectual security. That is one meaning of the idea of an intellectual common denominator: men can state their strongest convictions in its terms; other terms and other styles of reflection seem mere vehicles of escape and obscurity.

That a common denominator prevails does not of course mean that no other styles of thought or modes of sensibility exist. But it does mean that more general intellectual interests tend to slide into this area, to be formulated there most sharply, and when so formulated, to be thought somehow to have reached, if not a solution, at least a profitable way of being carried along.

The sociological imagination is becoming, I believe, the major common denominator of our cultural life and its signal feature. This quality of mind is found in the social and psychological sciences, but it goes far beyond these studies as we now know them. Its acquisition by individuals and by the cultural community at large is slow and often fumbling; many social scientists are themselves quite unaware of it. They do not seem to know that the use of this imagination is central to the best work that they might do, that by failing to develop and to use it they are failing to meet the cultural expectations that are coming to be demanded of them and that the classic traditions of their several disciplines make available to them.

Yet in factual and moral concerns, in literary work and in political analysis, the qualities of this imagination are regularly demanded. In a great variety of expressions, they have become central features of intellectual endeavor and cultural sensibility. Leading critics exemplify these qualities as do serious journalists—in fact the work of both is often judged in these terms. Popular categories of criticism—high, middle, and low-brow, for example—are now at least as much sociological as aesthetic. Novelists—whose serious work embodies the most widespread definitions of human reality—frequently possess this imagination, and do much to meet the demand for it. By means of it, orientation to the present as history is sought. As images of 'human nature' become more problematic, an increasing need is felt to pay closer yet more imaginative attention to the social routines and catastrophes which reveal (and which shape) man's nature in this time of civil unrest and ideological conflict. Although fashion is often revealed by attempts to use it, the sociological imagination is not merely a fashion. It is a quality of mind that seems most dramatically to promise an understanding of the intimate realities of ourselves in connection with larger social realities. It is not merely one quality of mind among the contemporary range of cultural sensibilities—it is *the* quality whose wider and more adroit use offers the promise that all such sensibilities—and in fact, human reason itself—will come to play a greater role in human affairs.

The cultural meaning of physical science—the major older common denominator—is becoming doubtful. As an intellectual style, physical science is coming to be thought by many as somehow inadequate. The adequacy of scientific styles of thought and feeling, imagination and sensibility, has of course from their beginnings been subject to religious doubt and theological controversy, but our scientific grandfathers and fathers beat down such religious doubts. The current doubts are secular, humanistic —and often quite confused. Recent developments in physical science—with its technological climax in the H-bomb and the means of carrying it about the earth—have not been experienced as a solution to any problems widely known and deeply pondered by larger intellectual communities and cultural publics. These developments have been correctly seen as a result of highly specialized inquiry, and improperly felt to be wonderfully mysterious. They have raised more problems—both intellectual and moral—than they have solved, and the problems they have raised lie almost entirely in the area of social not physical affairs. The obvious conquest of nature, the overcoming of scarcity, is felt by men of the overdeveloped societies to be virtually complete. And now in these societies, science—the chief instrument of this conquest—is felt to be footloose, aimless, and in need of re-appraisal.

The modern esteem for science has long been merely assumed, but now the technological ethos and the kind of engineering imagination associated with science are more likely to be frightening and ambiguous than hopeful and progressive. Of course this is not all there is to 'science,' but it is feared that this could become all that there is to it. The felt need to reappraise physical science reflects the need for a new common denominator. It is the human meaning and the social role of science, its military and commercial issue, its political significance that are undergoing confused re-appraisal. Scientific developments of weaponry may lead to the 'necessity' for world political rearrangements—but such 'necessity' is not felt to be solvable by physical science itself.

Much that has passed for 'science' is now felt to be dubious philosophy; much that is held to be 'real science' is often felt to provide only confused fragments of the realities among which men live. Men of science, it is widely felt, no longer try to picture reality as a whole or to present a true outline of human destiny. Moreover, 'science' seems to many less a creative ethos and a manner of orientation than a set of Science Machines, operated by technicians and controlled by economic and military men who neither embody nor understand science as ethos and orientation. In the meantime, philosophers who speak in the name of science often transform it into 'scientism,' making out its experience to be identical with human experience, and claiming that only by its method can the problems of life be solved. With all this, many cultural workmen have come to feel that 'science' is a false and pretentious Messiah, or at the very least a highly ambiguous element in modern civilization.

But there are, in C. P. Snow's phrase, 'two cultures': the scientific and the humanistic. Whether as history or drama, as biography, poetry or fiction, the essence of the humanistic culture has been literature. Yet it is now frequently suggested that serious literature has in many ways become a minor art. If this is so, it is not merely because of the development of mass publics and mass media of communication, and all that these mean for serious literary production. It is also owing to the very quality of the history of our times and the kinds of need men of sensibility feel to grasp that quality.

What fiction, what journalism, what artistic endeavor can compete with the historical reality and political facts of our time? What dramatic vision of hell can compete with the events of twentieth-century war? What moral denunciations can measure up to the moral insensibility of men in the agonies of primary accumulation? It is social and historical reality that men want to know, and often they do not find contemporary literature an adequate means for knowing it. They yearn for facts, they search for their meanings, they want 'a big picture' in which they can believe and within which they can come to understand themselves. They want orienting values too, and suitable ways of feeling and styles of emotion and vocabularies of motive. And they do not readily find these in the literature of today. It does not matter whether or not these qualities *are* to be found there; what matters is that men do not often find them there.

In the past, literary men as critics and historians made notes on England and on journeys to America. They tried to characterize societies as wholes, and to discern their moral meanings. Were Tocqueville or Taine alive today, would they not be sociologists? Asking this question about Taine, a reviewer in *The Times* (London) suggests:

> Taine always saw man primarily as a social animal and society as a collection of groups: he could observe minutely, was a tireless field worker and possessed a quality . . . particularly valuable for perceiving relationships between social phenomena—the quality of springliness. He was too interested in the present to be a good historian, too much of a theorist to try his hand as a novelist, and he thought of literature too much as documents in the culture of an age or country to achieve first-class status as a critic. . . His work on English literature is less about English literature than a commentary on the morality of English society and a vehicle for his positivism. He is a social theorist before all else.[1]

That he remained a 'literary man' rather than a 'social scientist' testifies perhaps to the domination of much nineteenth-cen-

[1] Times Literary Supplement, 15 November 1957.

tury social science by the zealous search for 'laws' presumably comparable to those imagined to be found by natural scientists. In the absence of an adequate social science, critics and novelists, dramatists and poets have been the major, and often the only, formulators of private troubles and even of public issues. Art does express such feelings and often focuses them—at its best with dramatic sharpness—but still not with the intellectual clarity required for their understanding or relief today. Art does not and cannot formulate these feelings as problems containing the troubles and issues men must now confront if they are to overcome their uneasiness and indifference and the intractable miseries to which these lead. The artist, indeed, does not often try to do this. Moreover, the serious artist is himself in much trouble, and could well do with some intellectual and cultural aid from a social science made sprightly by the sociological imagination.

5

It is my aim in this book to define the meaning of the social sciences for the cultural tasks of our time. I want to specify the kinds of effort that lie behind the development of the sociological imagination; to indicate its implications for political as well as for cultural life; and perhaps to suggest something of what is required to possess it. In these ways, I want to make clear the nature and the uses of the social sciences today, and to give a limited account of their contemporary condition in the United States.[2]

[2] I feel the need to say that I much prefer the phrase, 'the social studies' to 'the social sciences'—not because I do not like physical scientists (on the contrary, I do, very much), but because the word 'science' has acquired great prestige and rather imprecise meaning. I do not feel any need to kidnap the prestige or to make the meaning even less precise by using it as a philosophical metaphor. Yet I suspect that if I wrote about 'the social studies,' readers would think only of high school civics, which of all fields of human learning is the one with which I most wish to avoid association. 'The Behavioral Sciences' is simply impossible; it was thought up, I suppose, as a propaganda device to get money for social research from Foundations and Congressmen who confuse 'social science' with 'socialism.' The best term would include history (and psychology, so far as it is concerned with human beings), and should be as non-controversial as possible, for we should argue *with* terms, not fight *over* them. Perhaps 'the human disciplines' would do.

At any given moment, of course, 'social science' consists of what duly recognized social scientists are doing—but all of them are by no means doing the same thing, in fact not even the same sort of thing. Social science is also what social scientists of the past have done—but different students choose to construct and to recall different traditions in their discipline. When I speak of 'the promise of social science,' I hope it is clear that I mean the promise as I see it.

Just now, among social scientists, there is widespread uneasiness, both intellectual and moral, about the direction their chosen studies seem to be taking. This uneasiness, as well as the unfortunate tendencies that contribute to it, are, I suppose, part of a general malaise of contemporary intellectual life. Yet perhaps the uneasiness is more acute among social scientists, if only because of the larger promise that has guided much earlier work in their fields, the nature of the subjects with which they deal, and the urgent need for significant work today.

Not everyone shares this uneasiness, but the fact that many do not is itself a cause for further uneasiness among those who

---

But never mind. With the hope of not being too widely misunderstood, I bow to convention and use the more standard 'social sciences.'

One other point: I hope my colleagues will accept the term 'sociological imagination.' Political scientists who have read my manuscript suggest 'the political imagination'; anthropologists, 'the anthropological imagination'—and so on. The term matters less than the idea, which I hope will become clear in the course of this book. By use of it, I do not of course want to suggest merely the academic discipline of 'sociology.' Much of what the phrase means to me is not at all expressed by sociologists. In England, for example, sociology as an academic discipline is still somewhat marginal, yet in much English journalism, fiction, and above all history, the sociological imagination is very well developed indeed. The case is similar for France: both the confusion and the audacity of French reflection since World War Two rest upon its feeling for the sociological features of man's fate in our time, yet these trends are carried by men of letters rather than by professional sociologists. Nevertheless, I use 'sociological imagination' because: (1) every cobbler thinks leather is the only thing, and for better or worse, I am a sociologist; (2) I do believe that historically the quality of mind has been more frequently and more vividly displayed by classic sociologists than by other social scientists; (3) since I am going to examine critically a number of curious sociological schools, I need a counter term on which to stand.

are alert to the promise and honest enough to admit the pretentious mediocrity of much current effort. It is, quite frankly, my hope to increase this uneasiness, to define some of its sources, to help transform it into a specific urge to realize the promise of social science, to clear the ground for new beginnings: in short, to indicate some of the tasks at hand and the means available for doing the work that must now be done.

Of late the conception of social science I hold has not been ascendant. My conception stands opposed to social science as a set of bureaucratic techniques which inhibit social inquiry by 'methodological' pretensions, which congest such work by obscurantist conceptions, or which trivialize it by concern with minor problems unconnected with publicly revelant issues. These inhibitions, obscurities, and trivialities have created a crisis in the social studies today without suggesting, in the least, a way out of that crisis.

Some social scientists stress the need for 'research teams of technicians,' others for the primacy of the individual scholar. Some expend great energy upon refinements of methods and techniques of investigation; others think the scholarly ways of the intellectual craftsmen are being abandoned and ought now to be rehabilitated. Some go about their work in accordance with a rigid set of mechanical procedures; others seek to develop, to invite, and to use the sociological imagination. Some—being addicts of the high formalism of 'theory'—associate and disassociate concepts in what seems to others a curious manner; these others urge the elaboration of terms only when it is clear that it enlarges the scope of sensibility and furthers the reach of reasoning. Some narrowly study only small-scale milieux, in the hope of 'building up' to conceptions of larger structures; others examine social structures in which they try 'to locate' many smaller milieux. Some, neglecting comparative studies altogether, study only one small community in one society at a time; others in a fully comparative way work directly on the national social structures of the world. Some confine their exact research to very short-run sequences of human affairs; others are concerned with issues which are only apparent in long historical perspective.

Some specialize their work according to academic departments; others, drawing upon all departments, specialize according to topic or problem, regardless of where these lie academically. Some confront the variety of history, biography, society; others do not.

Such contrasts, and many others of similar kind, are not necessarily true alternatives, although in the heat of statesman-like controversy or the lazy safety of specialization they are often taken to be. At this point I merely state them in inchoate form; I shall return to them toward the end of this book. I am hopeful of course that all my own biases will show, for I think judgments should be explicit. But I am also trying, regardless of my own judgments, to state the cultural and political meanings of social science. My biases are of course no more or no less biases than those I am going to examine. Let those who do not care for mine use their rejections of them to make their own as explicit and as acknowledged as I am going to try to make mine! Then the moral problems of social study—the problem of social science as a public issue—will be recognized, and discussion will become possible. Then there will be greater self-awareness all around—which is of coure a pre-condition for objectivity in the enterprise of social science as a whole.

In brief, I believe that what may be called classic social analysis is a definable and usable set of traditions; that its essential feature is the concern with historical social structures; and that its problems are of direct relevance to urgent public issues and insistent human troubles. I also believe that there are now great obstacles in the way of this tradition's continuing—both within the social sciences and in their academic and political settings—but that nevertheless the qualities of mind that constitute it are becoming a common denominator of our general cultural life and that, however vaguely and in however a confusing variety of disguises, they are coming to be felt as a need.

Many practitioners of social science, especially in America, seem to me curiously reluctant to take up the challenge that now confronts them. Many in fact abdicate the intellectual and the political tasks of social analysis; others no doubt are simply not up to the role for which they are nevertheless being cast. At times they seem almost deliberately to have brought forth old ruses and developed new timidities. Yet despite this reluctance, intellectual as well as public attention is now so obviously upon the social worlds which they presumably study that it must be agreed that they are uniquely confronted with an opportunity. In this opportunity there is revealed the intellectual promise of the social sciences, the cultural uses of the sociological imagination, and the political meaning of studies of man and society.

6

Embarrassingly enough for an avowed sociologist, all the unfortunate tendencies (except possibly one) that I shall consider in the following chapters fall into what is generally thought to be 'the field of sociology,' although the cultural and political abdication implicit in them no doubt characterize much of the daily work in other social sciences. Whatever may be true in such disciplines as political science and economics, history and anthropology, it is evident that in the United States today what is known as sociology has become the center of reflection about social science. It has become the center for interest in methods; and in it one also finds the most extreme interest in 'general theory.' A truly remarkable variety of intellectual work has entered into the development of the sociological tradition. To interpret this variety as A Tradition is in itself audacious. Yet perhaps it will be generally agreed that what is now recognized as sociological work has tended to move in one or more of three general directions, each of which is subject to distortion, to being run into the ground.

Tendency I: Toward a theory of history. For example, in the hands of Comte, as in those of Marx, Spencer, and Weber, sociology is an encyclopedic endeavor, concerned with the whole of man's social life. It is at once historical and systematic—historical, because it deals with and uses the materials of the past; systematic, because it does so in order to discern 'the stages' of the course of history and the regularities of social life.

The theory of man's history can all too readily become distorted into a trans-historical strait-jacket into which the materials of human history are forced and out of which issue prophetic views (usually gloomy ones) of the future. The works of Arnold Toynbee and of Oswald Spengler are well-known examples.

Tendency II: Toward a systematic theory of 'the nature of man and society.' For example, in the works of the formalists, notably Simmel and Von Weise, sociology comes to deal in conceptions intended to be of use in classifying all social relations and providing insight into their supposedly invariant features. It is, in short, concerned with a rather static and abstract view of the components of social structure on a quite high level of generality.

Perhaps in reaction to the distortion of Tendency I, history can be altogether abandoned: the systematic theory of the nature of man and of society all too readily becomes an elaborate and arid formalism in which the splitting of Concepts and their endless rearrangement becomes the central endeavor. Among what I shall call Grand Theorists, conceptions have indeed become Concepts. The work of Talcott Parsons is the leading contemporary example in American sociology.

Tendency III: Toward empirical studies of contemporary social facts and problems. Although Comte and Spencer were mainstays of American social science until 1914 or thereabout, and German theoretical influence was heavy, the empirical survey became central in the United States at an early time. In part this resulted from the prior academic establishment of economics and political science. Given this, in so far as sociology is defined as a study of some special area of society, it readily becomes a sort of odd job man among the social sciences, consisting of miscellaneous studies of academic leftovers. There are studies of cities and families, racial and ethnic relations, and of course 'small groups.' As we shall see, the resulting miscellany was transformed into a style of thought, which I shall examine under the term 'liberal practicality.'

Studies of contemporary fact can easily become a series of rather unrelated and often insignificant facts of milieu. Many course offerings in American sociology illustrate this; perhaps textbooks in the field of social disorganization reveal it best. On the other hand, sociologists have tended to become specialists in the technique of research into almost anything; among them methods have become Methodology. Much of the work—and more of the ethos—of George Lundberg, Samuel Stouffer, Stuart Dodd, Paul F. Lazarsfeld are present-day examples. These tendencies—to scatter one's attention and to cultivate method for its own sake—are fit companions, although they do not necessarily occur together.

The peculiarities of sociology may be understood as distortions of one or more of its traditional tendencies. But its promises may also be understood in terms of these tendencies. In the United States today there has come about a sort of Hellenistic amalgamation, embodying various elements and aims from the sociologies of the several Western societies. The danger is that amidst such sociological abundance, other social scientists will become so impatient, and sociologists be in such a hurry for 'research,' that they will lose hold of a truly valuable legacy. But there is also an opportunity in our condition: the sociological tradition contains the best statements of the full promise of the social sciences as a whole, as well as some partial fulfillments of it. The nuance and suggestion that students of sociology can find in their traditions are not to be briefly summarized, but any social scientist who takes them in hand will be richly rewarded. His mastery of them may readily be turned into new orientations for his own work in social science.

I shall return to the promises of social science (in chapters Seven through Ten), after an examination of some of its more habitual distortions (chapters Two through Six).

2

Grand Theory

LET US BEGIN with a sample of grand theory, taken from Talcott Parsons' *The Social System*—widely regarded as a most important book by a most eminent representative of the style.

An element of a shared symbolic system which serves as a criterion or standard for selection among the alternatives of orientation which are intrinsically open in a situation may be called a value. . . But from this motivational orientation aspect of the totality of action it is, in view of the role of symbolic systems, necessary to distinguish a 'value-orientation' aspect. This aspect concerns, not the meaning of the expected state of affairs to the actor in terms of his gratification-deprivation balance but the content of the selective standards themselves. The concept of value-orientations in this sense is thus the logical device for formulating one central aspect of the articulation of cultural traditions into the action system.

It follows from the derivation of normative orientation and the role of values in action as stated above, that all values involve what may be called a social reference. . . It is inherent in an action system that action is, to use one phrase, 'normatively oriented.' This follows, as was shown, from the concept of expectations and its place in action theory, especially in the 'active' phase in which the actor pursues goals. Expectations then, in combination with th 'double contingency' of the process of interaction as it has been called, create a crucially imperative problem of order. Two aspects of this problem of order may in turn be distinguished, order in the symbolic systems which make communication possible, and order in the mutuality of motivational orientation to the normative aspect of expectations, the 'Hobbesian' problem of order.

The problem of order, and thus of the nature of the integration of stable systems of social interaction, that is, of social structure, thus focuses on the integration of the motivation of actors with the normative cultural standards which integrate the action system, in our context interpersonally. These standards are, in the terms used in the preceding chapter, patterns of value-orientation, and as such are a particularly crucial part of the cultural tradition of the social system.[1]

Perhaps some readers will now feel a desire to turn to the next chapter; I hope they will not indulge the impulse. Grand Theory —the associating and dissociating of concepts—is well worth considering. True, it has not had so important an effect as the methodological inhibition that is to be examined in the next chapter, for as a style of work its spread has been limited. The fact is that it is not readily understandable; the suspicion is that it may not be altogether intelligible. This is, to be sure, a protective advantage, but it is a disadvantage in so far as its *pronunciamentos* are intended to influence the working habits of social scientists. Not to make fun but to report factually, we have to admit that its productions have been received by social scientists in one or more of the following ways:

To at least some of those who claim to understand it, and who like it, it is one of the greatest advances in the entire history of social science.

To many of those who claim to understand it, but who do not like it, it is a clumsy piece of irrelevant ponderosity. (These are rare, if only because dislike and impatience prevent many from trying to puzzle it out.)

To those who do not claim to understand it, but who like it very much—and there are many of these—it is a wondrous maze, fascinating precisely because of its often splendid lack of intelligibility.

Those who do not claim to understand it and who do not like it—if they retain the courage of their convictions—will feel that indeed the emperor has no clothes.

Of course there are also many who qualify their views, and many more who remain patiently neutral, waiting to see the professional outcome, if any. And although it is, perhaps, a dreadful

[1] Talcott Parsons, *The Social System*, Glencoe, Illinois, The Free Press, 1951, pp. 12, 36-7.

thought, many social scientists do not even know about it, except as notorious hearsay.

Now all this raises a sore point—intelligibility. That point, of course, goes beyond grand theory,[2] but grand theorists are so deeply involved in it that I fear we really must ask: Is grand theory merely a confused verbiage or is there, after all, also something there? The answer, I think, is: Something is there, buried deep to be sure, but still something is being said. So the question becomes: After all the impediments to meaning are removed from grand theory and what is intelligible becomes available, what, then, is being said?

1

There is only one way to answer such a question: we must translate a leading example of this style of thought and then consider the translation. I have already indicated my choice of example. I want now to make clear that I am not here trying to judge the value of Parsons' work as a whole. If I refer to other writings of his, it is only in order to clarify, in an economical way, some point contained in this one volume. In translating the contents of *The Social System* into English, I do not pretend that my translation is excellent, but only that in the translation no explicit meaning is lost. This—I am asserting—contains all that is intelligible in it. In particular, I shall attempt to sort out statements about something from definitions of words and of their wordy relations. Both are important; to confuse them is fatal to clarity. To make evident the sort of thing that is needed, I shall first translate several passages; then I shall offer two abbreviated translations of the book as a whole.

To translate the example quoted at the opening of this chapter: People often share standards and expect one another to stick to them. In so far as they do, their society may be orderly. (end of translation)

Parsons has written:

There is in turn a two-fold structure of this 'binding in.' In the first place, by virtue of internalization of the standard, conformity with it

[2] See Appendix, section 5.

tends to be of personal, expressive and/or instrumental significance to ego. In the second place, the structuring of the reactions of alter to ego's action as sanctions is a function of his conformity with the standard. Therefore conformity as a direct mode of the fulfillment of his own need-dispositions tends to coincide with conformity as a condition of eliciting the favorable and avoiding the unfavorable reactions of others. In so far as, relative to the actions of a plurality of actors, conformity with a value-orientation standard meets *both* these criteria, that is from the point of view of any given actor in the system, it is both a mode of the fulfillment of his own need-dispositions and a condition of 'optimizing' the reactions of other significant actors, that standard will be said to be 'institutionalized.'

A value pattern in this sense is always institutionalized in an *inter-action* context. Therefore there is always a double aspect of the expectation system which is integrated in relation to it. On the one hand there are the expectations which concern and in part set standards for the behavior of the actor, ego, who is taken as the point of reference; these are his 'role-expectations.' On the other hand, from his point of view there is a set of expectations relative to the contingently probable *re*actions of others (alters)—these will be called 'sanctions,' which in turn may be subdivided into positive and negative according to whether they are felt by ego to be gratification-promoting or depriving. The relation between role-expectations and sanctions then is clearly reciprocal. What are sanctions to ego are role-expectations to alter and vice versa.

A role then is a sector of the total orientation system of an individual actor which is organized about expectations in relation to a particular interaction context, that is integrated with a particular set of value-standards which govern interaction with one or more alters in the appropriate complementary roles. These alters need not be a defined group of individuals, but can involve any alter if and when he comes into a particular complementary interaction relationship with ego which involves a reciprocity of expectations with reference to common standards of value-orientation.

The institutionalization of a set of role-expectations and of the corresponding sanctions is clearly a matter of degree. This degree is a function of two sets of variables; on the one hand those affecting the actual sharedness of the value-orientation patterns, on the other those determining the motivational orientation or commitment to the fulfillment of the relevant expectations. As we shall see a variety of factors can influence this degree of institutionalization through each of these channels. The polar antithesis of full institutionalization is, however, *anomie*, the absence of structured complementarity of the interaction process or, what is the same thing, the complete breakdown of normative order in both senses. This is, however, a limiting concept which is never descriptive of a concrete social system. Just as there are degrees of institutionalization so are there also degrees of *anomie*. The one is the obverse of the other.

An *institution* will be said to be a complex of institutionalized role integrates which is of strategic structural significance in the social system in question. The institution should be considered to be a higher order unit of social structure than the role, and indeed it is made up of a plurality of interdependent role-patterns or components of them.[3]

Or in other words: Men act with and against one another. Each takes into account what others expect. When such mutual expectations are sufficiently definite and durable, we call them standards. Each man also expects that others are going to react to what he does. We call these expected reactions sanctions. Some of them seem very gratifying, some do not. When men are guided by standards and sanctions, we may say that they are playing roles together. It is a convenient metaphor. And as a matter of fact, what we call an institution is probably best defined as a more or less stable set of roles. When within some institution— or an entire society composed of such institutions—the standards and sanctions no longer grip men, we may speak, with Durkheim, of *anomie*. At one extreme, then, are institutions, with standards and sanctions all neat and orderly. At the other extreme, there is *anomie*: as Yeats says, the center does not hold; or, as I say, the normative order has broken down. (end of translation)

In this translation, I must admit, I have not been altogether faithful; I have helped out a little because these are very good ideas. In fact, many of the ideas of grand theorists, when translated, are more or less standard ones available in many textbooks of sociology. But in connection with 'institutions' the definition given above is not quite complete. To what is translated, we must add that the roles making up an institution are not usually just one big 'complementarity' of 'shared expectations.' Have you ever been in an army, a factory—or for that matter a family? Well, those are institutions. Within them, the expectations of some men seem just a little more urgent than those of anyone

[3] Parsons, op. cit. pp. 38-9.

else. That is because, as we say, they have more power. Or to put it more sociologically, although not yet altogether so: an institution is a set of roles graded in authority.

Parsons writes:

Attachment to common values means, motivationally considered, that the actors have common 'sentiments' in support of the value patterns, which may be defined as meaning that conformity with the relevant expectations is treated as a 'good thing' relatively independently of any specific instrumental 'advantage' to be gained from such conformity, e.g., in the avoidance of negative sanctions. Furthermore, this attachment to common values, while it may fit the immediate gratificational needs of the actor, always has also a 'moral' aspect in that to some degree this conformity defines the 'responsibilities' of the actor in the wider, that is, social action systems in which he participates. Obviously the specific focus of responsibility is the collectivity which is constituted by a particular common value-orientation.

Finally, it is quite clear that the 'sentiments' which support such common values are not ordinarily in their specific structure the manifestation of constitutionally given propensities of the organism. They are in general learned or acquired. Furthermore, the part they play in the orientation of action is not predominantly that of cultural objects which are cognized and 'adapted to' but the culture patterns have come to be internalized; they constitute part of the structure of the personality system of the actor itself. Such sentiments or 'value-attitudes' as they may be called are therefore genuine need-dispositions of the personality. It is only by virtue of internalization of institutionalized values that a genuine motivational integration of behavior in the social structure takes place, that the 'deeper' layers of motivation become harnessed to the fulfillment of role-expectations. It is only when this has taken place to a high degree that it is possible to say that a social system is highly integrated, and that the interests of the collectivity and the private interests of its constituent members can be said to approach° coincidence.

°Exact coincidence should be regarded as a limiting case like the famous frictionless machine. Though complete integration of a social system of motivation with a fully consistent set of cultural patterns is empirically unknown, the conception of such an integrated social system is of high theoretical significance. (Parsons' footnote: CWM).

This integration of a set of common value patterns with the internalized need-disposition structure of the constituent personalities is the core phenomenon of the dynamics of social systems. That the stability of any social system except the most evanescent interaction process is dependent on a degree of such integration may be said to be the fundamental dynamic theorem of sociology. It is the major point of reference for all analysis which may claim to be a dynamic analysis of social process.[4]

Or in other words: When people share the same values, they tend to behave in accordance with the way they expect one another to behave. Moreover, they often treat such conformity as a very good thing—even when it seems to go against their immediate interests. That these shared values are learned rather than inherited does not make them any the less important in human motivation. On the contrary, they become part of the personality itself. As such, they bind a society together, for what is socially expected becomes individually needed. This is so important to the stability of any social system that I am going to use it as my chief point of departure if I ever analyze some society as a going concern. (end of translation)

In a similar fashion, I suppose, one could translate the 555 pages of *The Social System* into about 150 pages of straightforward English. The result would not be very impressive. It would, however, contain the terms in which the key problem of the book, and the solution it offers to this problem, are most clearly statable. Any idea, any book can of course be suggested in a sentence or expounded in twenty volumes. It is a question of how full a statement is needed to make something clear and of how important that something seems to be: how many experiences it makes intelligible, how great a range of problems it enables us to solve or at least to state.

To suggest Parsons' book, for example, in two or three phrases: 'We are asked: How is social order possible? The answer we are given seems to be: Commonly accepted values.' Is that all there is to it? Of course not, but it is the main point. But isn't this unfair? Can't any book be treated this way? Of course. Here is a book of my own treated in this way: 'Who, after all, runs America? No one runs it altogether, but in so far as any group does, the power elite.' And here is the book in your hand: 'What are the social sciences all about? They ought to be about man and society and sometimes they are. They are attempts to help us understand

[4] Ibid. pp. 41-2.

biography and history, and the connections of the two in a variety of social structures.'

Here is a translation of Parsons' book in four paragraphs:

Let us imagine something we may call 'the social system,' in which individuals act with reference to one another. These actions are often rather orderly, for the individuals in the system share standards of value and of appropriate and practical ways to behave. Some of these standards we may call norms; those who act in accordance with them tend to act similarly on similar occasions. In so far as this is so, there are 'social regularities,' which we may observe and which are often quite durable. Such enduring and stable regularities I shall call 'structural.' It is possible to think of all these regularities within the social system as a great and intricate balance. That this is a metaphor I am now going to forget, because I want you to take as very real my Concept: The social equilibrium.

There are two major ways by which the social equilibrium is maintained, and by which—should either or both fail—disequilibrium results. The first is 'socialization,' all the ways by which the newborn individual is made into a social person. Part of this social making of persons consists in their acquiring motives for taking the social actions required or expected by others. The second is 'social control,' by which I mean all the ways of keeping people in line and by which they keep themselves in line. By 'line' of course, I refer to whatever action is typically expected and approved in the social system.

The first problem of maintaining social equilibrium is to make people want to do what is required and expected of them. That failing, the second problem is to adopt other means to keep them in line. The best classifications and definitions of these social controls have been given by Max Weber, and I have little to add to what he, and a few other writers since then, have said so well.

One point does puzzle me a little: given this social equilibrium, and all the socialization and control that man it, how is it possible that anyone should ever get out of line? This I cannot explain very well, that is, in the terms of my Systematic and General Theory of the social system. And there is another point that is not as clear as I should like it to be: how should I account for social change—that is, for history? About these two problems, I recommend that whenever you come upon them, you undertake empirical investigations. (end of translation)

Perhaps that is enough. Of course we could translate more fully, but 'more fully' does not necessarily mean 'more adequately,' and I invite the reader to inspect *The Social System* and find more. In the meantime, we have three tasks: first, to characterize the logical style of thinking represented by grand theory; second, to make clear a certain generic confusion in this particular example; third, to indicate how most social scientists now set up and solve Parsons' problem of order. My purpose in all this is to help grand theorists get down from their useless heights.

2

Serious differences among social scientists occur not between those who would observe without thinking and those who would think without observing; the differences have rather to do with what kinds of thinking, what kinds of observing, and what kinds of links, if any, there are between the two.

The basic cause of grand theory is the initial choice of a level of thinking so general that its practitioners cannot logically get down to observation. They never, as grand theorists, get down from the higher generalities to problems in their historical and structural contexts. This absence of a firm sense of genuine problems, in turn, makes for the unreality so noticeable in their pages. One resulting characteristic is a seemingly arbitrary and certainly endless elaboration of distinctions, which neither enlarge our understanding nor make our experience more sensible. This in turn is revealed as a partially organized abdication of the effort to describe and explain human conduct and society plainly.

When we consider what a word stands for, we are dealing with its *semantic* aspects; when we consider it in relation to other words, we are dealing with its *syntactic* features.[5] I introduce

[5] We can also consider it in relation to its users—the pragmatic aspect, about which we have no need to worry here. These are three 'dimensions of meaning' which Charles M. Morris has so neatly systematized in his useful 'Foundations of the Theory of Signs,' *International Encyclopedia of United Science*, Vol. I, No. 2. University of Chicago Press, 1938.

these shorthand terms because they provide an economical and precise way to make this point: Grand theory is drunk on syntax, blind to semantics. Its practitioners do not truly understand that when we define a word we are merely inviting others to use it as we would like it to be used; that the purpose of definition is to focus argument upon fact, and that the proper result of good definition is to transform argument over terms into disagreements about fact, and thus open arguments to further inquiry.

The grand theorists are so preoccupied by syntactic meanings and so unimaginative about semantic references, they are so rigidly confined to such high levels of abstraction that the 'typologies' they make up—and the work they do to make them up—seem more often an arid game of Concepts than an effort to define systematically—which is to say, in a clear and orderly way—the problems at hand, and to guide our efforts to solve them.

One great lesson that we can learn from its systematic absence in the work of the grand theorists is that every self-conscious thinker must at all times be aware of—and hence be able to control—the levels of abstraction on which he is working. The capacity to shuttle between levels of abstraction, with ease and with clarity, is a signal mark of the imaginative and systematic thinker.

Around such terms as 'capitalism' or 'middle class' or 'bureaucracy' or 'power elite' or 'totalitarian democracy,' there are often somewhat tangled and obscured connotations, and in using these terms, such connotations must be carefully watched and controlled. Around such terms, there are often 'compounded' sets of facts and relations as well as merely guessed-at factors and observations. These too must be carefully sorted out and made clear in our definition and in our use.

To clarify the syntactic and the semantic dimensions of such conceptions, we must be aware of the hierarchy of specificity under each of them, and we must be able to consider all levels of this hierarchy. We must ask: Do we mean by 'capitalism,' as we are going to use it, merely the fact that all means of production are privately owned? Or do we also want to include under the term the further idea of a free market as the determining mechanism of price, wages, profit? And to what extent are we entitled to assume that, by definition, the term implies assertions about the political order as well as economic institutions?

Such habits of mind I suppose to be the keys to systematic thinking and their absence the keys to the fetishism of the Concept. Perhaps one result of such an absence will become clearer as we consider, more specifically now, a major confusion of Parsons' book.

3

Claiming to set forth 'a general sociological theory,' the grand theorist in fact sets forth a realm of concepts from which are excluded many structural features of human society, features long and accurately recognized as fundamental to its understanding. Seemingly, this is deliberate in the interest of making the concern of sociologists a specialized endeavor distinct from that of economists and political scientists. Sociology, according to Parsons, has to do with 'that aspect of the theory of social systems which is concerned with the phenomena of the institutionalization of patterns of value-orientation in the social system, with the conditions of that institutionalization; and of changes in the patterns, with conditions of conformity with and deviance from a set of such patterns, and with motivational processes in so far as they are involved in all of these.' [6] Translated and unloaded of assumption, as any definition should be, this reads: Sociologists of my sort would like to study what people want and cherish. We would also like to find out why there is a variety of such values and why they change. When we do find a more or less unitary set of values, we would like to find out why some people do and others do not conform to them. (end of translation)

As David Lockwood has noted,[7] such a statement delivers the sociologist from any concern with 'power,' with economic and political institutions. I would go further than that. This statement, and, in fact, the whole of Parsons' book, deals much more

[6] Parsons, op. cit. p. 552.
[7] Cf. his excellent 'Some Remarks on "The Social System," ' *The British Journal of Sociology*, Vol. VII, 2 June 1956.

with what have been traditionally called 'legitimations' than with institutions of any sort. The result, I think, is to transform, by definition, all institutional structures into a sort of moral sphere— or more accurately, into what has been called 'the symbol sphere.'[8] In order to make the point clear, I should like first to explain something about this sphere; second to discuss its alleged autonomy; and third, to indicate how Parsons' conceptions make it quite difficult even to raise several of the most important problems of any analysis of social structure.

Those in authority attempt to justify their rule over institutions by linking it, as if it were a necessary consequence, with widely believed-in moral symbols, sacred emblems, legal formulae. These central conceptions may refer to a god or gods, the 'vote of the majority,' 'the will of the people,' 'the aristocracy of talent or wealth,' to the 'divine right of kings,' or to the allegedly extraordinary endowment of the ruler himself. Social scientists, following Weber, call such conceptions 'legitimations,' or sometimes 'symbols of justification.'

Various thinkers have used different terms to refer to them: Mosca's 'political formula' or 'great superstitions,' Locke's 'principle of sovereignty,' Sorel's 'ruling myth,' Thurman Arnold's 'folklore,' Weber's 'legitimations,' Durkheim's 'collective representations,' Marx's 'dominant ideas,' Rousseau's 'general will,' Lasswell's 'symbols of authority,' Mannheim's 'ideology,' Herbert Spencer's 'public sentiments'—all these and others like them testify to the central place of master symbols in social analysis.

Similarly in psychological analysis, such master symbols, relevant when they are taken over privately, become the reasons and often the motives that lead persons into roles and sanction their enactment of them. If, for example, economic institutions are publicly justified in terms of them, then references to self-interest may be acceptable justification for individual conduct. But, if it is felt publicly necessary to justify such institutions in terms of 'public service and trust,' the old self-interest motives and reasons may

[8] H. H. Gerth and C. Wright Mills, *Character and Social Structure*, New York, Harcourt, Brace, 1953, pp. 274-7, upon which I am drawing freely in this section and in section 5, below.

lead to guilt or at least to uneasiness among capitalists. Legitimations that are publicly effective often become, in due course, effective as personal motives.

Now, what Parsons and other grand theorists call 'value-orientations' and 'normative structure' has mainly to do with master symbols of legitimation. This is, indeed, a useful and important subject. The relations of such symbols to the structure of institutions are among the most important problems of social science. Such symbols, however, do not form some autonomous realm within a society; their social relevance lies in their use to justify or to oppose the arrangement of power and the positions within this arrangement of the powerful. Their psychological relevance lies in the fact that they become the basis for adherence to the structure of power or for opposing it.

We may not merely assume that some such set of values, or legitimations, *must* prevail lest a social structure come apart, nor may we assume that a social structure must be made coherent or unified by any such 'normative structure.' Certainly we may not merely assume that any such 'normative structure' as may prevail is, in any meaning of the word, autonomous. In fact, for modern Western societies—and in particular the United States—there is much evidence that the opposite of each of these assumptions is the more accurate. Often—although not in the United States since World War II—there are quite well organized symbols of opposition which are used to justify insurgent movements and to debunk ruling authorities. The continuity of the American political system is quite unique, having been threatened by internal violence only once in its history; this fact may be among those that have misled Parsons in his image of The Normative Structure of Value-Orientation.

'Governments' do not necessarily, as Emerson would have it, 'have their origin in the moral identity of men.' To believe that government does is to confuse its legitimations with its causes. Just as often, or even more often, such moral identities as men of some society may have rest on the fact that institutional rulers successfully monopolize, and even impose, their master symbols.

Some hundred years ago, this matter was fruitfully discussed in terms of the assumptions of those who believe that symbol spheres are self-determining, and that such 'values' may indeed dominate history: The symbols that justify some authority are separated from the actual persons or strata that exercise the authority. The 'ideas,' not the strata or the persons using the ideas, are then thought to rule. In order to lend continuity to the sequence of these symbols, they are presented as in some way connected with one another. The symbols are thus seen as 'self-determining.' To make more plausible this curious notion, the symbols are often 'personalized' or given 'self-consciousness.' They may then be conceived of as The Concepts of History or as a sequence of 'philosophers' whose thinking determines institutional dynamics. Or, we may add, the Concept of 'normative order' may be fetishized. I have, of course, just paraphrased Marx and Engels speaking of Hegel.[9]

Unless they justify institutions and motivate persons to enact institutional roles, 'the values' of a society, however important in various private milieux, are historically and sociologically irrelevant. There is of course an interplay between justifying symbols, institutional authorities, and obedient persons. At times we should not hesitate to assign causal weight to master symbols—but we may not misuse the idea as *the* theory of social order or of the unity of society. There are better ways to construct a 'unity,' as we shall presently see, ways that are more useful in the formulation of significant problems of social structure and closer to observable materials.

So far as 'common values' interest us, it is best to build up our conception of them by examining the legitimations of each institutional order in any given social structure, rather than to *begin* by attempting first to grasp them, and in their light 'explain' the society's composition and unity.[10] We may, I suppose, speak of 'common values' when a great proportion of the members of an

[9] Cf. Karl Marx and Frederick Engels, *The German Ideology*, New York, International Publishers, 1939, pp. 42 ff.
[10] For a detailed and empirical account of the 'values' which American businessmen, for example, seek to promulgate, see Sutton, Harris, Kaysen and Tobin, *The American Business Creed*, Cambridge, Mass., Harvard University Press, 1956.

institutional order have taken over that order's legitimations, when such legitimations are the terms in which obedience is successfully claimed, or at least complacency secured. Such symbols are then used to 'define the situations' encountered in various roles and as yardsticks for the evaluations of leaders and followers. Social structures that display such universal and central symbols are naturally extreme and 'pure' types.

At the other end of the scale, there are societies in which a dominant set of institutions controls the total society and super-imposes its values by violence and the threat of violence. This need not involve any breakdown of the social structure, for men may be effectively conditioned by formal discipline; and at times, unless they accept institutional demands for discipline, they may have no chance to earn a living.

A skilled compositor employed by a reactionary newspaper, for example, may for the sake of making a living and holding his job conform to the demands of employer discipline. In his heart, and out-side the shop, he may be a radical agitator. Many German socialists allowed themselves to become perfectly disciplined soldiers under the Kaiser's flag—despite the fact that their subjective values were those of revolutionary Marxism. It is a long way from symbols to conduct and back again, and not all integration is based on symbols.[11]

To emphasize such conflict of value is not to deny 'the force of rational consistencies.' The discrepancy between word and deed is often characteristic, but so is the striving for consistency. Which is predominant in any given society cannot be decided *a priori* on the basis of 'human nature' or on the 'principles of sociology' or by the fiat of grand theory. We might well imagine a 'pure type' of society, a perfectly disciplined social structure, in which the dominated men, for a variety of reasons, cannot quit their prescribed roles, but nevertheless share none of the dominator's values, and thus in no way believe in the legitimacy of the order. It would be like a ship manned by galley slaves, in which the disciplined movement of the oars reduces the rowers to cogs in a machine, and the violence of the whipmaster is only rarely needed. The galley slaves need not even be aware of the ship's

[11] Gerth and Mills, op. cit. p. 300.

direction, although any turn of the bow evokes the wrath of the master, the only man aboard who is able to see ahead. But perhaps I begin to describe rather than to imagine.

Between these two types—a 'common value system' and a superimposed discipline—there are numerous forms of 'social integration.' Most occidental societies have incorporated many divergent 'value-orientations'; their unities involve various mixtures of legitimation and coercion. And that, of course, may be true of any institutional order, not only of the political and economic. A father may impose demands upon his family by threatening to withhold inheritance, or by the use of such violence as the political order may allow him. Even in such sacred little groups as families, the unity of 'common values' is by no means necessary: distrust and hatred may be the very stuff needed to hold a loving family together. A society as well may of course flourish quite adequately without such a 'normative structure' as grand theorists believe to be universal.

I do not here wish to expound any solution to the problem of order, but merely to raise questions. For if we cannot do that, we must, as demanded by the fiat of quite arbitary definition, *assume* the 'normative structure' which Parsons imagines to be the heart of 'the social system.'

4

'Power,' as the term is now generally used in social science, has to do with whatever decisions men make about the arrangements under which they live, and about the events which make up the history of their period. Events that are beyond human decision do happen; social arrangements do change without benefit of explicit decision. But in so far as such decisions are made (and in so far as they could be but are not) the problem of who is involved in making them (or not making them) is the basic problem of power.

We cannot assume today that men must in the last resort be governed by their own consent. Among the means of power that now prevail is the power to manage and to manipulate the consent of men. That we do not know the limits of such power— and that we hope it does have limits—does not remove the fact that much power today is successfully employed without the sanction of the reason or the conscience of the obedient.

Surely in our time we need not argue that, in the last resort, coercion is the 'final' form of power. But then we are by no means constantly at the last resort. Authority (power justified by the beliefs of the voluntarily obedient) and manipulation (power wielded unbeknown to the powerless) must also be considered, along with coercion. In fact, the three types must constantly be sorted out when we think about the nature of power.

In the modern world, I think we must bear in mind, power is often not so authoritative as it appeared to be in the medieval period; justifications of rulers no longer seem so necessary to their exercise of power. At least for many of the great decisions of our time—especially those of an international sort—mass 'persuasion' has not been 'necessary'; the fact is simply accomplished. Furthermore, such ideologies as are available to the powerful are often neither taken up nor used by them. Ideologies usually arise as a response to an effective debunking of power; in the United States such opposition has not been recently effective enough to create a felt need for new ideologies of rule.

Today, of course, many people who are disengaged from prevailing allegiances have not acquired new ones, and so are inattentive to political concerns of any kind. They are neither radical nor reactionary. They are inactionary. If we accept the Greek's definition of the idiot as an altogether private man, then we must conclude that many citizens of many societies are indeed idiots. This—and I use the word with care—this spiritual condition seems to me the key to much modern malaise among political intellectuals, as well as the key to much political bewilderment in modern society. Intellectual 'conviction' and moral 'belief' are not necessary, in either the rulers or the ruled, for a structure of power to persist and even to flourish. So far as the role of ideologies is concerned, the frequent absence of engaging legitimation and the prevalence of mass apathy are surely two of the central political facts about the Western societies today.

In the course of any substantive research, many problems do confront those who hold the view of power that I have been suggesting. But we are not at all helped by the deviant assumptions of Parsons, who merely assumes that there is, presumably in every society, such a 'value hierarchy' as he imagines. Moreover, its implications systematically impede the clear formulation of significant problems:

To accept his scheme we are required to read out of the picture the facts of power and indeed of all institutional structures, in particular the economic, the political, the military. In this curious 'general theory,' such structures of domination have no place.

In the terms provided, we cannot properly pose the empirical question of the extent to which, and in what manner, institutions are, in any given case, legitimated. The idea of the normative order that is set forth, and the way it is handled by grand theorists, leads us to assume that virtually all power is legitimated. In fact: that in the social system, 'the maintenance of the complementarity of role-expectations, once established, is not problematical. . . . No special mechanisms are required for the explanation of the maintenance of complementary interaction-orientation.' [12]

In these terms, the idea of conflict cannot effectively be formulated. Structural antagonisms, large-scale revolts, revolutions— they cannot be imagined. In fact, it is assumed that 'the system,' once established, is not only stable but intrinsically harmonious; disturbances must, in his language, be 'introduced into the system.' [13] The idea of the normative order set forth leads us to assume a sort of harmony of interests as the natural feature of any society; as it appears here, this idea is as much a metaphysical anchor point as was the quite similar idea among the eighteenth-century philosophers of natural order.[14]

The magical elimination of conflict, and the wondrous achievement of harmony, remove from this 'systematic' and 'general' theory the possibilities of dealing with social change, with history. Not only does the 'collective behavior' of terrorized masses and excited mobs, crowds and movements—with which our era is so filled—find no place in the normatively created social structures

[12] Parsons, op. cit. p. 205.
[13] Ibid. p. 262.
[14] Cf. Carl Becker, *The Heavenly City;* and Lewis A. Coser, *Conflict,* Glencoe, Illinois, The Free Press, 1956.

of grand theorists. But any systematic ideas of how history itself occurs, of its mechanics and processes, are unavailable to grand theory, and accordingly, Parsons believes, unavailable to social science: 'When such a theory is available the millennium for social science will have arrived. This will not come in our time and most probably never.' [15] Surely this is an extraordinarily vague assertion.

Virtually any problem of substance that is taken up in the terms of grand theory is incapable of being clearly stated. Worse: its statement is often loaded with evaluations as well as obscured by sponge-words. It is, for example, difficult to imagine a more futile endeavor than analyzing American society in terms of 'the value pattern' of 'universalistic-achievement' with no mention of the changing nature, meaning and forms of success characteristic of modern capitalism, or of the changing structure of capitalism itself; or, analyzing United States stratification in terms of 'the dominant value system' without taking into account the known statistics of life-chances based on levels of property and income.[16]

I do not think it too much to say that in so far as problems are dealt with realistically by grand theorists, they are dealt with in terms that find no place in grand theory, and are often contradictory to it. 'Indeed,' Alvin Gouldner has remarked, 'the extent to which Parsons' efforts at theoretical and empirical analysis of change suddenly lead him to enlist a body of Marxist concepts and assumptions is nothing less than bewildering. . . . It almost seems as if two sets of books were being kept, one for the analysis of equilibrium and another for the investigation of change.' [17] Gouldner goes on to remark how in the case of defeated Germany, Parsons recommends attacking the Junkers at their base, as 'a case of exclusive class privilege' and analyzes the civil service in terms of 'the class basis of recruitment.' In short, the whole economic and occupational structure—conceived in quite Marxian

---

[15] Parsons, taken from Alvin W. Gouldner, 'Some observations on Systematic Theory, 1945-55,' *Sociology in the United States of America*, Paris, UNESCO, 1956, p. 40.

[16] Cf. Lockwood, op. cit. p. 138.

[17] Gouldner, op. cit. p. 41.

terms, not in terms of the normative structure projected by grand theory—suddenly rises into view. It makes one entertain the hope that grand theorists have not lost all touch with historical reality.

5

I now return to the problem of order, which in a rather Hobbesian version, seems to be the major problem in Parsons' book. It is possible to be brief about it because in the development of social science it has been re-defined, and in its most useful statement might now be called the problem of social integration; it does of course require a working conception of social structure and of historical change. Unlike grand theorists, most social scientists, I think, would give answers running something like this:

First of all, there is no *one* answer to the question, What holds a social structure together? There is no one answer because social structures differ profoundly in their degrees and kinds of unity. In fact, types of social structure are usefully conceived in terms of different modes of integration. When we descend from the level of grand theory to historical realities, we immediately realize the irrelevance of its monolithic Concepts. With these we cannot think about the human variety, about Nazi Germany in 1936, Sparta in seventh century B.C., the United States in 1836, Japan in 1866, Great Britain in 1950, Rome at the time of Diocletian. Merely to name this variety is surely to suggest that whatever these societies may have in common must be discovered by empirical examination. To predicate anything beyond the most empty formalities about the historical range of social structure is to mistake one's own capacity to talk for all that is meant by the work of social investigation.

One may usefully conceive types of social structure in terms of such institutional orders as the political and kinship, the military and economic, and the religious. Having defined each of these in such a way as to be able to discern their outlines in a given historical society, one asks how each is related to the others, how, in short, they are composed into a social structure. The answers are conveniently put as a set of 'working models' which are used to make us more aware, as we examine specific societies at specific times, of the links by which they are 'tied together.'

One such 'model' may be imagined in terms of the working out in each institutional order of a similar structural principle; think for example of Tocqueville's America. In that classical liberal society each order of institutions is conceived as autonomous, and its freedom demanded from any co-ordination by other orders. In the economy, there is *laissez faire;* in the religious sphere, a variety of sects and churches openly compete on the market for salvation; kinship institutions are set up on a marriage market in which individuals choose one another. Not a family-made man, but a self-made man, comes to ascendancy in the sphere of status. In the political order, there is party competition for the votes of the individual; even in the military zone there is much freedom in the recruitment of state militia, and in a wide sense—a very important sense—one man means one rifle. The principle of integration—which is also the basic legitimation of this society—is the ascendancy within each order of institutions of the free initiative of independent men in competition with one another. It is in this fact of correspondence that we may understand the way in which a classic liberal society is unified.

But such 'correspondence' is only one type, only one answer to the 'problem of order.' There are other types of unity. Nazi Germany, for example, was integrated by 'co-ordination.' The general model can be stated as follows: Within the economic order, institutions are highly centralized; a few big units more or less control all operations. Within the political order there is more fragmentation: Many parties compete to influence the state, but no one of them is powerful enough to control the results of economic concentration, one of these results—along with other factors —being the slump. The Nazi movement successfully exploits the mass despair, especially that of its lower middle classes, in the economic slump and brings into close correspondence the political, military, and economic orders. One party monopolizes and remakes the political order, abolishing or amalgamating all other parties that might compete for power. To do this requires that the Nazi party find points of coinciding interest with monopolies in the economic order and also with certain elites of the military order. In these main orders there is, first, a corresponding concentration of power; then each of them coincides and co-operates in the taking of power. President Hindenburg's army is not interested in defending the Weimar Republic, or in crushing the marching columns of a popular war party. Big business circles are willing to help finance the Nazi party, which, among other things, promises to smash the labor movement. And the three types of elite join in an often uneasy coalition to maintain power in their respective orders and to co-ordinate the rest of society. Rival political parties are either suppressed and outlawed, or they disband voluntarily. Kinship and religious institutions, as well as all organizations within and between all orders, are infiltrated and co-ordinated, or at least neutralized.

The totalitarian party-state is the means by which high agents of each of the three dominant orders co-ordinate their own and other institutional orders. It becomes the over-all 'frame organization' which imposes goals upon all institutional orders instead of merely guaranteeing 'government by law.' The party extends itself, prowling everywhere in 'auxiliaries' and 'affiliations.' It either breaks up or it infiltrates, and in either case it comes to control all types of organizations, including the family.

The symbol spheres of all institutions are controlled by the party. With the partial exception of the religious order, no rival claims to legitimate autonomy are permitted. There is a party monopoly of formal communications, including educational institutions. All symbols are recast to form the basic legitimation of the co-ordinated society. The principle of absolute and magical leadership (charismatic rule) in a strict hierarchy is widely promulgated, in a social structure that is to a considerable extent held together by a network of rackets.[18]

But surely that is enough to make evident what I should think an obvious point: that there is no 'grand theory,' no one universal scheme in terms of which we can understand the unity of social

[18] Franz Neumann, *Behemoth*, New York, Oxford, 1942, which is a truly splendid model of what a structural analysis of an historical society ought to be. For the above account, see Gerth and Mills, op. cit. pp. 363 ff.

structure, no one answer to the tired old problem of social order, taken *überhaupt*. Useful work on such problems will proceed in terms of a variety of such working models as I have outlined here, and these models will be used in close and empirical connection with a range of historical as well as contemporary social structures.

It is important to understand that such 'modes of integration' may also be conceived as working models of historical change. If, for example, we observe American society at the time of Tocqueville and again in the middle of the twentieth century, we see at once that the way the nineteenth century structure 'hangs together' is quite different from its current modes of integration. We ask: How have each of its instutional orders changed? How have its relations with each of the others changed? What have been the tempos, the varying rates at which these structural changes have occurred? And, in each case, what have been the necessary and sufficient causes of these changes? Usually, of course, the search for adequate cause requires at least some work in a comparative as well as an historical manner. In an over-all way, we can summarize such an analysis of social change, and thus formulate more economically a range of larger problems, by indicating that the changes have resulted in a shift from one 'mode of integration' to another. For example, the last century of American history shows a transition from a social structure largely integrated by correspondence to one much more subject to coordination.

The general problem of a theory of history can not be separated from the general problem of a theory of social structure. I think it is obvious that in their actual studies, working social scientists do not experience any great theoretical difficulties in understanding the two in a unified way. Perhaps that is why one *Behemoth* is worth, to social science, twenty *Social Systems*.

I do not, of course, present these points in any effort to make a definitive statement of the problems of order and change—that is, of social structure and history. I do so merely to suggest the outlines of such problems and to indicate something of the kind of work that has been done on them. Perhaps these remarks are also useful to make more specific one aspect of the promise of social science. And, of course, I have set them forth here in order to indicate how inadequately grand theorists have handled one major problem of social science. In *The Social System* Parsons has not been able to get down to the work of social science because he is possessed by the idea that the one model of social order he has constructed is some kind of universal model; because, in fact, he has fetishized his Concepts. What is 'systematic' about this particular grand theory is the way it outruns any specific and empirical problem. It is not used to state more precisely or more adequately any new problem of recognizable significance. It has not been developed out of any need to fly high for a little while in order to see something in the social world more clearly, to solve some problem that can be stated in terms of the historical reality in which men and institutions have their concrete being. Its problem, its course, and its solutions are grandly theoretical.

The withdrawal into systematic work on conceptions should be only a formal moment within the work of social science. It is useful to recall that in Germany the yield of such formal work was soon turned to encyclopedic and historical use. That use, presided over by the ethos of Max Weber, was the climax of the classic German tradition. In considerable part, it was made possible by a body of sociological work in which general conceptions about society were closely joined with historical exposition. Classical Marxism has been central to the development of modern sociology; Max Weber, like so many other sociologists, developed much of his work in a dialogue with Karl Marx. But the amnesia of the American scholar has always to be recognized. In grand theory we now confront another formalist withdrawal, and again, what is properly only a pause seems to have become permanent. As they say in Spain, 'many can shuffle cards who can't play.' [19]

[19] It must be evident that the particular view of society which it is possible to dig out of Parsons' texts is of rather direct ideological use; traditionally, such views have of course been associated with conservative styles of thinking. Grand theorists have not often descended into the political arena; cer-

¹⁹ *footnote continued*

tainly they have not often taken their problems to lie within the political contexts of modern society. But that of course does not exempt their work from ideological meaning. I shall not analyze Parsons in this connection, for the political meaning of *The Social System* lies so close to its surface, when it is adequately translated, that I feel no need to make it any plainer. Grand theory does not now play any direct bureaucratic role, and as I have noted, its lack of intelligibility limits any public favor it might come to have. This might of course become an asset: its obscurity does give it a great ideological potential.

The ideological meaning of grand theory tends strongly to legitimate stable forms of domination. Yet only if there should arise a much greater need for elaborate legitimations among conservative groups would grand theory have a chance to become politically relevant. I began this chapter with a question: Is grand theory, as represented in *The Social System,* merely verbiage or is it also profound? My answer to this question is: It is only about 50 per cent verbiage; 40 per cent is well-known textbook sociology. The other 10 per cent, as Parsons might say, I am willing to leave open for your own empirical investigations. My own investigations suggest that the remaining 10 per cent is of possible—although rather vague—ideological use.

3

Abstracted Empiricism

LIKE GRAND THEORY, abstracted empiricism seizes upon one juncture in the process of work and allows it to dominate the mind. Both are withdrawals from the tasks of the social sciences. Considerations of method and theory are of course essential to work upon our tasks, but in these two styles they have become hindrances: the methodological inhibition stands parallel to the fetishism of the Concept.

1

I am not of course attempting to summarize the results of all the work of abstracted empiricists, but only to make clear the general character of their style of work and some of its assumptions. Accredited studies in this style now tend regularly to fall into a more or less standard pattern. In practice the new school usually takes as the basic source of its 'data' the more or less set interview with a series of individuals selected by a sampling procedure. Their answers are classified and, for convenience, punched on Hollerith cards which are then used to make statistical runs by means of which relations are sought. Undoubtedly this fact, and the consequent ease with which the procedure is learned by any fairly intelligent person, accounts for much of its appeal. The results are normally put in the form of statistical assertions: on the simplest level, these specific results are assertions of proportion; on more complicated levels, the answers to various questions are combined in often elaborate cross-classifications, which are then, in various ways, collapsed to form scales. There are several complicated ways of manipulating such data, but these need not concern us here, for regardless of the degree of complication, they are still manipulations of the sort of material indicated.

Apart from advertising and media research, perhaps 'public opinion' is the subject-matter of most work in this style, although no idea which re-states the problems of public opinion and communications as a field of intelligible study has been associated with it. The framework of such studies has been the simple classification of questions: who says what to whom in which media and with what results? The going definitions of the key terms are as follows:

. . . By 'public' I mean to refer to the magnitude involved—that is, to non-private, non-individualized feelings and responses of large numbers of people. This characteristic of public opinion necessitates the use of sample surveys. By 'opinion' I mean to include not only the usual sense of opinion on topical, ephemeral, and typically political issues but also attitudes, sentiments, values, information, and related actions. To get at them properly necessitates the use not only of questionnaires and interviews but also of projective and scaling devices.[1]

In these assertions, there is a pronounced tendency to confuse whatever is to be studied with the set of methods suggested for its study. What is probably meant runs something like this: The word public, as I am going to use it, refers to any sizable aggregate and hence may be statistically sampled; since opinions are held by people, to find them you have to talk with people. Sometimes, however, they will not or cannot tell you; then you may try to use 'projective and scaling devices.'

Studies of public opinion have mostly been done within the one national social structure of the United States and of course concern only the last decade or so. Perhaps that is why they do not refine the meaning of 'public opinion,' or reformulate the major problems of this area. They cannot properly do so, even in a preliminary way, within the historical and structural confinement selected for them.

[1] Bernard Berelson, 'The Study of Public Opinion,' *The State of the Social Sciences*, edited by Leonard D. White, Chicago, Illinois, University of Chicago Press, 1956, p. 299.

The problem of 'the public' in Western societies arises out of the transformation of the traditional and conventional consensus of medieval society; it reaches its present-day climax in the idea of a mass society. What were called 'publics' in the eighteenth and nineteenth centuries are being transformed into a society of 'masses.' Moreover, the structural relevance of publics is declining, as men at large become 'mass men,' each trapped in quite power-less milieux. That, or something like it, may suggest the framework that is required for the selection and the design of studies of publics, public opinion, and mass communications. There is also required a full statement of the historical phases of democratic societies, and in particular, of what has been called 'democratic totalitarianism' or 'totalitarian democracy.' In short, in this area the problems of social science cannot be stated within the scope and terms of abstracted empiricism as now practiced.

Many problems with which its practitioners do try to deal—effects of the mass media, for example—cannot be adequately stated without some structural setting. Can one hope to understand the effects of these media—much less their combined meaning for the development of a mass society—if one studies, with what-ever precision, only a population that has been 'saturated' by these media for almost a generation? The attempt to sort out individuals 'less exposed' from those 'more exposed' to one or another medium may well be of great concern to advertising interests, but it is not an adequate basis for the development of a theory of the social meaning of the mass media.

In this school's study of political life, 'voting behavior' has been the chief subject matter, chosen, I suppose, because it seems so readily amenable to statistical investigation. The thinness of the results is matched only by the elaboration of the methods and the care employed. It must be interesting to political scientists to ex-amine a full-scale study of voting which contains no reference to the party machinery for 'getting out the vote,' or indeed to any political institutions. Yet that is what happens in *The Peoples' Choice*, a duly accredited and celebrated study of the 1940 elec-tion in Erie County, Ohio. From this book we learn that rich, rural, and Protestant persons tend to vote Republican; people of opposite type incline toward the Democrats; and so on. But we learn little about the dynamics of American politics.

The idea of legitimation is one of the central conceptions of political science, particularly as the problems of this discipline bear on questions of opinion and ideology. The research on 'political opinion' is all the more curious in view of the suspicion that American electoral politics is a sort of politics without opinion— if one takes the word 'opinion' seriously; a sort of voting without much political meaning of any psychological depth—if one takes the phrase 'political meaning' seriously. But no such questions— and I intend these remarks only as questions—can be raised about such 'political researches' as these. How could they be? They require an historical knowledge and a style of psychological reflection which is not duly accredited by abstracted empiricists, or in truth, available to most of its practitioners.

Perhaps the key event of the last two decades is World War Two; its historic and psychological consequences frame much of what, over the last decade, we have studied. It is curious, I think, that we do not yet happen to have a definitive work on the causes of this war, but then, we are still trying, with some success, to characterize it as an historically specific form of warfare, and to locate it as a pivot of our period. Apart from official histories of the War, the most elaborate body of research is probably the several-year inquiry made for the American Army under the direction of Samuel Stouffer. These studies, it seems to me, prove that it is possible for social research to be of administrative use without being concerned with the problems of social science. The results must surely be disappointing to anyone who wishes to understand something of the American soldier who was in the war—in particular, to those who ask: how was it possible to win so many battles with men of such 'low morale'? But attempts to answer such queries take one far outside the scope of the accredited style and into the flimsy realm of 'speculation.'

Alfred Vagts' one volume *History of Militarism* and the wonderful reportorial techniques for getting up close to men in battle, used by S. L. A. Marshall, in his *Men Under Fire,* are of greater substantive worth than Stouffer's four volumes.

In so far as studies of stratification have been done in the new style, no new conceptions have arisen. In fact, the key conceptions available from other styles of work have not been 'translated'; usually, quite spongy 'indices' of 'socio-economic status' have served. The very difficult problems of 'class consciousness' and of 'false consciousness'; of conceptions of status, as against class; and Weber's statistically challenging idea of 'social class,' have not been advanced by workers in this style. Moreover, and in many ways most grievously, the choice of smaller cities as 'the sample area' for studies persists mightily, despite the quite obvious fact that one cannot add up any aggregate of such studies to an adequate view of the national structure of class, status, and power.

In discussing changes in studies of public opinion, Bernard Berelson has provided a statement which holds, I believe, of most studies in the abstracted emipirical manner:

Put together, these differences [25 years ago vs today] spell a revolutionary change in the field of public opinion studies: the field has become technical and quantitative, a-theoretical, segmentalized, and particularized, specialized and institutionalized, 'modernized' and 'group-ized'—in short, as a characteristic behavioral science, Americanized. Twenty-five years ago and earlier, prominent writers, as part of their general concern with the nature and functioning of society, learnedly studied public opinion not 'for itself' but in broad historical, theoretical, and philosophical terms and wrote treatises. Today, teams of technicians do research projects on specific subjects and report findings. Twenty years ago the study of public opinion was part of scholarship. Today it is part of science.[2]

In this short attempt to characterize studies in the abstracted empirical style I have not merely been saying: 'These people have not studied the substantive problems in which I am interested,' or merely: 'They have not studied what most social scientists consider important problems.' What I have been saying is: They

2 Ibid. pp. 304-5.

have studied problems of abstracted empiricism; but only within the curiously self-imposed limitations of their arbitrary epistomology have they stated their questions and answers. And I have not—I think—used phrases without due care: they are possessed by the methodological inhibition. All of which means, in terms of the results, that in these studies the details are piled up with insufficient attention to form; indeed, often there is no form except that provided by typesetters and bookbinders. The details, no matter how numerous, do not convince us of anything worth having convictions about.

2

As a style of social science, abstracted empiricism is not characterized by any substantive propositions or theories. It is not based upon any new conception of the nature of society or of man or upon any particular facts about them. True, it is recognizable by the kinds of problems its practitioners typically select to study, and by the way in which they typically study them. But certainly these studies are no reason for such celebration as this style of social research may enjoy.

In itself, however, the character of this school's substantive results is not an adequate basis on which to judge it. As a school, it is new; as a method, it does take time; and as a style of work, it is only now spreading into a fuller range of 'problem areas.'

The most conspicuous—although not necessarily the most important—of its characteristics have to do with the administrative apparatus that it has come to employ and the types of intellectual workmen it has recruited and trained. This apparatus has now become large scale, and many signs point to its becoming more widespread and more influential. The intellectual administrator and the research technician—both quite new types of professional men—now compete with the more usual kinds of professors and scholars.

But again all these developments, although of enormous importance to the character of the future university, to the liberal arts tradition, and to the qualities of mind that may become ascendent in American academic life, do not constitute a sufficient basis upon which to judge this style of social research. These developments do go much farther than many of the adherents of abstracted empiricism would probably admit toward explaining the appeal and the prominence of their style. If nothing else, they provide employment for semi-skilled technicians on a scale and in a manner not known before; they offer to them careers having the security of the older academic life but not requiring the older sort of individual accomplishment. This style of research, in brief, is accompanied by an administrative demiurge which is relevant to the future of social study and to its possible bureaucratization.

But the intellectual characteristics of abstracted empiricism that are most important to grasp are the philosophy of science held by its practitioners, how they hold to it, and how they use it. It is this philosophy that underlies both the type of substantive research undertaken and its administrative and personnel apparatus. Both the substantive thinness of the actual studies and the felt need for the apparatus find their major intellectual justification in this particular philosophy of science.

It is important to get this point quite clear, for one would suppose that philosophical tenets would not be central to the shaping of an enterprise which is so emphatic in its claim to be Science. It is important also because the practitioners of the style do not usually seem aware that it is a philosophy upon which they stand. Probably no one familiar with its practitioners would care to deny that many of them are dominated by concern with their own scientific status; their most cherished professional self-image is that of the natural scientist. In their arguments about various philosophical issues of social science, one of their invariable points is that they *are* 'natural scientists,' or at least that they 'represent the viewpoint of natural science.' In the discourse of the more sophisticated, or in the presence of some smiling and exalted physicist, the self-image is more likely to be shortened to merely 'scientist.' [3]

[3] The following example happens to be ready at hand. In discussing various philosophical issues, in particular the nature of 'mental' phenomena and the bearing of his views of them on problems of epistemology, George A. Lundberg remarks: 'Because of this uncertainty of the definition of the "school," and more especially because of the many curious associations which the term

As a matter of practice, abstracted empiricists often seem more concerned with the philosophy of science than with social study itself. What they have done, in brief, is to embrace one philosophy of science which they now suppose to be The Scientific Method. This model of research is largely an epistemological construction; within the social sciences, its most decisive result has been a sort of methodological inhibition. By this I mean that the kinds of problems that will be taken up and the way in which they are formulated are quite severely limited by The Scientific Method. Methodology, in short, seems to determine the problems. And this, after all, is only to be expected. The Scientific Method that is projected here did not grow out of, and is not a generalization of, what are generally and correctly taken to be the classic lines of social science work. It has been largely drawn, with expedient modifications, from one philosophy of natural science.

Philosophies of the social sciences seem, broadly, to consist of two kinds of effort. (1) The philosophers can attempt to examine what actually goes on in the process of social study, then generalize and make consistent those procedures of inquiry that seem most promising. This is a difficult kind of work and can easily result in nonsense, but it is much less difficult if every working social scientist does it, and there is a sense in which each must do it. So far little of it has been done, and it has been applied to only certain kinds of method. (2) The style of social research I have called abstracted empiricism often seems to consist of efforts to restate and adopt *philosophies* of *natural* science in such a way as to form a program and a canon for work in social science.

Methods are the procedures used by men trying to understand

"positivism" has in many minds, I have always preferred to characterize my own viewpoint as that of *natural science* rather than attempt to identify it with any of the conventional schools of traditional philosophy, of which positivism has been one, at least since Comte.' And again: 'Dodd and I, in common, I believe, with all other natural scientists, do indeed proceed on the postulate that the data of empirical science consist of symbolized reactions through the media of the human senses (i.e., all our responses, including those of the "sense organs").' And again: 'In common with all natural scientists, we certainly reject the notion that...' 'The Natural Science Trend in Sociology,' *The American Journal of Sociology*, Vol. LXI, No. 3, November, 1955, pp. 191 and 192.

or explain something. Methodology is a study of methods; it offers theories about what men are doing when they are at work at their studies. Since there may be many methods, methodology tends necessarily to be rather general in character and, accordingly, does not usually—although of course it may—provide specific procedures for men at study. Epistomology is still more general than methodology, for its practitioners are occupied with the grounds and the limits, in brief, the character, of 'knowledge.' Contemporary epistemologists have tended to take their signals from what they believe to be the methods of modern physics. Having tended to ask and to answer general questions about knowledge in terms of their understanding of this science, they have in effect become philosophers of physics. Some natural scientists seem interested in this philosophical work, some seem merely amused; some agree with the current model most philosophers accept, some do not—and it is to be suspected that very many working scientists are quite unaware of it.

Physics, we are told, has arrived at a condition in which problems of rigorous and exact experimentation can be derived from rigorous and mathematical theory. It did not arrive at this condition because epistomologists set forth such an interplay within a model of inquiry that they had constructed. The sequence would seem to have been the other way around: the epistomology of science is parasitical upon the methods that physicists, theoretical and experimental, come to use.

Polykarp Kusch, Nobel Prize-winning physicist, has declared that there is no 'scientific method,' and that what is called by that name can be outlined for only quite simple problems. Percy Bridgman, another Nobel Prize-winning physicist, goes even further: 'There is no scientific method as such, but the vital feature of the scientist's procedure has been merely to do his utmost with his mind, *no holds barred.*' 'The mechanics of discovery,' William S. Beck remarks, 'are not known. . . I think that the creative process is so closely tied in with the emotional structure of an individual . . . that . . . it is a poor subject for generalization. . . .' [4]

[4] William S. Beck, *Modern Science and the Nature of Life,* New York, Harcourt, Brace, 1957.

3

Specialists in method tend also to be specialists in one or another species of social philosophy. The important point about them, in sociology today, is not that they are specialists, but that one of the results of their specialty is to further the process of specialization within the social sciences as a whole. Moreover, they further it in accordance with the methodological inhibition and in terms of the research institute in which it may be embodied. Theirs is not a proposal for any scheme of topical specialization according to 'intelligible fields of study' or a conception of problems of social structure. It is a proposed specialization based solely on use of The Method, regardless of content, problem, or area. These are not stray impressions; they are readily documented.

The most explicit and straightforward statement of abstracted empiricism as a style of work, and of the role within social science which the abstracted empiricist should perform, has been made by Paul F. Lazarsfeld, who is among the more sophisticated spokesmen of this school.[5]

Lazarsfeld defines 'sociology' as a specialty, not in terms of any methods peculiar to *it*, but in terms of its being the methodological specialty. In this view, the sociologist becomes the methodologist of all the social sciences.

'This then is the first function of the sociologist, which we can make fairly explicit. He is so to say the *pathfinder* of the advancing army of social scientists, when a new sector of human affairs is about to become an object of empirical scientific investigations. It is the sociologist who takes the first steps. He is the bridge between the social philosopher, the individual observer and commentator on the one hand and the organized team work of the empirical investigators and analyzers on the other hand ... historically speaking we then have to distinguish

[5] 'What Is Sociology?' Universitets Studentkontor, Skrivemaskinstua, Oslo, September, 1948 (mimeo). This paper was written for and delivered to a group of people who sought general guidance in setting up a research institution. Accordingly it is most suitable for my present purposes, being brief, clear, and authoritative. More elaborate and elegant statements can of course be found, for example, in *The Language of Social Research*, edited by Lazarsfeld and Rosenberg, Glencoe, Illinois, The Free Press, 1955.

three major ways of looking at social subject matters: social analysis as practiced by the individual observer; organized fullfledged empirical sciences; and a transitory phase which we call the sociology of any special area of social behavior... It should be helpful at this point to insert some comments on what is going on at the time of such a transition from social philosophy to empirical sociology.' [6]

'The individual observer,' please note, is curiously equated with the 'social philosopher.' Note also that this is a statement not only of an intellectual program but also of an administrative plan: 'Certain areas of human behavior have become the object of organized social sciences which have names, institutes, budgets, data, personnel, and so on. Other areas have been left undeveloped in this respect.' Any area can be developed or 'sociologized.' For example: 'As a matter of fact we don't even have a name for a social science which would be concerned with the happiness of the population. But there is nothing which would make such a science impossible. It would not be more difficult and not even more expensive to collect happiness ratings than to collect data on income, savings and prices.'

Sociology, then, as mid-wife to a series of specialized 'social sciences' stands between any topical area that has not yet become the object of The Method and 'the fully developed social sciences.' It is not altogether clear what are considered 'the fully developed social sciences,' but it is implied that only demography and economics qualify: 'No one will doubt any more that it is necessary and possible to deal with human affairs in a scientific way. For 100 or more years we have had fully developed sciences like economics and demography, which deal with various sectors of human behavior.' I find no other specifications of 'full-fledged social sciences' in the twenty pages of this essay.

When sociology is assigned the task of converting philosophy into sciences, it is assumed or implied that the genius of The Method is such that it does not require traditional scholarly knowledge of the area to be converted. Surely such knowledge would require a little more time than is implied in this statement. Perhaps what is meant is made clear by a chance remark about

[6] Ibid. pp. 4-5.

political science: '... The Greeks had a science of politics, the Germans talk of *Staatslehr* and the Anglosaxons of political science. No one has yet made a good content analysis so that one could really know what the books in this field deal with ...' [7]

Here, then, are the organized teams of full-fledged, empirical social scientists; there are the unorganized, individual social philosophers. As The Methodologist, the sociologist converts the latter into the former. He is, in short, the science-maker, at once intellectual, or rather, Scientific, and administrative.

'The transition [from 'social philosophies' and 'the individual observer' to 'organised, full-fledged empirical science'] is usually characterized by four turns in the work of the students concerned.'

(1) 'There is first the shift of emphasis from the history of institutions and ideas to the concrete behavior of peoples.' This is not quite so simple; abstracted empiricism, as we shall see in chapter 6, is not everyday empiricism. 'The concrete behavior of people' is not its unit of study. Presently I shall show that in practice the choice that is involved often reveals a distinct tendency to what is called 'psychologism,' and, moreover, a persistent avoidance of problems of structure in favor of those of milieux.

(2) 'There is secondly,' Lazarsfeld continues, 'a tendency not to study one sector of human affairs alone but to relate it to other sectors.' This I do not believe is true; to see that it is not, one need only compare the productions of Marx or Spencer or Weber with those of any abstracted empiricist. What is probably meant, however, rests on a special meaning of 'relate': it is confined to the statistical.

(3) 'There is third a preference for studying social situations and problems which repeat themselves rather than those which occur only once.' This might be thought an attempt to point toward structural considerations, for 'repetitions' or 'regularities' of social life are, of course, anchored in established structures. That is why to understand, for example, American political cam-

---

[7] Ibid. p. 5. 'A content analysis of a set of materials consists essentially of classifying small units of the documents (words, sentences, themes) according to some set of *a priori* categories.' Peter H. Rossi, 'Methods of Social Research, 1945-55,' *Sociology in the United States of America,* edited by Hans L. Zetterberg, Paris, France, UNESCO, 1956, p. 33.

paigns one needs to understand the structure of parties, their roles within the economy, etc. But this is not what is meant by Lazarsfeld; what is meant is that elections require many people to engage in a similar act, and that elections recur: hence the voting behavior of individuals may be studied statistically, and re-studied, and re-studied.

(4) 'And finally there is a greater emphasis on contemporary rather than on historical social events...' This a-historical emphasis is due to an epistomological preference: '...The sociologist will therefore have a tendency to deal mainly with contemporaneous events for which he is likely to get the kind of data he needs...' Such an epistomological bias stands in contrast with the formulation of substantive problems as the orienting point of work in social science.[8]

Before considering these points further I must complete my report of this statement of sociology, which is conceived to have two further tasks:

... sociological research consists in applying scientific procedures to new areas. They [Lazarsfeld's observations] are just designed to characterize crudely the atmosphere which is likely to prevail during the transition from social philosophy to empirical social research... As a sociologist starts to study new sectors of human affairs, he has to collect the data he wants all by himself... It is in connection with this situation that the second major function of the sociologist has developed. He is at the moment something of a *toolmaker* for the other social sciences. Let me remind you of a few of the many problems the social scientist meets when he has to collect his own data. Very often he has to ask people themselves what they did or saw or wanted. This people often won't remember easily; or they are reluctant to tell us; or they don't exactly understand what we want to know. Thus the important and difficult art of interviewing has developed...
... But [the sociologist] has had historically still a third function as an *interpreter* ... it is helpful to distinguish between the description and the interpretation of social relationships. On the interpretative level we would mainly raise questions which every day language covers by the word 'why.' Why do people have less children now than before? Why do they have a tendency to move from the country to the city? Why are elections won or lost? ...

[8] All quotations in the above paragraphs are from Lazarsfeld, op. cit., pp. 5-6.

The basic techniques of finding such explanations are statistical. We have to compare families who have many and who have few children; we have to compare workers who often stay away from work with those who come regularly. But *what* about them should we compare? [9]

The sociologist seems suddenly to assume a truly encyclopedic posture: Every division of social science contains interpretations and theories, but here we are told that 'interpretation' and 'theory' are the sociologist's domain. What is meant becomes clear when we realize that these other interpretations are not yet scientific. The kinds of 'interpretations' with which the sociologist is to work, as he transforms philosophies into sciences, are 'interpretive variables' useful in statistical inquiry. Moreover, note the tendency to reduce sociological realities to psychological variables, in the immediate continuation of the above quotation: 'We have to assume that there is something in the personality, experience and the attitude of people, which makes them act differently in what seem from the outside to be the same situations. What is needed is explanatory ideas and conceptions which can be tested by empirical research . . .'

'Social theory' as a whole becomes a systematic collection of such concepts, that is, of variables useful in interpretations of statistical findings:

We do call these concepts sociological *because* they apply to many varieties of social behavior. . . We assign to the sociologist the task to collect and analyze these concepts, which are useful for the interpretation of empirical results found in specific areas like the analysis of price or crime or suicide or voting statistics. Sometimes the term social theory is used for a systematic presentation of such concepts and their interrelationships. [10]

It is not, I must note in passing, altogether clear whether this statement as a whole is a theory of the historical role that sociologists have actually played—in which case it is surely inadequate; or whether it is merely a suggestion that sociologists ought to be technicians-as-midwives and keepers of the interpretation of everything—in which case, of course, any sociologist is free to

[9] Ibid. pp. 7-8, 12-13.
[10] Ibid. p. 17.

decline the invitation in the interests of his own substantive problems. But is it fact or precept, statement or program?

Perhaps it is propaganda for a philosophy of technique and an
admiration for administrative energy, disguised as part of the
natural history of science.

This conception of the sociologist, well housed in research institutes, as science-maker, tool-maker, and keeper of the interpretations—as well as the whole style of work, of which this is the
clearest statement I know—involves several problems which I
shall now take up more systematically.

4

There are two current apologies for abstracted empiricism
which, if accepted, would mean that the thinness of its result is
due less to any feature inherent in The Method than to causes
of an 'accidental nature,' namely, money and time.

It might, first, be said that as such studies are usually quite expensive, they have had to be shaped by some concern for the
problems of the interests that have paid for them; and moreover,
that the aggregate of these interests has had rather scattered
problems. Accordingly, the researchers have not been able to
select problems in such a way as to allow a true accumulation of
results—that is, one that would add up in a more significant way.
They have done the best they could; they could not be concerned
with a fruitful series of substantive problems, so they have had to
specialize in developing methods that could be put to work regardless of the substantive issues.

In brief, the economics of truth—the costs of research—seem to
conflict with the politics of truth—the use of research to clarify
significant issues and to bring political controversy closer to realities. The conclusion is that if only social research institutions had,
say, 25 per cent of the total scientific funds of the nation and if
they were free to do with this money as they like, things would be
ever so much better. I must admit that I do not know whether or
not this is a reasonable expectation. Nor does anyone else, although it must be the conviction of the administrative intellectuals
among us who have frankly given up work in social science for
promotional activities. But to take this as *the* issue would be to

eliminate the relevance of any intellectual criticism. One thing, moreover, is surely clear: because of the expensiveness of The Method, its practitioners have often become involved in the commercial and bureaucratic uses of their work, and this indeed has affected their style.

It might be thought, secondly, that critics are merely impatient, and I am aware of magisterial discourse about 'the requirements of science' being on the order of centuries rather than decades. It might be said that 'in due course' such studies will accumulate in such a way as to permit significant results about society to be generalized from them. This line of justification, it seems to me, assumes a view of the development of social science as a strange building-block endeavor. It assumes that such studies as these are by their nature capable of being 'units' which at some point in the future can be 'added up' or 'fitted together' to 'build up' a reliable and verified image of some whole. It is not merely an assumption; it is an explicit policy. 'Empirical sciences,' Lazarsfeld asserts, 'have to work on specific problems and build up broader knowledge by putting together the results of many minute, careful, and time-consuming investigations. It is certainly desirable that more students turn to social sciences. But not because this will save the world overnight; it is rather because this will somewhat accelerate the hard task of developing in the end an integrated social science, which can help us to understand and control social affairs.' [11]

Ignoring for the moment its political ambiguities, the program suggested is to narrow the work to 'minute' investigations on the assumption that their findings can be 'put together,' and that this, in turn, will be 'an integrated social science.' To explain why this is an inadequate view, I must go beyond extrinsic reasons for the thinness of result achieved by these researchers, and turn to reasons inherent in their style and program.

My first point has to do with the relation between theory and research, with the policy social scientists should adopt about

[11] Op. cit. p. 20.

the priority of larger conceptions and of areas for detailed exposition.

There is of course much generous comment in all schools of social science about the blindness of empirical data without theory and the emptiness of theory without data. But we do better to examine the practice and its results, as I am trying to do here, than the philosophical embroidery. In the more forthright statements, such as Lazarsfeld's, the working ideas of 'theory' and of 'empirical data' are made quite plain: 'Theory' becomes the variables useful in interpreting statistical findings; 'empirical data,' it is strongly suggested and made evident in practice, are restricted to such statistically determined facts and relations as are numerous, repeatable, measurable. With both theory and data so restricted, the generosity of comment about their interplay appears to shrink to a miserly acknowledgment, in fact, to no acknowledgment at all. There are no philosophical grounds, and certainly no grounds in the work of social science, as I have already indicated, so to restrict these terms.

To check and to re-shape a broad conception, one must have detailed expositions, but the detailed expositions cannot necessarily be put together to constitute a broad conception. What should one select for detailed exposition? What are the criteria for selection? And what does 'put together' mean? It is not so mechanical a task as the easy phrase makes it seem. We speak of the interplay of broader conception and detailed information (theory and research), but we must also speak of problems. The problems of social science are stated in terms of conceptions that usually relate to social-historical structures. If we take such problems as real, then it does seem foolish to undertake any detailed studies of smaller-scale areas before we have good reason to believe that, whatever the results, they will permit us to draw inferences useful in solving or clarifying problems of structural significance. We are not 'translating' such problems when we merely assume a perspective in which all problems are seen as a scatter of requests for scattered information, statistical or otherwise, about a scatter of individuals and their scattered milieux.

So far as ideas are concerned, you seldom get out of any truly detailed research more than you have put into it. What you get out of empirical research as such is information, and what you can do with this information depends a great deal upon whether or not in the course of your work you have selected your specific empirical studies as check points of larger constructions. As the science-maker goes about transforming social philosophies into empirical sciences, and erecting research institutions in which to house them, a vast number of studies result. There is, in truth, no principle or theory that guides the selection of what is to be the subject of these studies. 'Happiness,' as we have seen, might be one; marketing behavior, another. It is merely assumed that if only The Method is used, such studies as result—scattered from Elmira to Zagreb to Shanghai—will add up finally to a 'full-fledged, organized' science of man and society. The practice, in the meantime, is to get on with the next study.

In contending that these studies probably cannot be 'added up' to more significant results, I am taking into account the theory of society toward which abstracted empiricism actually tends. Any style of empiricism involves a metaphysical choice—a choice as to what is most real—and now we must see something of the choice required by this particular style. A rather convincing case, I believe, might be made for the contention that these studies are very often examples of what is known as psychologism.[12] The argument might be based on the fact that their fundamental source of information is a sample of individuals. The questions asked in these studies are put in terms of the psychological reactions of individuals. Accordingly, the assumption is required that the institutional structure of society, in so far as it is to be

[12] 'Psychologism' refers to the attempt to explain social phenomena in terms of facts and theories about the make-up of individuals. Historically, as a doctrine, it rests upon an explicit metaphysical denial of the reality of social structure. At other times, its adherents may set forth a conception of structure which reduces it, so far as explanations are concerned, to a set of milieux. In a still more general way, and of more direct interest to our concern with the current research policies of social science, psychologism rests upon the idea that if we study a series of individuals and their milieux, the results of our studies in some way can be added up to knowledge of social structure.

studied in this way, can be understood by means of such data about individuals.

To become aware of problems of structure, and of their explanatory significance for even individual behavior, requires a much broader style of empiricism. For example, within the structure of even American society—and especially of one American town at one time, which is usually the 'sample area'—there are so many common denominators, social and psychological, that the variety of conduct which social scientists must take into account is simply not available. That variety, and hence the very formulation of problems, becomes available only when our view is broadened to include comparative and historical social structures. Yet because of epistemological dogma, abstracted empiricists are systematically a-historical and non-comparative; they deal with small-scale areas and they incline to psychologism. Neither in defining their problems nor in explaining their own microscopic findings do they make any real use of the basic idea of historical social structure.

Even as studies of milieux, such research cannot be expected to be very perceptive. By definition, as well as on the basis of our studies, we know that the causes of many changes in milieux are often unknown to the people (the interviewees) in specific milieux, and that these changes can be understood only in terms of structural transformations. This general view, of course, is the polar opposite of psychologism. Its implications for our methods seem clear and simple: the selection of milieux for detailed study ought to be made in accordance with problems of structural significance. The kinds of 'variables' to be isolated and observed within milieux ought to be those that have been found to be important by our examination of structure. There should of course be a two-way interaction between studies of milieux and studies of structure. The development of social science cannot very well be thought of as resulting from a scattered group of women each making a part of some great quilt: the little pieces, no matter how precisely defined, are not to be so mechanically and so externally linked.

But it is not at all unusual, in the practice of abstracted empiricists, to 'get the data' and 'run it' through a more or less stand-ardized statistical analysis, usually conducted by semi-skilled analysts. Then a sociologist is hired, or even a series of them, 'really to analyze it.' Which brings me to my next point.

Among abstracted empiricists, there is a recent tendency to preface empirical studies with a chapter or two in which they summarize 'the literature of the problem.' This is of course a good sign and is, I think, in some part a response to criticism from the established social disciplines. But in actual practice this work is all too often done after the data are collected and 'written up.' Furthermore, since it requires considerable time and patience, in the busy research institutions it is often given over to the busy assistant. The memorandum which he produces is then reshaped in an effort to surround the empirical study with 'theory' and to 'give it meaning,' or—as is frequently said—to 'get a better story out of it.' Even this, perhaps, is better than nothing. But it does often mislead the outsider who may hastily assume that this particular empirical study was selected and designed and executed in such a way as empirically to test broader conceptions or assumptions.

I do not believe that this is the usual practice. It could, in fact, become usual only in the hands of men who took seriously 'the literature' of social science—on its own terms and for long enough to grasp the conceptions and theories and problems it contains. Only then would it be conceivable that, without abandonment of the problems and conceptions, their meanings could be trans-lated into more specific and smaller scale problems readily amenable to The Method. Such translation, of course, is what all working social scientists do, although they do not confine the term 'empirical' to abstracted, statistical information about a series of contemporary individuals, or 'theory' to a collection of 'interpretative variables.'

Interesting tricks are used in such discussion. Studies of the type I am examining, when analyzed from a logical standpoint, reveal that the 'interesting concepts' used to interpret and explain 'the data' almost always point to: (1) structural and historical 'factors' above the level made available by the interview; (2)

psychological 'factors' below the depth open to the interviewer. But the important point is that conceptions neither of structure nor of psychological depth are typically among the terms with which the research has been formulated and 'the data' collected. These terms may point in a gross way in one or the other of these directions, but they are not among those specific and 'clean' variables which are duly accredited by this style of work.

The main reason for this seems clear: in practice, the more or less set interview—the basic source of information—usually requires a curious sort of social behaviorism. Given the administrative and financial facts of research, this is almost inevitable. For is it not obvious that interviewers at best semi-skilled cannot obtain—in fact, no one regardless of skill can obtain—in a twenty-minute or even a day-long interview the kinds of depth materials which we know, from the most skilled and prolonged interviews, are there to be gotten? [13] Nor is it possible to obtain by the usual sort of sample survey the kind of information on structure which we know is available from studies properly oriented to history.

Yet conceptions of structure and of depth psychology are dragged into studies in the abstracted empirical style. Particular observations are explained by appealing *ad hoc* to general conceptions. General conceptions are used to formulate structural or psychological problems for the 'front-end' of 'the write-up' of a study.

In some research shops the term 'bright' is sometimes used when detailed facts or relations are persuasively 'explained' by broader suppositions. When minute variables, whose meanings are stretched, are used to explain broad questions, the result may be referred to as 'cute.' I mention this to indicate that there is emerging a 'shop language' to cover the procedures I am reporting.

[13] In passing I must note that one reason for the thin formality or even emptiness of these fact-cluttered studies is that they contain very little or no direct observation by those who are in charge of them. The 'empirical facts' are facts collected by a bureaucratically guided set of usually semi-skilled individuals. It has been forgotten that social observation requires high skill and acute sensibility; that discovery often occurs precisely when an imaginative mind sets itself down in the middle of social realities.

What all this amounts to is the use of statistics to illustrate general points and the use of general points to illustrate statistics. The general points are neither tested nor made specific. They are adapted to the figures, as the arrangement of the figures is adapted to them. The general points and explanations can be used with other figures too; and the figures can be used with other general points. These logical tricks are used to give apparent structural and historical and psychological meaning to studies which by their very style of abstraction have eliminated such meanings. In the ways indicated, as well as in others, it is possible to cling to The Method and yet attempt to cover up the triviality of its results.

Examples of such procedures are available quite usually in the lead paragraphs of given chapters, in 'the general introductions,' and sometimes in an 'interpretative' chapter or section which is 'spliced in.' My purpose here cannot be the detailed examination of given studies; I wish only to alert the reader in such a way that he will sharpen his own examination of studies.

The point is simply this: Social research of any kind is advanced by ideas; it is only disciplined by fact. That is just as true of abstracted empirical surveys of 'why people vote as they do' as it is of an historian's account of the position and outlook of the nineteenth-century Russian intelligentsia. The ritual of the first is usually more elaborate and certainly more pretentious. The logical status of the result is not different.

There is, finally, one explanation of abstracted empiricism's usual thinness of result that may best be put as a question: Is there any necessary tension between that which is true but unimportant, and that which is important but not necessarily true? A better way to ask the question is: For what level of verification ought workers in social science be willing to settle? We could of course become so exacting in our demands that we should necessarily have nothing but very detailed exposition; we could also become so inexacting that we should have only very grand conceptions indeed.

Those in the grip of the methodological inhibition often refuse to say anything about modern society unless it has been through the fine little mill of The Statistical Ritual. It is usual to say that what they produce is true even if unimportant. I do not agree with this; more and more I wonder how true it is. I wonder how much exactitude, or even pseudo-precision, is here confused with 'truth'; and how much abstracted empiricism is taken as the only 'empirical' manner of work. If you have ever seriously studied, for a year or two, some thousand hour-long interviews, carefully coded and punched, you will have begun to see how very malleable the realm of 'fact' may really be. Moreover, as for 'importance,' surely it is important when some of the most energetic minds among us use themselves up in the study of details because The Method to which they are dogmatically committed does not allow them to study anything else. Much of such work, I am now convinced, has become the mere following of a ritual— which happens to have gained commercial and foundation value —rather than, in the words of its spokesmen, a 'commitment to the hard demands of science.'

Precision is not the sole criterion for choice of method; certainly precision ought not to be confused, as it so often is, with 'empirical' or 'true.' We should be as accurate as we are able to be in our work upon the problems that concern us. But no method, as such, should be used to delimit the problems we take up, if for no other reason than that the most interesting and difficult issues of *method* usually begin where established techniques do not apply.

If we have a sense of real problems, as they arise out of history, the question of truth and significance tends to answer itself: we should work on such problems as carefully and as exactly as we can. The important work in social science has usually been, and usually is, carefully elaborated hypotheses, documented at key points by more detailed information. There is, in fact, no other way, at least as yet, to confront the topics and themes that are widely acknowledged as important.

What is meant by the demand that our studies be concerned with important, or as it is more usually put, significant, problems? Significant for what? At this point it must be said that I do not mean merely that they should have political or practical or moral meaning—in any of the senses that may be given to any such terms. What we should mean in the first instance is that they should have genuine relevance to our conception of a social structure and to what is happening within it. By 'genuine relevance' I mean that our studies be logically connected with such conceptions. And by 'logically connected' I mean that there is an open and clear shuttle between broader expositions and more detailed information, within the problem phase, and within the explanatory phase of our work. The political meaning of 'significant' I shall take up later. In the meantime, surely it is evident that an empiricism as cautious and rigid as abstracted empiricism eliminates the great social problems and human issues of our time from inquiry. Men who would understand these problems and grapple with these issues will then turn for enlightenment to other ways of formulating beliefs.

5

The specific methods—as distinct from the philosophy—of empiricism are clearly suitable and convenient for work on many problems, and I do not see how anyone could reasonably object to such use of them. We can of course, by suitable abstraction, be exact about anything. Nothing is inherently immune to measurement.

If the problems upon which one is at work are readily amenable to statistical procedures, one should always try to use them. If, for example, in working out a theory of elites, we need to know the social origins of a group of generals, naturally we try to find out the proportions coming from various social strata. If we need to know the extent to which the real income of white-collar people has gone up or down since 1900, we run a time-series of income by occupation, controlled in terms of some price index. No one, however, need accept such procedures, when generalized, as the only procedure available. Certainly no one need accept this model as a total canon. It is not the only empirical manner.

We should choose particular and minute features for intensive and exact study in accordance with our less exact view of the whole, and in order to solve problems having to do with structural wholes. It is a choice made according to the requirements of our problems, not a 'necessity' that follows from an epistomological dogma.

I do not suppose that anyone has a right to object to detailed studies of minor problems. The narrowed focus they require might be part of an admirable quest for precision and certainty; it might also be part of a division of intellectual labor, of a specialization to which, again, no one ought to object. But surely we are entitled to ask: If it is claimed that these studies are parts of some division of labor which as a whole constitutes the social science endeavor, where are the other divisions of which these studies are parts? And where is the 'division' wherein just such studies as these are put into some larger picture?

Practitioners of almost all styles of work, it should be noted, tend to use similar slogans. Everyone counting outhouses (and this old joke is by no means only a joke) is today very much aware of his conceptual implications; everyone elaborating distinctions (and many are doing just that) is altogether aware of 'the paradigm of empirical verification.' It is commonly recognized that any systematic attempt to understand involves some kind of alternation between (empirical) intake and (theoretical) assimilation, that concepts and ideas ought to guide factual investigation, and that detailed investigations ought to be used to check up on and re-shape ideas.

What has happened in the methodological inhibition is that men have become stuck, not so much in the empirical intake, as in what are essentially epistomological problems of method. Since many of these men, especially the younger, do not know very much about epistomology, they tend to be quite dogmatic about the one set of canons that dominate them.

What has happened in the fetishism of the Concept is that men have become stuck way up on a very high level of generalization, usually of a syntactical nature, and they cannot get down to fact. Both of these tendencies or schools exist and flourish within what ought to be pauses in the working process of social science. But in them what ought to be a little pause has become, if I may put it so, the entrance into fruitlessness.

Intellectually these schools represent abdications of classic social science. The vehicle of their abdication is pretentious over-elaboration of 'method' and 'theory'; the main reason for it is their lack of firm connection with substantive problems. Were the rise and fall of doctrines and methods due altogether to some purely intellectual competition among them (the more adequate and fruitful winning out, the less adequate and less fruitful falling by the wayside), grand theory and abstracted empiricism would not have gained such ascendancy as they have. Grand theory would be a minor tendency among philosophers—and perhaps something young academic men go through; abstracted empiricism would be one theory among philosophers of science, and as well a useful accessory among the several methods of social inquiry.

Were there nothing else but these two, standing supreme and alongside each other, our condition would indeed be a sad one: As practices, they may be understood as insuring that we do not learn too much about man and society—the first by formal and cloudy obscurantism, the second by formal and empty ingenuity.

4

Types of Practicality

THE CONFUSION in the social sciences is moral as well as 'scientific,' political as well as intellectual. Attempts to ignore this fact are among the reasons for the continuing confusion. In order to judge the problems and methods of various schools of social science, we must make up our minds about a great many political values as well as intellectual issues, for we cannot very well state any problem until we know *whose* problem it is. A problem to one man is no problem at all to another; it depends upon what each is interested in, and upon how aware he is of his interests. Moreover, an unfortunate ethical issue arises: Men are not always interested in what is to their interests. Everyone is not so rational as social scientists often believe themselves to be. All of which means that by their work all students of man and society assume and imply moral and political decisions.

1

Work in social science has always been accompanied by problems of evaluation. The traditions of these sciences contain a long sequence of often dogmatic resolutions, much attempted straddling of fences, and also a number of well-reasoned and sensible views. Often the problem has not been faced directly at all but scattered answers merely assumed—or adopted—as in the applied sociology of the research technician available for hire. Such a practitioner does not, by the assumed neutrality of his techniques, escape this problem—in effect, he allows other types of men to solve it for him. But surely the intellectual craftsman

will try to do his work in awareness of its assumptions and implications, not the least of which are its moral and political meaning
for the society in which he works and for his role within that
society.

Agreement is now wide enough to make commonplace the
notion that one cannot infer judgments of value from statements
of fact or from definitions of conceptions. But this does not mean
that such statements and definitions are irrelevant to judgment.
It is easy to see that most social issues involve a tangled-up mess
of factual errors and unclear conceptions, as well as evaluative
bias. Only after they have been logically untangled is it possible
to know whether issues really do involve a conflict of values.

To determine whether or not such a conflict exists, and if it
does, to sort out fact from value, is of course one of the prime
tasks often assumed by social scientists. Such an untangling
sometimes leads readily to a re-statement of the issue in such a
way as to open it for solution, for it may reveal an inconsistency
of values held by the same interest: an emerging value cannot
be realized if an older one is not sacrificed, and so, in order to act,
the interested must get straight what it is they value most.

But when there are values so firmly and so consistently held
by genuinely conflicting interests that the conflict cannot be
resolved by logical analysis and factual investigation, then the
role of reason in that human affair seems at an end. We can clarify
the meaning and the consequences of values, we can make them
consistent with one another and ascertain their actual priorities,
we can surround them with fact—but in the end we may be reduced to mere assertion and counter-assertion; then we can only
plead or persuade. And at the very end, if the end is reached,
moral problems become problems of power, and in the last resort,
if the last resort is reached, the final form of power is coercion.

We cannot deduce—Hume's celebrated dictum runs—how we
ought to act from what we believe is. Neither can we deduce
how anyone else ought to act from how we believe we ought
to act. In the end, if the end comes, we just have to beat those
who disagree with us over the head; let us hope the end comes
seldom. In the meantime, being as reasonable as we are able to
be, we ought all to argue.

Values are involved in the selection of the problems we study; values are also involved in certain of the key conceptions we use in our formulation of these problems, and values affect the course of their solution. So far as conceptions are concerned, the aim ought to be to use as many 'value-neutral' terms as possible and to become aware of and to make explicit the value implications that remain. So far as problems are concerned, the aim ought to be, again, to be clear about the values in terms of which they are selected, and then to avoid as best one can evaluative bias in their solution, no matter where that solution takes one and no matter what its moral or political implications may be.

Certain types of critics, by the way, judge work in social science according to whether or not its conclusions are gloomy or sunshiny, negative or constructive. These sunshine moralists want a lyric upsurge, at least at the end: they are made happy by a sturdy little mood of earnest optimism, out of which we step forward fresh and shining. But the world we are trying to understand does not always make all of us politically hopeful and morally complacent, which is to say, that social scientists sometimes find it difficult to play the cheerful idiot. Personally, I happen to be a very optimistic type, but I must confess that I have never been able to make up my mind about whether something is so or not in terms of whether or not it leads to good cheer. First, one tries to get it straight, to make an adequate statement—if it is gloomy, too bad; if it leads to hope, fine. In the meantime, to cry for 'the constructive program' and 'the hopeful note' is often a sign of an incapacity to face facts as they are even when they are decidedly unpleasant—and it is irrelevant to truth or falsity and to judgments of proper work in social science.

The social scientist who spends his intellectual force on the details of small-scale milieux is not putting his work outside the political conflicts and forces of his time. He is, at least indirectly and in effect, 'accepting' the framework of his society. But no one who accepts the full intellectual tasks of social science can merely assume that structure. In fact, it is his job to make that structure explicit and to study it as a whole. To take on this job *is* his major judgment. And because there are so many falsifications of American society, merely to describe it neutrally is often considered a 'savage naturalism.' It is, of course, not very difficult to hide such values as the social scientist may assume or accept or imply. As we all know, an ungainly apparatus is at hand for that: much of the jargon of social science, and especially of sociology, results from the curious passion for the mannerism of the non-committed.

Whether he wants it or not, or whether he is aware of it or not, anyone who spends his life studying society and publishing the results *is* acting morally and usually politically as well. The question is whether he faces this condition and makes up his own mind, or whether he conceals it from himself and from others and drifts morally. Many, I should say most, social scientists in America today are easily or uneasily liberal. They conform to the prevailing fear of any passionate commitment. *This,* and not 'scientific objectivity,' is what is really wanted by such men when they complain about 'making value judgments.'

Teaching, by the way, I do not regard as altogether in the same case as writing. When one publishes a book it becomes a public property; the author's only responsibility to his reading public, if any, is to make it as good a book as he can and he is the final judge of that. But the teacher has further responsibilities. To some extent, students are a captive audience; and to some extent they are dependent upon their teacher, who is something of a model to them. His foremost job is to reveal to them as fully as he can just how a supposedly self-disciplined mind works. The art of teaching is in considerable part the art of thinking out loud but intelligibly. In a book the writer is often trying to persuade others of the result of his thinking; in a classroom the teacher ought to be trying to show others how one man thinks—and at the same time reveal what a fine feeling he gets when he does it well. The teacher ought then, it seems to me, to make very explicit the assumptions, the facts, the methods, the judgments. He ought not to hold back anything, but ought to take it very slowly and at all times repeatedly make clear the full range of moral alternatives before he gives his own choice. To write that way would be enormously dull, and impossibly self-conscious. That is one reason why very successful lectures usually do not print well.

It is difficult to be as optimistic as Kenneth Boulding, who writes: 'For all the attempts of our positivists to dehumanize the sciences of man, a moral science it remains.' But it is even more difficult not to agree with Lionel Robbins, who writes: 'It is not an exaggeration to say that, at the present day, one of the main dangers of civilization arises from the inability of minds trained in the natural sciences to perceive the difference between the economic and the technical.' [1]

2

In itself all this is nothing to upset one; it is widely acknowledged, even when it is not confronted. Nowadays social research is often of direct service to army generals and social workers, corporation managers and prison wardens. Such *bureaucratic use* has been increasing; no doubt it will continue to increase. Studies are also used—by social scientists and by other people—in *ideological ways*. In fact the ideological relevance of social science is inherent in its very existence as social fact. Every society holds images of its own nature—in particular, images and slogans that justify its system of power and the ways of the powerful. The images and ideas produced by social scientists may or may not be consistent with these prevailing images, but they always carry implications for them. In so far as these implications become known, they usually come to be argued over—and used:

By justifying the arrangement of power and the ascendancy of the powerful, images and ideas transform power into authority.

By criticizing or debunking prevailing arrangements and rulers, they strip them of authority.

By distracting attention from issues of power and authority, they distract attention from the structural realities of the society itself.

[1] I have taken these two quotes from Barzun and Graff, *The Modern Researcher*, New York, Harcourt, Brace, 1957, p. 217.

Such uses are not necessarily a matter of the intentions of social scientists. That is as it may be, yet it has been quite usual for social scientists to become aware of the political meanings of their work. If one of them does not, in this age of ideology, another is very likely to.

The demand for explicit ideological justifications has been greatly enlarged, if only because new institutions of enormous power have arisen but have not been legitimated, and because older powers have outrun their old sanctions. The power of the modern corporation, for example, is not automatically justified in terms of the liberal doctrines inherited from the eighteenth century that are the main line of legitimate authority in the United States. Every interest and power, every passion and bias, every hatred and hope tends to acquire an ideological apparatus with which to compete with the slogans and symbols, the doctrines and appeals of other interests. As public communications are expanded and speeded up, their effectiveness is worn out by repetition; so there is a continuous demand for new slogans and beliefs and ideologies. In this situation of mass communication and intensive public relations, it would indeed be strange were the social studies immune from the demand for ideological ammunition, and stranger still were social researchers to fail to provide it.

But whether the social scientist is aware of it or not, merely by working as a social scientist he is to some extent enacting a bureaucratic or an ideological role. Moreover, either role readily leads to the other. The use of the most formal research techniques for bureaucratic purposes easily leads to justifications of decisions presumably made on the basis of such research. In turn, ideological uses of the findings of social science readily become part of bureaucratic operations: nowadays attempts to make power legitimate, and to make specific policies palatable, are often very much a part of 'personnel administration' and 'public relations.'

Historically, social science has been used more ideologically than bureaucratically; even now that is probably so, although the balance often seems to be shifting. In some part, ideological uses have been due to the fact that so very much of modern social science has been a frequently unacknowledged debate with the work of Marx, and a reflection as well of the challenge of socialist movements and communist parties.

Classical economics has been the major ideology of capitalism as a system of power. In this, it has often been 'fruitfully misunderstood'—even as the work of Marx is used by Soviet publicists today. That economists have clung tenaciously to the metaphysics of natural law and the moral philosophy of utilitarianism has been made clear by the criticisms of classical and neo-classical doctrine set forth by historical and institutional schools of economics. But these schools themselves can be understood only by reference to conservative, liberal, or radical 'social philosophies.' Especially since the 'thirties, economists—having become advisers to governments and corporations—have set forth administrative techniques, pronounced upon policy, and established routines of detailed economic reportage. Very actively, although not always explicitly, all this involves ideological as well as bureaucratic use.

The present-day confusion of economics is a confusion involving questions of policy as well as of methods and views. Equally eminent economists pronounce quite contradictory views. Gardiner C. Means, for example, attacks his colleagues for clinging to 'eighteenth century' images of atomistic enterprises, and calls for a new model of the economy in which huge corporations make and control prices. Wassily Leontief, on the other hand, attacks the split among his colleagues into pure theorists and fact-grubbers, and calls for intricate schemes of input and output. But Colin Clark thinks such schemes 'pointlessly detailed and time-wasting analyses,' and calls upon economists to think about how to improve 'the material welfare of mankind'—and demands that taxes be reduced. Yet John K. Galbraith asserts that economists should stop being so concerned with increasing material welfare, that America is already too rich, and that to increase production still further is stupid. He calls upon his colleagues to demand that public services be increased and that taxes (indeed, sales taxes) be increased.[2]

[2] Compare the report on economists in *Business Week*, 2 August 1958, p. 48.

Even demography, a quite statistical specialty, has been deeply involved in the conflicts of policy and the factual controversies first aroused by Thomas Malthus. Many of these issues now center upon formerly colonial areas in which we find that, in several ways, cultural anthropology has been deeply concerned with the facts and the ethos of colonialism. From a liberal or a radical point of view, the economic and political problems of these countries are generally defined as the need for rapid economic progress—in particular, industrialization and all that this means. Anthropologists have generally joined the discussion with cautions which, like those of the old colonial powers, have seemed to avoid the upheaval and tensions that nowadays almost inevitably accompany change in underdeveloped areas. The content and history of cultural anthropology is of course not to be 'explained' by any facts of colonialism, although such facts are not irrelevant to it. It has also served liberal and even radical purposes, especially by its insistence upon the integrity of peoples of simpler societies, upon the social relativity of man's character, and by its anti-parochial propaganda among westerners.

Some historians seem eager to re-write the past in order to serve what can only be recognized as ideological purposes of the present. One current example is the American 're-appraisal' of the post-Civil War era of corporate and other business life. Examining carefully much American history of the last few decades, we have to realize that whatever history is or ought to be it easily becomes also a ponderous re-making of national and class myths. As new bureaucratic uses of social science have come about, there has been, especially since World War Two, an attempt to celebrate 'the historical meaning of America,' and in this celebration some historians have made history useful to the conservative mood and to its spiritual and material beneficiaries.

Political scientists, especially in dealing with international relations since World War Two, certainly cannot be accused of having examined United States policy with any oppositional vigor. Perhaps Professor Neal Houghton goes too far when he asserts that 'too much of what has been passing for political science scholarship has been little more than footnoted rationalization and huckstering of these policies,'[3] but the case he makes out cannot be set aside without very thorough examination. Neither can Professor Arnold Rogow's question: 'Whatever Happened to the Great Issues?'[4] be answered without realizing that much political science has of late been irrelevant to understanding important political realities, but not irrelevant to the scientific applauding of official policies and defaults.

I mention these few uses and implications neither in criticism nor in an attempt to prove bias. I do so merely to remind the reader that social science is inevitably relevant to bureaucratic routines and ideological issues, that this relevance is involved in the variety and confusion of the social sciences today, and that their political meanings might better be made explicit than left hidden.

3

In the last half of the nineteenth century, social science in the United States was directly linked with reform movements and betterment activities. What is known as 'the social science movement—organized in 1865 as 'the American Social Science Association'—was a late nineteenth-century attempt 'to apply science' to social problems without resort to explicit political tactics. Its members, in brief, sought to turn the troubles of lower-class people into issues for middle-class publics. By the early decades of the twentieth century, this movement had run its course. It did not remain the bearer of any radical middle-class ideology of reform; its larger urge to welfare was transformed into the limited concerns of social work, associated charities, child welfare, and prison reform. But out of 'The American Social Science Association,' there also arose the several professional associations, and in due course the several academic disciplines, of the social sciences.

Thus, what happened to the early middle-class sociology of reform is that it split, on the one hand into academic specialties,

[3] Speech to Western Political Science Association, 12 April 1958.
[4] *American Political Science Review*, September, 1957.

and on the other into more specific and institutional welfare activities. This split, however, did not mean that the academic specialties became morally neutral and scientifically antiseptic.

In the United States, liberalism has been the political common denominator of virtually all social study as well as the source of virtually all public rhetoric and ideology. This is widely recognized as due to well-known historical conditions, perhaps above all to the absence of feudalism and thus of an aristocratic basis for anti-capitalist elites and intellectuals. The liberalism of classical economics, which still shapes the outlook of important sections of the business elite, has been of continuous political use; even among the most sophisticated economic portrayals, the idea of balance or equilibrium is clung to mightily.

In a somewhat more diffuse way, liberalism has also informed sociology and political science. In contrast to their European forebears, American sociologists have tended strongly to take up one empirical detail, one problem of milieu, at a time. In a word, they have tended to scatter their attention. According to the 'democratic theory of knowledge' they have assumed all facts are created equal. Moreover, they have insisted that for any social phenomenon there surely must be a very great number of minute causes. Such 'pluralistic causation' as it is called, is quite serviceable to a liberal politics of 'piecemeal' reform. In fact, the idea that the causes of social events are necessarily numerous, scattered and minute, readily falls into the perspective of what may be called liberal practicality.[5]

If there is any one line of orientation historically implicit in American social science, surely it is the bias toward scattered studies, toward factual surveys and the accompanying dogma of a pluralist confusion of causes. These are essential features of liberal practicality as a style of social study. For if everything is caused by innumerable 'factors,' then we had best be very careful in any practical actions we undertake. We must deal with many details, and so it is advisable to proceed to reform this little piece and see what happens, before we reform that little

[5] Cf. Mills, 'The Professional Ideology of Social Pathologists,' *American Journal of Sociology*, September, 1943.

piece too. And surely we had better not be dogmatic and set forth too large a plan of action: We must enter the all-interacting flux with a tolerant awareness that we may well not yet know, and perhaps will never know, all the multiple causes at work. As social scientists of milieux, we must become aware of many little causes; to act intelligently, as practical men, we must be piecemeal reformers of milieux, one here and one there.

Walk carefully, someone must once have said, things are not so simple. If we break a society into tiny 'factors,' naturally we shall then need quite a few of them to account for something and we can never be sure that we have hold of them all. A merely formal emphasis upon 'the organic whole,' plus a failure to consider the adequate causes—which are usually structural—plus a compulsion to examine only one situation at a time—such ideas do make it difficult to understand the structure of the *status quo*. For the sake of balance, perhaps we should remind ourselves of other views:

First of all, is it not evident that 'principled pluralism' may be as dogmatic as 'principled monism'? Second, is it not possible to study causes without becoming overwhelmed? In fact, is not this just what social scientists ought to be doing when they examine social structure? By such studies, surely we are trying to find out the adequate causes of something, and having found them out, to open up a view of those strategic factors which as objects of political and administrative action offer men a chance to make reason available in the shaping of human affairs.

But in the 'organic' metaphysics of liberal practicality, whatever tends to harmonious balance is likely to be stressed. In viewing everything as a 'continuous process,' sudden changes of pace and revolutionary dislocations—so characteristic of our time—are missed, or, if not missed, merely taken as signs of the 'pathological,' the 'maladjusted.' The formality and the assumed unity implied by such innocent phrases as 'the mores' or 'the society' decrease the possibility of seeing what a modern social structure may be all about.

What are the reasons for the fragmentary character of liberal practicality? Why this sociology of scattered milieux? The curious division of academic departments may have helped social scientists fragment their problems. Sociologists in particular often seem to feel that representatives of older social sciences are not ready to admit that there is a place for sociology. Perhaps, like August Comte—and like such grand theorists as Talcott Parsons —sociologists have wanted something of their very own, quite distinct from economics and political science. But I do not believe that the restrictions of departments in academic struggle—or general lack of ability—is an altogether adequate explanation of liberal practicality's low level of abstraction and the accompanying failure of its adherents to consider problems of social structure.

Consider the publics for which so many books of sociology have been written: Most of the 'systematic' or 'theoretical' work in this discipline has been performed by teachers in textbooks for classroom purposes. The fact, just noted, that sociology has often won its academic right to existence in opposition to other departments may have increased the necessity for textbooks. Now, textbooks organize facts in order to make them available to youngsters, not around the growing points of research and discovery. Accordingly textbooks readily become a rather mechanical gathering of facts to illustrate more or less settled conceptions. The research possibilities of new ideas, the interplay of ideas and facts, are not usually considered very important in putting accumulated detail into some sort of textbook order. Old ideas and new facts are often more important than new ideas—which are often felt dangerously to restrict the number of 'adoptions' of a textbook for classroom use. In adopting or not adopting a text, professors judge it and so determine what is considered its success. After all, we must remember, it does take time to work up new lecture notes.

But who are the students for whom these books are written? They have been mainly middle-class youngsters; many of them— in the midwestern schools especially—of farm or small-business origin; and they are on their way to becoming professional people and junior executives. To write for them is to write for a rather specific kind of ascending, middle-class public. Author and public, teacher and student, have had similar social experience.

They share where they have come from, where they are going, and what might stand in their way.

In the older practical sociology of milieux, problems of politics are seldom radically considered. Liberal practicality tends to be a-political or to aspire to a kind of democratic opportunism. When its adherents touch upon something political, its 'pathological' features are usually stated in such terms as 'the anti-social,' or 'corruption.' In other contexts, 'the political' seems to be identified with the proper functioning of the political *status quo*, and is readily identified with law or administration. The political order itself is seldom examined; it is merely assumed as a quite fixed and distant framework.

Liberal practicality is congenial to people who by virtue of their social positions handle, usually with a degree of authority, a series of individual cases. Judges, social workers, mental hygienists, teachers, and local reformers tend to think in terms of 'situations.' Their outlook tends to be limited to existing standards, and their professional work tends to train them for an occupational incapacity to rise above a series of 'cases.' Their experience and the points of view from which each of them views society are too similar, too homogeneous, to permit the competition of ideas and the controversy of opinions which might lead to an attempt to construct the whole. Liberal practicality is a moralizing sociology of milieux.

The notion of 'cultural lag' is very much a part of this 'utopian' and progressive style of thought. The idea suggests the need to change something in order to 'bring it into line' with the state of progressive technology. Whatever is thought to be 'lagging' exists in the present, but its reasons-for-being are held to lie in the past. Judgments are thus disguised as statements about a time sequence. As an evaluative assertion of unequal 'progress,' cultural lag is of great use to men in a liberal and optative mood: it tells them what changes are 'called for,' and what changes 'ought' to have come about but have not. It tells them where they have made progress and where they have not done so well. The detection of a pathological 'lag' is, of course, somewhat complicated by the historical guise in which it is presented, and by the little programs that are so crudely shoved into such pseudo-objective phrases as 'called for.'

To state problems in terms of cultural lag is to disguise evaluations, but the more important question is: What kinds of evaluations have been readily used by the liberally practical? The idea that 'institutions' in general lag behind 'technology and science' in general is a very popular idea. It involves a positive evaluation of Science and of orderly progressive change; in brief, it is a liberal continuation of The Enlightenment with its full rationalism, its messianic and now politically naïve admiration of physical science as a model of thinking *and* action, and of the conception of time as progress. This notion of progress was carried into American colleges by the once prevalent Scottish moral philosophy. From after the Civil War until only a generation or so ago, the urban middle class of America was, in part, composed of men with expanding businesses, who were taking over instruments of production *and* gaining political power as well as social prestige. Many of the academic men of the older generation of sociologists were either recruited from these rising strata or actively mingled with them. Their students—the public of their thought—have been the products of such strata. Notions of progress, it has often been noted, are usually congenial to those who are rising in the scale of income and position.

Those who use the notion of cultural lag do not usually examine the positions of the interest groups and decision-makers which might be back of varying 'rates of change' in different areas of a society. One might say that in terms of the rates of change at which sectors of culture *could* move, it is often technology that is 'lagging.' Certainly that was the case during the 'thirties, and it is still very much the case in, for example, household technology and personal transportation.

In contrast to many sociologists' use of 'lag,' Thorstein Veblen's phrase 'lag, leak and friction' led him to a structural analysis of 'industry versus business.' He asked: where does 'the lag' pinch? And he attempted to reveal how the trained incapacity of businessmen acting in accordance with entrepreneurial canons resulted in an efficient sabotage of production and productivity. He

was also somewhat aware of the role of profit-making within a
system of private ownership, and he did not especially care for
the 'unworkman-like results.' But the great point is that he revealed the structural mechanics of 'the lag.' Many social scientists, however, use the politically washed-out notion of 'cultural
lag,' which has lost any such specific and structural anchorage:
they have generalized the idea in order to apply it to everything,
always in a fragmenting manner.

4

To detect practical problems is to make evaluations. Often
what is taken by the liberally practical to be a 'problem' is whatever (1) deviates from middle-class, small-town ways of life,
(2) is not in line with rural principles of stability and order, (3)
is not in concurrence with the optimistic progressive slogans of
'cultural lag,' and (4) does not conform with appropriate 'social
progress.' But in many ways the nub of liberal practicality is
revealed by (5) the notion of 'adjustment' and of its opposite,
'maladjustment.'

This notion is often left empty of any specific content; but often,
too, its content is in effect a propaganda for conformity to those
norms and traits ideally associated with the small-town middle
class. Yet these social and moral elements are masked by the
biological metaphor implied by the term 'adaptation'; in fact the
term is accompanied by an entourage of such socially bare terms
as 'existence' and 'survival.' The Concept of 'adjustment,' by biological metaphor, is made formal and universal. But the actual use
of the term often makes evident the acceptance of the ends and
the means of the smaller community milieux. Many writers
suggest techniques believed to be less disruptive than otherwise in order to attain goals as given; they do not usually
consider whether or not certain groups or individuals, caught in
underprivileged situations, can possibly achieve these goals without modification of the institutional framework as a whole.

The idea of adjustment seems most directly applicable to
a social scene in which, on the one hand, there is 'the society'
and, on the other, 'the individual immigrant.' The immigrant must
then 'adjust' to the society. The 'immigrant problem' was early

in the sociologist's center of attention, and the notions used to state it may well have become part of the general model for the formulation of all 'problems.'

From detailed examination of specific illustrations of maladjustment, it is easy to infer the type of person who is judged to be ideally 'adjusted':

The ideal man of the earlier generation of sociologists, and of the liberally practical in general, is 'socialized.' Often this means that he is the ethical opposite of 'selfish.' Being socialized, he thinks of others and is kindly toward them; he does not brood or mope; on the contrary, he is somewhat extrovert, eagerly 'participating' in the routines of his community, helping this community 'to progress' at a neatly adjustable rate. He is in and of and for quite a few community organizations. If not an outright 'joiner,' he certainly does get around a lot. Happily, he conforms to conventional morality and motives; happily, he participates in the gradual progress of respectable institutions. His mother and father were never divorced; his home never cruelly broken. He is 'successful,' at least in a modest way, since he is modestly ambitious; but he does not dwell upon matters too far above his means, lest he become a 'fantasy thinker.' As a proper little man, he does not scramble after the big money. Some of his virtues are very general, and then we cannot tell what they mean. But some are very specific, and then we come to know that the virtues of this adjusted man of local milieu correspond with the expected norms of the smaller, independent middle class verbally living out Protestant ideals in the small towns of America.

This pleasant little world of liberal practicality—I am ready to agree—must have existed somewhere, else surely it would have had to be invented. For its invention, no set of men seem more ideally suited than the rank and file of the last generation of American sociologists, and no conceptions more serviceable to the task than those of liberal practicality.

5

During the last several decades, alongside the older practicality a new kind has arisen—in fact, several new kinds. Liberalism has become less a reform movement than the administration of social services in a welfare state; sociology has lost its reforming push; its tendencies toward fragmentary problems and scattered causation have been conservatively turned to the use of corporation, army, and state. As such bureaucracies have become more dominant in the economic, the political, the military orders, the meaning of 'practical' has shifted: that which is thought to serve the purposes, of these great institutions is held to be 'practical.' [6]

Perhaps 'the human relations in industry' school will do as a brief example of the new illiberal practicality.[7] When we examine all the terms in 'the literature' of this style referring to managers and to workmen, we find that the managers are most frequently talked about along such lines as 'intelligent-unintelligent,' 'rational-irrational,' 'knowledge-ignorance'; whereas the workmen are talked about most frequently along such lines as 'happy-unhappy,' 'efficient-inefficient,' 'good morale-bad morale.' Much of the advice of these scholars—explicit and tacit—can be neatly summerized in this simple formula: To make the worker happy, efficient, and co-operative we need only make the managers intelligent, rational, knowledgeable. Is this the political formula of human relations in industry? If it is not, what else is involved? If it is, does not this formula, speaking practically, constitute a 'psychologizing' of the problems of industrial relations? Does it not rest upon the classic formulae of a natural harmony of interests, now unfortunately interfered with by the frailty of human relations, as revealed by the unintelligence of managers and the unhappy irrationality of workmen? To what extent is the advice, when summed up from these studies, advice to the personnel

[6] Even the specialty of 'social problems'—a major academic seat of liberal practicality—has reflected this shift from the old to the new practicality. The course in 'social disorganization' has not remained what it was. As of 1958, there is a more sophisticated awareness on the part of its practitioners of the values in which they deal. Politically the field has become, to some extent, part of the general ideology and one of the critical pressure groups and administrative adjuncts of the welfare state.

[7] For a detailed account of 'The Mayo School,' see Mills, 'The Contributions of Sociology to Studies of Industrial Relations,' in *Proceedings of First Annual Meeting of Industrial Relations Research Association*, Cleveland, Ohio, 1948.

manager to relax his authoritative manner and widen his manipulative grip over the employees by understanding them better and countering their informal solidarities against management in order to secure smoother and less troublesome managerial efficiency? All this is brought into quite sharp focus by the Concept of morale.

Work in modern industry is work within a hierarchy: there is a line of authority and hence, from the under-side, a line of obedience. A great deal of work is semi-routine—which means that for higher output the operations of each worker are slivered and stereotyped. If we combine these two facts—the hierarchical nature of the industrial structure and the semi-routine character of much of the work—it becomes evident that work in a modern factory involves discipline: quick and rather stereotyped obedience to authority. The factor of power, so coyly handled by human relations experts, is thus central to an adequate understanding of problems of morale.

Since factories, after all, are places where work is done, as well as social relations formed, to define morale we must consider both objective and subjective criteria. *Subjectively*, morale would seem to mean a willingness to do the work at hand, to do it with good cheer and even to enjoy doing it. *Objectively*, morale would seem to mean that the work gets done effectively, that the most work is done in the least time with the least trouble for the least money. Accordingly, morale in a modern American factory has to do with cheerful obedience on the part of the worker, resulting in efficient prosecution of the work at hand, as judged by the management.

Any clear notion of 'morale' requires that the values used as criteria be stated. Two relevant values would seem to be the cheerfulness or satisfaction of the worker, and the extent of his power to determine the course of his work life. If we broaden our consideration a bit, we will remember that there is one kind of 'morale' characteristic of the self-managing craftsman who participates in decisions about his work and is happy to do so. Here is the Adam Smith-Jeffersonian unalienated man, or as Whitman called him, 'man in the open air.' We will also remember that all the assumptions required to imagine such a man have been made absurd by the introduction of a large-scale hierarchical organization of work. Classic socialism, in point of fact, can be deduced, in rather strict logic, from classic liberalism by the introduction of this one factor. A second type, then, of 'morale' may be projected, and in fact has been, in classic notions of 'workers' control.' It is the form imagined for unalienated man under the objective conditions of large-scale collective work.

In contrast to both these types the 'morale' of the human relations expert is the morale of a worker who is powerless but nevertheless cheerful. Of course a very great variety of people fall into this category, but the point is that without changing the structure of power, no collective craftsmanship or self-direction is possible. The morale projected by the 'human relations' experts is the morale of men who are alienated but who have conformed to managed or conventional expectations of 'morale.' Assuming that the existing framework of industry is unalterable and that the aims of the managers are the aims of everyone, the experts of 'human relations' do not examine the authoritarian structure of modern industry and the role of the worker in it. They define the problem of morale in very limited terms, and by their techniques seek to reveal to their managerial clients how they can improve employee morale within the existing framework of power. Their endeavor is manipulative. They would allow the employee to 'blow off steam' without changing the structure within which he is to live out his working life. What they have 'discovered' is: (1) that within the authoritative structure of modern industry ('formal organization') there are status formations ('informal organizations'); (2) that often these resist the authorities and operate to protect the workers against the exercise of authority; (3) that therefore, for the sake of efficiency and to ward off 'uncollaborative' tendencies (unions and worker solidarity), managers should not try to break up these formations but rather should try to exploit them for their own ends ('in the collective purposes of the total organization'); and (4) that this might be done by recognizing and studying them, in order to manipulate the workers involved in them rather than merely authoritatively order them. In a word, the human relations experts have extended the general tendency for modern society to be rationalized in an intelligent way and in the service of a managerial elite.[8]

6

The new practicality leads to new images of social science—and of social scientists. New institutions have arisen in which this illiberal practicality is installed: industrial relations centers, research bureaus of universities, new research branches of corporation, air force and government. They are not concerned with the battered human beings living at the bottom of society—the bad boy, the loose woman, the migrant worker, the un-Americanized immigrant. On the contrary, they are connected, in fact and in fantasy, with the top levels of society, in particular, with enlightened circles of business executives and with generals having sizable budgets. For the first time in the history of their disciplines, social scientists have come into professional rela-

[8] It should not of course be supposed that social scientists have done no better with this area of investigation than the one school of human relations in industry. On the contrary, much excellent work has been done and more is currently under way. For example, the work of Charles E. Lindblom, John T. Dunlap, William Form, Delbert Miller, Wilbert Moore, V. L. Allen, Seymour Lipset, Ross Stagner, Arthur Kornhauser, William F. Whyte, Robert Dubin, Arthur M. Ross—to mention only a few.

One of the great nineteenth-century theses of social science is that in the evolution of modern capitalism people are moved by structural changes into a condition of powerlessness, and that simultaneously they become insurgent and demanding in psychological ways. Accordingly, the central line of historical development is projected: with the spread of rational awareness and knowledge, the worker will spring, in a new collective synthesis, from alienation into the morale of the triumphant proletariat. Karl Marx was quite right about much of the structural change; he was mistaken and inadequate about its psychological consequences.

The theoretical problem of industrial sociology, as it comes to an intellectual and political climax in the conception of morale, is a problem of exploring the several types of alienation and morale which we come upon as we consider systematically the structure of power and its meanings for the individual lives of workmen. It requires us to examine the extent to which psychological shifts have accompanied structural shifts; and in each case, why. In such directions lies the promise of a social science of modern man's working life.

tions with private and public powers well above the level of the welfare agency and the county agent.

Their positions change—from the academic to the bureaucratic; their publics change—from movements of reformers to circles of decision-makers; and their problems change—from those of their own choice to those of their new clients. The scholars themselves tend to become less intellectually insurgent and more administratively practical. Generally accepting the *status quo*, they tend to formulate problems out of the troubles and issues that administrators believe they face. They study, as we have seen, workers who are restless and without morale, and managers who 'do not understand' the art of managing human relations. They also diligently serve the commercial and corporate ends of the communications and advertising industries.

The new practicality is an academic response to a greatly increased demand for administrative technicians who will deal with 'human relations,' and for new justifications of corporate business as a system of power. These new demands, for personnel and ideology, result from such changes in American society as the rise of unions as competing centers of loyalty and the public hostility toward business during the slump; from the enormous scale and concentration of the power of modern corporations; from the enlargement of the welfare state, its public acceptance, and its increased intervention in economic affairs. Such developments as these are involved in the shift within the higher business world from what may be called economically practical to politically sophisticated conservatism.

The practical conservatives, with their *laissez-faire* image of utopian capitalism, have never really accepted labor unions as necessary or useful features of the political economy. Whenever possible, they have urged that unions be broken up or restricted. The public target of practical conservatives has been freedom for private gains, here and now. This plain-spoken view is still dominant in many smaller business circles—especially among retailers —and in larger businesses as well. General Motors and U.S. Steel, among the biggest of them all, often seem conspicuous among large business in the 'practicality' of their asserted conservatism.

Historically, practical conservatism has rested on the fact that businessmen have not felt the need for any newly created or more sophisticated ideology: the content of their ideology has coincided too closely with the content of widespread and unchallenged public ideas.

It is when new centers of power, not yet legitimated, not able to cloak themselves in established symbols of authority, arise, that there is a need for new ideologies of justification. The sophisticated conservatives—who are characterized by their use of liberal symbols for conservative purposes—may be traced back at least to the turn of this century, when business was being attacked by muckraking investigators and crusading journalists. In the atmosphere of the great slump, and with the passage of the Wagner Act, they came forth again; during and after World War Two, they became ascendant.

In contrast with the practical rank-and-file of the right, sophisticated conservatives are very alert to the political conditions of profit-making in an economy in which powerful labor unions confront powerful business combinations within the administrative framework of the enlarged liberal state. They are alert to the need for new symbols of justification for their power in a time when unions and government are competing for the loyalties of workers and citizens.

The interest of businessmen in the new practicality usually seems clear. But what about the professors? What are their interests? In contrast with the business spokesmen, they are not primarily concerned with the pecuniary, the managerial, or the political meanings of practicality. For them, such results are primarily means to other ends, which center, I think, upon their own 'careers.' It is true that professors certainly welcome the small increases in salaries that may come with new research activities and consultantships. They may or may not feel gratified to be helping managers administer their plants more profitably and with less trouble; they may or may not be powerfully uplifted by building new and more acceptable ideologies for established business powers. But in so far as they remain scholars, their extra-intellectual aims do not necessarily center upon such gratifications.

Their participation is, in part, a response to the new job opportunities that are part of the general increase in the scale and the bureaucratic character of business and government, and of the newer institutional relations between corporation, government, and union. These developments mean increased demands for experts and accordingly the opening of careers outside as well as within the universities. In response to these outside demands, the centers of higher learning tend increasingly to produce seemingly a-political technicians.

For those who remain academic, a new sort of career, different from that of the old-fashioned professor has become available; it may be called the career of 'the new entrepreneur.' This ambitious type of consultant is able to further his career *in* the university by securing prestige and even small-scale powers outside it. Above all, he is able to set up on the campus a respectably financed research and teaching institution, which brings the academic community into live contact with men of affairs. Among his more cloistered colleagues, such a new entrepreneur may often become a leader of university affairs.

The academic profession in America, I think we must recognize, has often failed to make ambitious men contented with merely academic careers. The prestige of the profession has not been proportionate to the economic sacrifice often involved; the pay and hence the style of life have often been miserable, and the discontent of many scholars is heightened by their awareness that often they are far brighter than men who have attained power and prestige available in other fields. For such unhappy professors the new developments in the administrative uses of social science offer gratifying opportunities to become, so to speak, Executives without having to become Deans.

And yet there is evidence, here and there, even among younger men in a greater hurry, that these new careers, while lifting the professors out of the academic rut, may have dropped them into something at least as unsatisfactory. At any rate there is worry about all this, and the new academic entrepreneurs often seem unaware of just what their new goals may be; often indeed, they do not seem to have firmly in mind even the terms in which success in achieving these hazy goals may be defined. Is not this the source of their anxious state of animated distraction?

The academic community in America as a whole is morally open to the new practicality in which it has become involved. Both in and out of the university, men at the centers of learning become experts inside administrative machines. This undoubtedly narrows their attention and the scope of such political thinking as they might do. As a group, American social scientists have seldom, if ever, been politically engaged in any large way; the trend toward the technician's role has strengthened their a-political outlook, reduced (if that is possible) their political involvement, and often, by disuse, their ability even to grasp political problems. That is one reason why one often encounters journalists who are more politically alert and knowledgeable than sociologists, economists, and especially, I am sorry to say, political scientists. The American university system seldom if ever provides political education; it seldom teaches how to gauge what is going on in the general struggle for power in modern society. Most social scientists have had little or no sustained contacts with such sections of the community as have been insurgent; there is no left-wing press with which the average academic practitioner in the course of his career could come into mutually educative relations. There is no movement that would support or give prestige, not to speak of jobs, to political intellectuals, and the academic community has few if any roots in labor circles.

All this means that the American scholar's situation allows him to take up the new practicality without any shift of ideology and without any political guilt. Thus it would be naïve, as well as inappropriate, to suggest that anyone was 'selling out,' for surely that harsh phrase may properly be used only when there is something to be sold.

5

The Bureaucratic Ethos

DURING THE LAST quarter of a century, there has been a decisive shift in the administrative uses and political meanings of social science. The older liberal practicality of 'social problems' still goes on, but it has been overshadowed by newer conservative uses of a managerial and manipulative sort. This new and illiberal practicality assumes various forms, but it is a general trend affecting the human disciplines as a whole. I may as well introduce my discussion of its ethos with an example of its major rationalization: 'One final word of caution is needed to the student who plans to become a sociologist,' Paul Lazarsfeld has written.

He is likely to be worried about the state of the world. The danger of a new war, the conflict between social systems, the rapid social changes which he has observed in his country has probably made him feel that the study of social matters is of great urgency. The danger is that he may expect to be able to solve all current problems if he just studies sociology for a few years. This unfortunately will not be the case. He will learn to understand better what is going on around him. Occasionally he will find leads for successful social action. But sociology is not yet in the stage where it can provide a *safe basis for social engineering*... It took the natural sciences about 250 years between Galileo and the beginning of the industrial revolution before they had a major effect upon the history of the world. Empirical social research has a history of three or four decades. If we expect from it quick solutions to the world's greatest problems, if we demand of it nothing but immediately practical results, we will just corrupt its natural course.[1]

What in recent years has been called 'The New Social Science' refers not only to abstracted empiricism but also to the new and

[1] Paul Lazarsfeld, op. cit., pp. 19-20. Italics mine.

illiberal practicality. The phrase refers to both method and use, and quite correctly so: for the technique of abstracted empiricism and its bureaucratic use are now regularly joined. It is my contention that, so joined, they are resulting in the development of a bureaucratic social science.

In each and every feature of its existence and its influence, abstracted empiricism, as it is currently practiced, represents a 'bureaucratic' development. (1) In an attempt to standardize and rationalize each phase of social inquiry, the intellectual operations themselves of the abstracted empirical style are becoming 'bureaucratic.' (2) These operations are such as to make studies of man usually collective and systematized: in the kind of research institutions, agencies, and bureaus in which abstracted empiricism is properly installed, there is a development, for efficiency's sake if for no other, of routines as rationalized as those of any corporation's accounting department. (3) These two developments, in turn, have much to do with the selection and the shaping of new qualities of mind among the personnel of the school, qualities both intellectual and political. (4) As it is practiced in business—especially in the communication adjuncts of advertising—in the armed forces, and increasingly in universities as well, 'the new social science' has come to serve whatever ends its bureaucratic clients may have in view. Those who promote and practice this style of research readily assume the political perspective of their bureaucratic clients and chieftains. To assume the perspective is often in due course to accept it. (5) In so far as such research efforts are effective in their declared practical aims, they serve to increase the efficiency and the reputation —and to that extent, the prevalence—of bureaucratic forms of domination in modern society. But whether or not effective in these explicit aims (the question is open), they do serve to spread the ethos of bureaucracy into other spheres of cultural, moral, and intellectual life.

1

It might seem ironic that precisely the people most urgently concerned to develop morally antiseptic methods are among those most deeply engaged in 'applied social science' and 'human engineering.' Since work in the abstracted empirical manner is expensive, only large institutions can readily afford it. Among these are corporation, army, state, and also their adjuncts, especially advertising, promotion, and public relations. There are also the foundations, but the personnel in charge of these often tend to act under the new canons of the practical, that is to say, the bureaucratically relevant. As a result, the style has become embodied in definite institutional centers: since the 'twenties in advertising and marketing agencies; since the 'thirties in corporations and syndicated polling agencies; since the 'forties, in academic life, at several research bureaus; and during World War Two, in research branches of the federal government. The institutional pattern is now spreading, but these remain its strongholds.

The formalism of these costly techniques makes them especially serviceable in providing the very kind of information needed by those capable and willing to pay for it. The new applied focus has typically been upon specific problems, designed to clarify the alternatives for practical—which is to say, pecuniary and administrative—action. It is not at all true that only as 'general principles' are discovered can social science offer 'sound practical guidance'; often the administrator needs to know certain detailed facts and relations, and that is all he needs or wants to know. Since the practitioners of abstracted empiricism are often little concerned to set their own substantive problems, they are all the more ready to abdicate the choice of their specific problems to others.

The sociologist of applied social research does not usually address 'the public'; he has specific clients with particular interests and perplexities. This shift from public to client clearly undermines the idea of objectivity-as-aloofness, an idea which has probably rested upon responsiveness to vague, unfocused pressures—and thus more on the individual interests of the researcher, who, in a small way, could divide and hence not be ruled.

All 'schools of thought' have meaning for the career of the academic man. 'Good work' is defined in terms agreeable to given schools, and thus academic success comes to depend upon active acceptance of the tenets of a dominant school. As long as there are many or at least several differing 'schools,' and especially in an expanding professional market, this requirement need not burden anyone.

Very little except his own individual limitations has stood between the individual craftsman of social science and work of the highest order. But such unattached men cannot pursue abstracted empirical research on a suitable scale, for such work cannot proceed until an agency of research is sufficiently developed to provide the appropriate kind of material, or perhaps I ought to say, work-flow. To practice abstracted empiricism requires a research institution, and, academically speaking, large funds. As the costs of research increase, as the research team comes into being, as the style of work itself becomes expensive, there comes about a corporate control over a division of labor. The idea of a university as a circle of professorial peers, each with apprentices and each practicing a craft, tends to be replaced by the idea of a university as a set of research bureaucracies, each containing an elaborate division of labor, and hence of intellectual technicians. For the efficient use of these technicians, if for no other reason, the need increases to codify procedures in order that they may be readily learned.

The research institution is also very much a training center. Like other institutions, it selects certain types of mind, and by virtue of the rewards it offers it places a premium upon the development of certain mental qualities. Two types of men, rather new to the academic scene, have arisen in these institutions, alongside more old-fashioned scholars and researchers.

There are, first, the intellectual administrators and research promoters—about whom I cannot say anything that is not, I suppose, familiar in academic circles. Their academic reputations rest upon their academic power: they are the members of The Committee; they are on The Board of Directors; they can get you the job, the trip, the research grant. They are a strange new kind of bureaucrat. They are the executives of the mind, public relations men specializing in the foundations. For them, as for promoters and executives elsewhere, the memorandum is replacing the book. They can set up another research project or institute in a most efficient manner, and they administer the production of 'books.' The span of time in which they say they work is 'a billion man-hours of technical labor.' In the meantime, we should not expect much substantive knowledge: first there must be many methodological inquiries—into the methods and into the inquiry—and then there must be all the 'pilot studies.' Many foundation administrators like to give money for projects that are large-scale and hence easier 'to administer' than more numerous handicraft projects; and for projects that are Scientific with a capital S—which often only means made 'safe' by being made trivial—for they do not want to be made the subjects of political attention. Accordingly, the larger foundations tend to encourage large-scale bureaucratic research into small-scale problems, and to seek out intellectual administrators for the job.

Second, there are the younger recruits, better described as research technicians than as social scientists. This is, I am aware, a quite large assertion, but I make it with due care. To understand the social meaning of a style of thought, we must always distinguish the leaders from the followers, the innovators from the routine workers, the 'first generation' which sets it up, from the second and third generations which carry it out. All schools, if they are successful, contain both types of men; that this is so is indeed one criterion of a 'successful' school. It is also an important clue to the intellectual consequences of success.

There is often a difference between the qualities of mind characteristic of the run-of-the-mill followers and of the innovators and founders. On this point, schools of thought differ rather profoundly. To a considerable extent, the differences depend upon the type of social organization that each school's style of work permits or encourages. At least several of the inventors and administrators of the style we are examining have highly cultivated minds. In their youth, before this style flourished, they absorbed the leading models of thought of Western society; such men have had years of cultural and intellectual experience. They are in fact educated men: imaginatively aware of their own sensibilities and capable of continuous self-cultivation.

But the second generation, the young men who come from what, I suppose it will be agreed, is the intellectually impoverished background of the American High School, have not had comparable experience. As often as not they have not had adequate college work; at least there are reasons to suspect—although I do not know—that there is a selection of not quite the brightest for such research institutes.

I have seldom seen one of these young men, once he is well caught up, in a condition of genuine intellectual puzzlement. And I have never seen any passionate curiosity about a great problem, the sort of curiosity that compels the mind to travel anywhere and by any means, to re-make itself if necessary, in order *to find out*. These young men are less restless than methodical; less imaginative than patient; above all, they are dogmatic—in all the historical and theological meanings of the term. Some of this is of course merely part of the sorry intellectual condition of so many students now in American colleges and universities, but I do believe it is more evident among the research technicians of abstracted empiricism.

They have taken up social research as a career; they have come early to an extreme specialization, and they have acquired an indifference or a contempt for 'social philosophy'—which means to them 'writing books out of other books' or 'merely speculating.' Listening to their conversations, trying to gauge the quality of their curiosity, one finds a deadly limitation of mind. The social worlds about which so many scholars feel ignorant do not puzzle them.

Much of the propaganda force of bureaucratic social science is due to its philosophical claims to Scientific Method; much of its power to recruit is due to the relative ease of training individuals and setting them to work in a career with a future. In both instances, explicitly coded methods, readily available to the technicians, are the major keys to success. In some of the founders, empirical techniques serve an imagination which, it is true, has often been curiously suppressed, but which one always feels to be there. When you talk with one of the founders you are always dealing with a mind. But once a young man has spent three or four years at this sort of thing, you cannot really talk to him about the problems of studying modern society. His position and career, his ambition and his very self-esteem, are based in large part upon this one perspective, this one vocabulary, this one set of techniques. In truth, he does not know anything else.

In some of these students, intelligence itself is often disassociated from personality, and is seen by them as a kind of skilled gadget that they hope to market successfully. They are among the humanistically impoverished, living with reference to values that exclude any arising from a respect for human reason. They are among the energetic and ambitious technicians whom a defective educational routine and a corrupting demand have made incapable of acquiring the sociological imagination. One can only hope that when sufficient numbers of these young men reach the associate professor level of their careers, they will by some intellectual mutation become aware of the fact that they are no longer dependent upon emperors without clothing.

The abstracted empirical manner, the methodological inhibition it sustains, the focus of its practicality, the qualities of mind its institutions tend to select and to train—these developments make questions about the social policies of the social sciences all the more urgent. This bureaucratic style and its institutional embodiment are in line with the dominant trends of modern social structure and its characteristic types of thought. I do not believe that it can be explained, or even fully understood, without recognizing this. These same social trends, in fact, affect not only the social sciences, but the whole intellectual life of the United States, and indeed the very role of reason in human affairs today.

What is at issue seems plain: if social science is not autonomous, it cannot be a publicly responsible enterprise. As the means of research become larger and more expensive, they tend to be 'expropriated'; accordingly, only as social scientists, in some collective way, exercise full control over these means of research can social science in this style be truly autonomous. In so far as the individual social scientist is dependent in his work upon bureaucracies, he tends to lose his individual autonomy; in so far as social science consists of bureaucratic work, it tends to lose its social and political autonomy. I do want to emphasize the 'in so far as.' For clearly I have been discussing one tendency, although a major one, and not the complete state of our affairs.

2

If we are to understand what is going on in any area of cultural and intellectual work, we must understand its immediate social context. I must accordingly now make a brief excursus on academic cliques. Of course it is true that to the extent that an idea is durable and significant, any given personality or clique can be but its temporary symbol. Yet the whole business of 'cliques' and 'personalities' and 'schools' is rather more complicated than that; their importance in shaping the development of social science deserves more awareness on our part. We must confront them, if for no other reason, because any cultural activity requires financial support of some kind and also a public of some sort to give it the help of criticism. Neither the money nor the criticism is given solely on the basis of objective judgments of worth, and besides there is usually argument about the objectivity of the judgments themselves as well as about the worth.

The function of the academic clique is not only to regulate the competition, but to set the terms of competition and to assign rewards for work done in accordance with these terms at any given time. It is the canons by which men are judged and work criticized that are the most important intellectual feature of the clique. To my previous point about 'the ethos of the technicians' of the bureaucratic social science—their qualities of mind and their influence upon the making of reputations and hence upon dominant fashions in social science and upon the canons of critical judgment that prevail—I here need only add that the means by which the internal tasks of the clique are accomplished include: the giving of friendly advice to younger men; job offers and recommendations of promotion; the assignment of books to admiring reviewers; the ready acceptance of articles and books for publication; the allocation of research funds; arranging or politicking for honorific positions within professional associations and on editorial boards of professional journals. In so far as these means constitute assignments of prestige, which is, in turn, very much a determinant of academic careers, they affect the economic expectations of the individual scholar as well as his professional reputation.

Once upon a time academic reputations were generally expected to be based upon the productions of books, studies, monographs—in sum, upon the production of ideas and scholarly works, and upon the judgment of these works by academic colleagues and intelligent laymen. One reason why this has been so in social science and the humanities is that a man's competence or incompetence has been available for inspection, since the older academic world did not contain privileged positions of competence. It is rather difficult to know whether the alleged competence of a corporation president, for example, is due to his own personal abilities or to the powers and facilities available to him by virtue of his position. But there has been no room for such doubt about scholars working, as old-fashioned professors have worked, as craftsmen.

However, by his prestige, the new academic statesman, like the business executive and the military chieftain, has acquired means of competence which must be distinguished from his personal competence—but which in his reputation are not so distinguished. A permanent professional secretary, a clerk to run to the library, an electric typewriter, dictating equipment, and a mimeographing machine, and perhaps a small budget of three or four thousand dollars a year for purchasing books and periodicals—even such minor office equipment and staff enormously increases any scholar's appearance of competence. Any business executive will laugh at the pettiness of such means; college professors will not —few professors, even productive ones, have such facilities on a secure basis. Yet such equipment *is* a means of competence and of career—which secure clique membership makes much more likely than does unattached scholarship. The clique's prestige increases the chance to get them, and having them in turn increases the chance to produce a reputation.

This, then, I think, is one kind of situation which helps to explain how men may acquire considerable reputation without having, in all truth, produced very much. About one such man, a colleague interested in posterity recently remarked, in a quite friendly way: 'As long as he lives, he'll be the most eminent man in his field; two weeks after he dies, no one will remember him.' That the statement is so harsh perhaps testifies to the painfulness of the anxieties that must frequently haunt the statesmen in their world of academic cliques.

If there is competition among several cliques in a field of study, the relative positions of the several competitors tend to determine clique strategies. Cliques that are small and considered unimportant can in due course be expected by leading cliques to go out of business. Their members will be ignored or won over or rejected, and in the end die off without having trained the next generation. It must always be kept in mind that one important function of cliques is the shaping of the next academic generation. To say that a clique is unimportant is to say that it will not have much voice in this shaping. But if there are, for example, two leading schools, each with leaders who are quite powerful and enjoy much prestige, then the relations between the two often tend to become problems of merger, problems of building a larger cartel. And of course if a school is under effective attack by outsiders, or by other cliques, one of the first strategies of defense is the denial that there actually is a clique or even a school; it is on such occasions that the statesmen come into their own.

Tasks of importance to the clique often are confused with tasks of importance to the actual work of a school. Among younger men, this affects the chances of their careers; among older men, there is a clique premium upon administrative and promotional, political and friendship skills. Especially among these older men, reputations may thus become rather ambiguously based. Is this man's high reputation—outsiders may ask—due to the intellectual value of work actually accomplished or is it due to his position in the clique?

When we consider the relations between cliques we immediately encounter those who are not spokesmen for one clique, but for 'the field' as a whole. They are not merely executives of one firm, they are industrial spokesmen. One who aspires to play the role of statesman for an entire field must usually in effect deny that real intellectual differences exist between say, the two leading cliques of the field. In fact, as their joint spokesman, it is his prime intellectual task to show that 'they are really working toward the same goal.' He comes to be a prestige symbol of that which each clique claims to be its own speciality, and as well a symbol of their 'actual' or at least eventual unity. Borrowing prestige from each of the cliques, he bestows prestige upon both of them. He is a kind of broker, dealing in the allocation of prestige for both teams.

Suppose, for example, in some field of study there are two leading schools, one called Theory and one called Research. The successful statesman carries on a busy traffic with both; he is seen as in both and yet as standing between them as well. By his prestige, he seems to promise that Theory and Research are not only compatible but parts of an integrated model of work in social science as a whole. He is a symbol of that promise. The promise does not rest upon any actual books or studies he has done. What is going on is this: in any work of Research that is to be celebrated, the statesman seeks Theory—and in an altogether optative manner, invariably finds it there. In any duly celebrated work of Theory, the statesman seeks Research—and again, in an altogether optative way, finds it. These 'findings' are of the order of extended book reviews, having as much to do with the allocation of prestige to men than with examinations of studies in their own right. The accomplished study, in which Theory and Research are displayed truly as one, is, as I have noted, a promise, a symbol. In the meantime, the prestige of the statesman does not rest upon any such study, in fact it seldom rests upon any study at all.

There is, I think, a tragic fact inherent in all such statesmanlike roles. Often those who play them have first-rate minds—in fact, mediocrities cannot really play such a role, although many do of course imitate it in a verbal way. The role the statesman has come to play keeps him from actual work. The prestige he has accumulated is so disproportionate to what he has actually accomplished, the promise that he has held out is so grand, that he is often quite inhibited from getting down to 'The Study'; and when he does have a major part in some study or book, he is reluctant to finish it or to publish it, even when others think it is finished. He complains then about the committees and the other statesmanlike burdens that he is carrying, but at the same time he accepts —indeed, he often seeks—many more such burdens. His very role as statesman is at once the cause and the excuse for his not getting down to work. He is trapped, as he so frequently says; but also he really must continue to trap himself—else his very role as a statesman will be recognized by others and by himself as a mere excuse.

The world of cliques is not all there is in the academic world. There are also the unattached, who come in many varieties indeed and whose work is also varied. From the standpoint of a leading clique, the unattached may be seen as friendly or at least neutral about the cliques' school; perhaps they are 'eclectic' in their work or merely not 'socially inclined.' To the extent that their work is attracting favorable attention or they are judged to be of merit, use, or worth, members of the clique may seek to attract them, to show them the way, and eventually to recruit them. Celebration that is merely mutual celebration—by, of, and for clique members—that is not enough.

But among the unattached there may also be those who don't play the game, won't cash in the prestige claims. Of these some are merely indifferent and absorbed in their own work, and some are downright hostile. They are critics of the school's work. If it is possible, the clique will ignore both them and their work. But only if the clique enjoys truly great prestige, is this simple strategy suitable and safe. It can be done in a truly lordly way, moreover, only if the clique coincides with virtually the whole field of study, and is monolithically in control of it. This, of course, is not the usual case; usually there are many neutral people and eclectic workmen, and other cliques as well, within the same field. There are also associated fields of study; and beyond that, a variety of non-academic audiences and publics whose interest or acclaim upsets, at least as yet, monolithic control of prestige, reputation, and career by cliques.

Accordingly, if the critics cannot be ignored, other strategies must be adopted. All the means used for the internal management of a school's members are of course also used for dealing with hostile outsiders; I need only briefly to discuss one of them: book reviewing, the most common medium for prestige allocation. Suppose an unattached scholar produces a book to which sufficient attention is paid to make ignoring it inconvenient. The crude ploy is to give it to a leading member of the clique, especially to one known to be in competition with or even directly hostile to the author's views, or at least associated with contrary views. It is more subtle to assign it to a minor yet upcoming member of the clique who has not published much himself and whose views are therefore not widely known. This has many advantages. For the young man it is a pay-off for his loyalty and as well an opportunity to win recognition by his criticism of an older and better-known man. By implication it places the book in a position of less importance than if it has been assigned to an eminent scholar. It is also a safe role for the young man to play: the better-known man, out of a certain snobbery, may not wish to 'answer' the review; it is not conventional for the author of a book to answer criticisms of it by professorial reviewers, in fact, it is the policy of some learned journals to discourage it, or not to allow it. But even if the review is answered, it does not really matter too much. Everyone who has not only reviewed but also written books knows that one of the easiest of all intellectual tasks is to 'debunk' a book—any book—in a two- or three-column review, and that it is virtually impossible to 'answer' such a review in the same space. It would not be impossible if the book itself has been read with some care by all readers of the controversy; that this cannot be assumed gives to the reviewer an overwhelming advantage.

If however the book in question gains a very great deal of attention inside or outside the field or both, then the only thing to do is to assign it to a leading clique member, preferably a statesman who will duly praise it without too much attention to its content, and also show how it contributes in its way to the dominant and promising trends in the field as a whole. The one thing that any serious and dedicated clique must try to avoid is having the book assigned to another unattached scholar who would, first, state accurately and clearly what the book contains and, second, criticize it in terms altogether independent of schools and cliques and fashions.

3

Among the slogans used by a variety of schools of social science, none is so frequent as, 'The purpose of social science is the prediction and control of human behavior.' Nowadays, in some circles we also hear much about 'human engineering'—an undefined phrase often mistaken for a clear and obvious goal. It is believed to be clear and obvious because it rests upon an unquestioned analogy between 'the mastery of nature' and 'the mastery of society.' Those who habitually use such phrases are very likely to be among those who are most passionately concerned to 'make the social studies into real sciences,' and conceive of their own work as politically neutral and morally irrelevant. Quite usually, the basic idea is stated as 'the lag' of social science behind physical science and the consequent need to close up the gap. These technocratic slogans are a substitute for a political philosophy among many of The Scientists of whom I have just written. They are, they suppose, out to do with society what they suppose physicists have done with nature. Their political philosophy is contained in the simple view that if only The Methods of Science, by which man now has come to control the atom, were employed to 'control social behavior,' the problems of mankind would soon be solved, and peace and plenty assured for all.

Behind these phrases there are curious notions of power, of reason, of history—all of them unclear and all of them in a deplorable state of confusion. The use of such phrases reveals a rationalistic and empty optimism which rests upon an ignorance of the several possible roles of reason in human affairs, the nature of power and its relations to knowledge, the meaning of moral action and the place of knowledge within it, the nature of history and the fact that men are not only creatures of history but on occasion creators within it and even of it. Before I take up such issues, as they bear upon the political meanings of the social sciences, I want briefly to examine the key slogan of the techno-cratic philosophers—the one about prediction and control.

To talk so glibly as many do about prediction and control is to assume the perspective of the bureaucrat to whom, as Marx once remarked, the world is an object to be manipulated. To make the point clear, take an extreme example: If a man has an apparatus of control, both subtle and powerful, over an army division on an isolated island with no enemy, he is, you must agree, in a position of control. If he uses his powers fully and has made definite plans, he can predict, within quite narrow margins, what each man will be doing at a certain hour of a certain day in a certain year. He can predict quite well even the feelings of various of these men, for he manipulates them as he would inert objects; he has power to override many of the plans they may have, and occasionally may properly consider himself an all-powerful despot. If he can control, he can predict. He is in command of 'regularities.'

But we, as social scientists, may not assume that we are dealing with objects that are so highly manipulable, and we may not assume that among men we are enlightened despots. At least, to make either assumption is to take a political stand that for pro-fessors seems a rather curious one. No historical society is con-structed within a frame as rigid as that enclosing my hypothetical army division. Nor are social scientists—let us be grateful—gen-erals of history. Yet to speak of 'prediction and control' in the same breath, as so many do, is usually to assume some kind of one-sided control such as that of my imaginary general, whose powers I have somewhat exaggerated in order to make the point clear.

I want to make it clear in order to reveal the political meaning of the bureaucratic ethos. Its use has mainly been in and for non-democratic areas of society—a military establishment, a corpora-tion, an advertising agency, an administrative division of gov-ernment. It is in and for such bureaucratic organizations that many social scientists have been invited to work, and the problems with which they there concern themselves are the kinds of problems that concern the more efficient members of such administrative machines.

I do not see how anyone can reasonably disagree with Professor Robert S. Lynd's comment on *The American Soldier:*

These volumes depict science being used with great skill to sort out and to control men for purposes not of their own willing. It is a significant measure of the impotence of liberal democracy that it must increasingly use its social sciences not directly on democracy's own problems, but tangentially and indirectly; it must pick up the crumbs from private business research on such problems as how to gauge audience reaction so as to put together synthetic radio programs and movies, or, as in the present case, from Army research on how to turn frightened draftees into tough soldiers who will fight a war whose purposes they do not understand. With such socially extraneous purposes controlling the use of social science, each advance in its use tends to make it an instrument of mass control, and thereby a further threat to democracy.[2]

The slogans of the human engineers serve to carry the bureaucratic ethos beyond the actual use of this style of thought and method of inquiry. To use these slogans as a statement of 'what one is about' is to accept a bureaucratic role even when one is not enacting it. This role, in short, is very often assumed on an *as if* basis. Assuming the technocratic view, and as a social scientist trying to act upon it, is to act *as if* one were indeed a human engineer. It is within such a bureaucratic perspective that the public role of the social scientist is now frequently conceived. To act in this as-if-I-were-a-human-engineer manner might be merely amusing in a society in which human reason were widely and democratically installed, but the United States is not such a society. Whatever else it is, surely this is evident: it is a society in which functionally rational bureaucracies are increasingly used in human affairs and in history-making decisions. Not all periods are alike in the degree to which historical changes within them are independent of willful control, go on behind all men's backs. Ours seems to be a period in which key decisions or their lack by bureaucratically instituted elites are increasingly sources

2 'The Science of Inhuman Relations,' *The New Republic,* 27 August 1949.

of historical change. Moreover, it is a period and a society in which the enlargement and the centralization of the means of control, of power, now include quite widely the use of social science for whatever ends those in control of these means may assign to it. To talk of 'prediction and control' without confronting the questions such developments raise is to abandon such moral and political autonomy as one may have.

Is it possible to speak of 'control' in any perspective other than the bureaucratic? Yes, of course it is. Various kinds of 'collective self-control' have been conceived. Adequate statement of any such idea includes all the issues of freedom and of rationality, as ideas and as values. It also includes the idea of 'democracy'—as a type of social structure and as a set of political expectations. Democracy means the power and the freedom of those controlled by law to change the law, according to agreed-upon rules—and even to change these rules; but more than that, it means some kind of collective self-control over the structural mechanics of history itself. This is a complicated and difficult idea, which I shall later discuss in some detail. Here I want merely to suggest that if social scientists, in a society which contains democratic aspirations, wish to discuss seriously the issues of 'prediction and control,' they must consider such problems carefully.

Is it possible to speak of 'prediction' in any perspective other than the bureaucratic? Yes, of course it is. Predictions may rest upon 'unintended regularities' rather than upon prescriptive controls. Without having control, we can predict best about those areas of social life over which no one else has much control either, those in which 'voluntary' and nonroutine activities are at a minimum. The usages of language, for example, change and persist 'behind men's backs.' Perhaps such regularities also occur in connection with the structural mechanics of history. If we can grasp what John Stuart Mill called the 'principia media' of a society, if we can grasp its major trends; in brief, if we can understand the structural transformation of our epoch, we might have 'a basis for prediction.'

Yet we must remember that within specific milieux, men do often control how they act; the extent to which they can do so are among the objects of our study. There are real generals, we ought to remember, as well as hypothetical ones, and also corporate executives and heads of states. Moreover, as has often been remarked, the fact that men are not inert objects means that they may become aware of predictions made about their activities, and that accordingly they can and often do re-direct themselves; they may falsify or fulfill the predictions. Which they will do is not, as yet, subject to very good prediction. In so far as men have some degree of freedom, what they may do will not be readily predictable.

But the point is: To say that 'the real and final aim of human engineering' or of 'social science' is 'to predict' is to substitute a technocratic slogan for what ought to be a reasoned moral choice. That too is to assume the bureaucratic perspective within which —once it is fully adopted—there is much less moral choice available.

The bureaucratization of social study is a quite general trend; perhaps, in due course, it is likely to come about in any society in which bureaucratic routines are becoming paramount. It is naturally accompanied by a rather Jesuitical and high-flown theory, which does not interact as such with administrative research. Particular researches, generally statistical and bound to administrative uses, do not affect the great elaboration of Concepts; this elaboration in turn has nothing to do with the results of particular researches, but rather with the legitimation of the regime and of its changing features. To the bureaucrat, the world is a world of facts to be treated in accordance with firm rules. To the theorist, the world is a world of conceptions to be manipulated, often without any discernible rules. Theory serves, in a variety of ways, as ideological justification of authority. Research for bureaucratic ends serves to make authority more effective and more efficient by providing information of use to authoritative planners.

Abstracted empiricism is used bureaucratically, although it has of course clear ideological meanings, which are sometimes used as such. Grand theory, as I have indicated, has no direct bureaucratic utility; its political meaning is ideological, and such use as it may have lies there. Should these two styles of work —abstracted empiricism and grand theory—come to enjoy an intellectual 'duopoly,' or even become the predominant styles of work, they would constitute a grievous threat to the intellectual promise of social science and as well to the political promise of the role of reason in human affairs—as that role has been classically conceived in the civilization of the Western societies.

6

Philosophies of Science

THE CONFUSION in the social sciences—it should now be obvious—
is wrapped up with the long-continuing controversy about the
nature of Science. Most students of society will surely agree that
their grateful acceptance of 'Science' is usually as ambiguous as
it is formal. 'Scientific empiricism' means many things, and there
is no one accepted version, much less any systematic use of any
one version. Professional expectations are quite confused and the
sense of craftsmanship may be realized in terms of quite different models of inquiry. In some part, it is because of this situation
that the epistemological models of philosophers of natural science
have such appeal as they do.[1]

Recognizing the existence of several styles of work in the social
sciences, many students eagerly agree that 'we ought to get them
together.' Sometimes this program is put rather persuasively: the
task during the next decades, it is said, is to unite the larger problems and theoretical work of the nineteenth century, especially
that of the Germans, with the research techniques predominant in
the twentieth century, especially that of the Americans. Within
this great dialectic, it is felt, signal and continuous advances in
masterful conception and rigorous procedure will be made.

As a problem in philosophy, it is not very difficult 'to get them
together.'[2] But the pertinent question is: suppose we do 'get them

[1] Cf. chapter 3, section 1.
[2] Cf. for example, the rather playful effort, 'Two Styles of Research in Current Social Studies,' *Philosophy of Science*, Vol. 20, No. 4, October, 1953,
pp. 266-75.

together' in one or another grand model of inquiry—of what use is such a model for work in social science, for the handling of its leading tasks?

Such philosophical work *is*, I believe, of some use to working social scientists. Awareness of it enables us to become more conscious of our conceptions and our procedures, and to clarify them. It provides a language with which we can do these things. But its use ought to be of a general nature; no working social scientist need take any such model very seriously. And above all, we ought to take it as a liberation of our imagination and a source of suggestion for our procedures, rather than as a limit upon our problems. To limit, in the name of 'natural science,' the problems upon which we shall work seems to me a curious timidity. Of course, if semi-skilled researchers wish to confine themselves to such problems, that may be a wise self-restraint; beyond that, such limitation is without significant basis.

1

The classic social analyst has avoided any rigid set of procedures; he has sought to develop and to use in his work the sociological imagination. Repelled by the association and disassociation of Concepts, he has used more elaborated terms only when he has had good reason to believe that by their use he enlarges the scope of his sensibilities, the precision of his references, the depth of his reasoning. He has not been inhibited by method and technique; the classic way has been the way of the intellectual craftsman.

Useful discussions of method as well as of theory usually arise as marginal notes on work-in-progress or work about to get under way. 'Method' has to do, first of all, with how to ask and answer questions with some assurance that the answers are more or less durable. 'Theory' has to do, above all, with paying close attention to the words one is using, especially their degree of generality and their logical relations. The primary purpose of both is clarity of conception and economy of procedure, and most importantly just now, the release rather than the restriction of the sociological imagination.

To have mastered 'method' and 'theory' is to have become a self-conscious thinker, a man at work and aware of the assumptions and the implications of whatever he is about. To be mastered by 'method' or 'theory' is simply to be kept from working, from trying, that is, to find out about something that is going on in the world. Without insight into the way the craft is carried on, the results of study are infirm; without a determination that study shall come to significant results, all method is meaningless pretense.

For the classic social scientists, neither method nor theory is an autonomous domain; methods are methods for some range of problems; theories are theories of some range of phenomena. They are like the language of the country you live in: it is nothing to brag about that you can speak it, but it is a disgrace and an inconvenience if you cannot.

The working social scientist must always keep uppermost a full sense of the problem at hand. This obviously means that he must be very well acquainted in a substantive way with the state of knowledge in the area with which the studies being examined are concerned. It also means, to an extent which I do not think can be made explicit, that such work is best done when the several studies examined are concerned with a similar area of study. Finally, such work is not best done as the sole specialty of one person, much less of a young man who has in fact done little if any actual work, or who may have taken part only in studies done in one or another particular style.

When we pause in our studies to reflect on theory and method, the greatest yield is a re-statement of our problems. Perhaps that is why, in actual practice, every working social scientist must be his own methodologist and his own theorist, which means only that he must be an intellectual craftsman. Every craftsman can of course learn something from over-all attempts to codify methods, but it is often not much more than a general kind of awareness. That is why 'crash programs' in methodology are not likely to help social science to develop. Really useful accounts of methods cannot be forced in that way, if they are not very firmly related to the actual working of social study, a sense of significant problem and the passion to solve it—nowadays so often lost—cannot be allowed full play in the mind of the working social scientist.

Advance in methods, then, is most likely to occur as modest generalizations stemming from work in progress. Accordingly, we should maintain in our individual practice, and in the organization of our discipline, a very close state of interaction between method and work under way. Serious attention should be paid to general discussions of methodology only when they are in direct reference to actual work. Such discussions of method do occur among social scientists, and I shall later, in an appendix, try to demonstrate one way in which they may be carried on.

Statements of method and arguments about them, distinctions of theory and further distinctions—however stimulating and even entertaining—are merely promises. Statements of method promise to guide us to better ways of studying something, often in fact of studying almost anything. Elaborations of theories, systematic and unsystematic, promise to alert us to distinctions in what we may see, or in what we may make of what we see, when we come to interpret it. But neither Method nor Theory alone can be taken as part of the actual work of the social studies. In fact, both are often just the opposite: they are statesmanlike withdrawals from the problems of social science. Usually, we have seen, they are based on some grand model of inquiry with which other people are beat on the head. That this grand model is not capable of altogether full use is not, perhaps, too important, for it may still be used ritualistically. Usually it is made up, as I have explained, out of some philosophy of natural science, and quite usually, of all things, from a philosophical gloss on physics, perhaps somewhat out of date. This little game, and others having similar rules, leads less to further work than to the kind of scientific know-nothingism, of which Max Horkheimer has written: 'The constant warning against premature conclusions and foggy generalities implies, unless properly qualified, a possible taboo against all thinking. If every thought has to be held in abeyance until it has been completely corroborated, no basic approach seems possible and we would limit ourselves to the level of mere symptoms.' [3]

The young, it has frequently been noticed, are often corruptible, but is it not curious to see older scholars of social science also made uneasy by the pretensions of the philosophers of science among us? How much more sensible and enlightening than the loud proclamations of some American sociologists is the conversational statement of a Swiss and an English economist, which illustrates well the classic view of the place of method: 'Many authors instinctively set about tackling these problems in the right way. But after studying the methodology they become conscious of the numerous pitfalls and other dangers which are waiting for them. The result is that they lose their former sure touch, and are led astray or in unsuitable directions. Scholars of this type are warned off methodology.' [4]

The slogans we ought to raise are surely these:

Every man his own methodologist!

Methodologists! Get to work!

Although we may not take such slogans too literally, as working social scientists we do need to defend ourselves; and given the curious and unscholarly zeal of some of our colleagues, perhaps we may be pardoned for our own exaggerations.

2

The everyday empiricism of common sense is filled with assumptions and stereotypes of one or another particular society; for common sense determines what is seen and how it is to be explained. If you attempt to escape from this condition by abstracted empiricism, you will end up on the microscopic or sub-historical level and you will try slowly to pile up the abstracted details with which you are dealing. If you attempt to

[3] *Tensions That Cause Wars*, ed. by Hadley Cantril, Urbana, Illinois, University of Illinois Press, 1950, p. 297.
[4] W. A. Johr and H. W. Singer, *The Role of the Economist as Official Adviser*, London, George Allen & Unwin, 1955, pp. 3-4. This book, by the way, is a model of the proper way of going about discussions of method in social science. Significantly, it was written out of a kind of conversation between two experienced craftsmen.

escape from common sense empiricism by grand theory, you will empty the concepts with which you are dealing of clear and present empirical reference and, if you are not careful, in the trans-historical world you are building, you will be quite alone.

A conception is an idea with empirical content. If the idea is too large for the content, you are tending toward the trap of grand theory; if the content swallows the idea, you are tending toward the pitfall of abstracted empiricism. The general problem involved here is often stated as 'the need for indices,' and it is among the leading technical challenges of actual work in social science today. Members of all schools are aware of it. Abstracted empiricists often solve the problem of indices by eliminating the scope and the meanings of that which is supposedly being indexed. Grand theory does not confront the problem usefully; it just goes on elaborating the Concept in terms of others equally abstract.

What abstracted empiricists call empirical 'data' represent a very abstracted view of everyday social worlds. They normally deal, for example, with an age-level of a sex-category of an income-bracket of middle-sized cities. That is four variables, rather more than many abstracted empiricists manage to get into any one of their snapshots of the world. And of course, there is another 'variable' in it too: these people live in the United States. But that is not, as a 'datum,' among the minute, precise, abstracted variables which make up the empirical world of abstracted empiricism. To get 'The United States' in would require a conception of social structure, and as well, a less rigid idea of empiricism.

Most classic work (in this connection sometimes called *macroscopic*) lies between abstracted empiricism and grand theory. Such work also involves an abstraction from what may be observed in everyday milieux, but the direction of its abstraction is toward social and historical structures. It is on the level of historical reality—which is merely to say that it is in terms of specific social and historical structures that the classic problems of social science have been formulated, and in such terms solutions offered.

Such work is no less empirical than abstracted empiricism: in fact, often it is more so; often it is closer to the world of everyday meanings and experiences. The point is quite simple: Franz Neumann's account of Nazi social structure is at least as 'empirical'—and 'systematic'—as Samuel Stouffer's account of the morale of army unit number 10079; Max Weber's account of the Chinese mandarin or Eugene Staley's study of underdeveloped countries or Barrington Moore's examinations of Soviet Russia are as 'empirical' as Paul Lazarsfeld's studies of opinion in Erie County or in the small town of Elmira.

It is out of classic work, moreover, that most of the *ideas* being used on the sub-historical and on the trans-historical levels of work have in fact arisen. What really fruitful idea, what conception of man and society and of their relations, has resulted from abstracted empiricism or grand theory? So far as ideas are concerned, both of these schools are parasites living off the classic social science tradition.

3

The problem of empirical verification is 'how to get down to facts' yet not get overwhelmed by them; how to anchor ideas to facts but not to sink the ideas. The problem is first *what* to verify and second *how* to verify it.

In grand theory, verification is hopefully deductive; neither what to verify nor how to verify it seems, as yet, a very definite problem.

In abstracted empiricism, what to verify often does not seem to be taken as a serious issue. How to verify is almost automatically provided by the terms in which the problem is stated: these feed into correlational and other statistical procedures. In fact, the dogmatic requirement for such verification often seems the sole concern, and hence limits or even determines the Concepts used and the problems taken up by those committed to this microscopic style.

In classical practice, what to verify is usually considered as important or perhaps more important than how to verify it. Ideas are elaborated in close connection with some set of substantive problems; the choice of what to verify is determined in accordance with some such rule as this one: Try to verify those features of the idea elaborated which seem to promise the most inferences of relevance to the elaboration. These features we call 'pivotal,'—if *this* is so, then it follows that this and this and this must also be so. If this is not so, then—another series of inferences follows. One reason for such a procedure is the felt need for economy of work: empirical verification, evidence, documentation, the determination of fact—they are very time-consuming and often tedious. Accordingly, one wants such work to make the most difference for the ideas and theories with which one is working.

The classic craftsman does not usually make up one big design for one big empirical study. His policy is to allow and to invite a continual shuttle between macroscopic conceptions and detailed expositions. He does this by designing his work as a series of smaller-scale empirical studies (which may of course include microscopic and statistical work), each of which seems to be pivotal to some part or another of the solution he is elaborating. That solution is confirmed, modified, or refuted, according to the results of these empirical studies.

How to verify statements, propositions, putative facts, does not seem to the classic practitioner as difficult as it is often made out to be by microscopic workers. The classic practitioner verifies a statement by detailed exposition of whatever empirical materials are relevant, and of course, I repeat, if we have felt the need to choose and to handle our conceptions in connection with our problems in this way, we may often be able to perform the detailed exposition in the abstracted and more precise manner of statistical inquiry. For other problems and conceptions, our verification will be like that of the historian; it is the problem of evidence. Of course it is true that we are never certain; in fact, that often we are 'guessing,' but it is not true that all guesses have an equal chance of being correct. Classic social science, it may be said in tribute, is, among other things, an attempt to improve the chances that our guesses about important matters may be right.

Verification consists of rationally convincing others, as well as ourselves. But to do that we must follow the accepted rules, above all the rule that work be presented in such a way that it is open at every step to the checking up by others. There is no One Way to do this; but it does always require a developed carefulness and attention to detail, a habit of being clear, a skeptical perusal of alleged facts, and a tireless curiosity about their possible meanings, their bearings on other facts and notions. It requires orderliness and system. In a word, it requires the firm and consistent practice of the ethics of scholarship. If that is not present, no technique, no method, will serve.

4

Every way of working on social studies, every choice of studies and of the methods of studying them, implies 'a theory of scientific progress.' Everyone, I suppose, agrees that scientific advance is cumulative: that it is not the creation of one man but the work of many men revising and criticizing, adding to and subtracting from one another's efforts. For one's own work to count, one must relate it to what has been done before and to other work currently in progress. This is needed in order to communicate, and it is needed for 'objectivity.' One must state what one has done in such a way that others may check it.

The policy for progress of abstracted empiricists is very specific and quite hopeful: Let us accumulate many microscopic studies; slowly and minutely, like ants dragging many small crumbs into a great pile, we shall 'build up the science.'

The policy of grand theorists seems to be: Somewhere and someday, we shall come into lively contact with empirical materials; when that day comes we shall be prepared to handle them 'systematically'; then we shall know what it means to make systematic theory logically available to the scientific way of empirical verification.

The theory of scientific progress held by those who would fulfill the promise of classic social science does not allow them to suppose that a series of microscopic studies will necessarily accumulate into a 'fully developed' social science. They are not willing to assume that such materials will necessarily become useful for any purposes other than their present ones. They do not, in short, accept the building-block (or old-ladies-putting-together-a-quilt) theory of social science development. They do not think that out of such work a Newton or a Darwin will arise to put it all together. Nor do they think that what Darwin or Newton did was to 'put together' such microscopic facts as are being piled up by microscopic social science today. The classic practitioner is also unwilling to assume, with the grand theorists, that judicious elaboration and distinction of Concepts will in due course somehow become relevant in a systematic way to empirical materials. There is no reason, they hold, to believe that these conceptual elaborations will ever be more than what they now are.

Classic social science, in brief, neither 'builds up' from microscopic study nor 'deduces down' from conceptual elaboration. Its practitioners try to build and to deduce at the same time, in the same process of study, and to do so by means of adequate formulation and re-formulation of problems and of their adequate solutions. To practice such a policy—and I am sorry for the repetition but it is the key point—is to take up substantive problems on the historical level of reality; to state these problems in terms appropriate to them; and then, no matter how high the flight of theory, no matter how painstaking the crawl among detail, in the end of each completed act of study, to state the solution in the macroscopic terms of the problem. The classic focus, in short, is on substantive problems. The character of these problems limits and suggests the methods and the conceptions that are used and how they are used. Controversy over different views of 'methodology' and 'theory' is properly carried on in close and continuous relation with substantive problems.

5

Whether he knows it or not, the line-up of a man's problems—how he states them and what priority he assigns to each—rests upon methods, theories, and values.

Yet, it must be admitted, some men working in social science do not have any ready answer to the signal question of the line-up of their problems. They do not feel the need of any, for they do not, in fact, determine the problems upon which they work. Some allow the immediate troubles of which ordinary men in their everyday milieux are aware to set the problems upon which they work; others accept as their points of orientation the issues defined officially or unofficially by authorities and interests. About this, our colleagues of Eastern Europe and Russia will know much more than we, for most of us have never lived under a political organization which officially controls the intellectual and cultural sphere. But by no means is the phenomenon absent in the West, certainly not in America. The political, but more especially the commercial, orientation of problems for social scientists may come about by their willing, even eager, self-co-ordination.

Among the old liberally practical sociologists, troubles have been taken too much on their own level; the values in terms of which their problems have been detected have not been clarified; and the structural conditions under which they might be realized have been neither worked out nor confronted. The work has been clogged by undigested facts; the scholars have not had the intellectual techniques to assimilate and order these facts; and this has led to the idea of a romantic pluralism of causes. At any rate, the values, whether espoused or not, that have been assumed by liberally practical social scientists have now been largely incorporated into the administrative liberalism of the welfare state.

In bureaucratic social science—of which abstracted empiricism is the most suitable tool and grand theory the accompanying lack of theory—the whole social science endeavor has been pinned down to the services of prevailing authorities. Neither the old liberal practicality nor bureaucratic social science handle public issues and private troubles in such a way as to incorporate both within the problems of social science. The intellectual character and the political uses of these schools (for that matter of any school of social science) cannot readily be separated: it is their political uses as well as their intellectual character (and their academic organization) that have led to the position they occupy in contemporary social science.

In the classic tradition of social science, problems are formulated in such a way that their very statement incorporates a number of specific milieux and the private troubles encountered there by a variety of individuals; these milieux, in turn, are located in terms of larger historical and social structures.

No problem can be adequately formulated unless the values involved and the apparent threat to them are stated. These values and their imperilment constitute the terms of the problem itself. The values that have been the thread of classic social analysis, I believe, are freedom and reason; the forces that imperil them today seem at times to be co-extensive with the major trends of contemporary society, if not to constitute the characterizing features of the contemporary period. The leading problems of the social studies today have this in common: they concern conditions and tendencies that seem to imperil these two values and the consequences of that imperilment for the nature of man and the making of history.

But I am less concerned here with any particular array of problems, including my own choice, than with the need for social scientists to reflect upon the actual problems that they do in fact assume by their work and in their plans. Only in view of such reflection can they consider their problems as well as possible alternatives to them, explicitly and carefully. Only in this way can they proceed objectively. For objectivity in the work of social science requires the continuous attempt to become explicitly aware of all that is involved in the enterprise; it requires wide and critical interchange of such attempts. It is neither by dogmatic models of Scientific Method nor by pretentious proclamations of The Problems of Social Science that social scientists may hope to develop their disciplines in a fruitfully cumulative way.

The formulation of problems, then, should include explicit attention to a range of public issues and of personal troubles; and they should open up for inquiry the causal connections between milieux and social structure. In our formulation of problems we must make clear the values that are really threatened in the troubles and issues involved, who accepts them as values, and by whom or by what they are threatened. Such formulations are often greatly complicated by the fact that the values found to be imperiled are not always those which individuals and publics believe to be imperiled, or at any rate not the only ones. Accordingly we must also ask such questions as these: What values do the actors believe to be imperiled? By whom or by what do they believe them to be imperiled? Were they fully aware of the values really involved, would they be disturbed by their imperilment? It is quite necessary to take these values and feelings, arguments and fears, into our formulation of the problem, for such beliefs and expectations, however inadequate and mistaken they may be, are the very stuff of issues and troubles. Moreover, the answer to the problem, if any, is to be tested in part by its usefulness in explaining troubles and issues as they are experienced.

The 'basic problem,' by the way, and its answer, usually require attention both to uneasiness arising from the 'depth' of biography, and to indifference arising from the very structure of an historical society. By our choice and statement of problems, we must first translate indifference into issues, uneasiness into trouble, and second, we must admit both troubles and issues in the statement of our problem. In both stages, we must try to state in as simple and precise a manner as we can, the several values and threats involved, and try to relate them.

Any adequate 'answer' to a problem, in turn, will contain a view of the strategic points of intervention—of the 'levers' by which the structure may be maintained or changed; and an assessment of those who are in a position to intervene but are not doing so. There is more—much more—involved in the formulation of problems, but I have wanted here only to indicate one outline.

7

The Human Variety

HAVING CRITICIZED at considerable length several prevailing tendencies in social science, I want now to return to more positive—even programmatic—ideas of the promise of social science. Social science may be confused, but its confusion should be exploited rather than bemoaned. It may be sick, but recognition of this fact can and should be taken as a call for diagnosis and perhaps even as a sign of coming health.

1

What social science is properly about is the human variety, which consists of all the social worlds in which men have lived, are living, and might live. These worlds contain primitive communities that, so far as we know, have changed little in a thousand years; but also great power states that have, as it were, come suddenly into violent being. Byzantine and Europe, classical China and ancient Rome, the city of Los Angeles and the empire of ancient Peru—all the worlds men have known now lie before us, open to our scrutiny.

Within these worlds there are open-country settlements and pressure groups and boys' gangs and Navajo oil men; air forces pointed to demolish metropolitan areas a hundred miles wide; policemen on a corner; intimate circles and publics seated in a room; criminal syndicates; masses thronged one night at the crossroads and squares of the cities of the world; Hopi children and slave dealers in Arabia and German parties and Polish classes and Mennonite schools and the mentally deranged in Tibet and radio networks reaching around the world. Racial stocks and ethnic groups are jumbled up in movie houses and also segregated; married happily and also hating systematically; a thousand detailed occupations are seated in businesses and industries, in governments and localities, in near-continent-wide nations. A million little bargains are transacted every day, and everywhere there are more 'small groups' than anyone could ever count.

The human variety also includes the variety of individual human beings; these too the sociological imagination must grasp and understand. In this imagination an Indian Brahmin of 1850 stands alongside a pioneer farmer of Illinois; an eighteenth-century English gentleman alongside an Australian aboriginal, together with a Chinese peasant of one hundred years ago, a politician in Bolivia today, a feudal knight of France, an English suffragette on hunger strike in 1914, a Hollywood starlet, a Roman patrician. To write of 'man' is to write of all these men and women—also of Goethe, and of the girl next door.

The social scientist seeks to understand the human variety in an orderly way, but considering the range and depth of this variety, he might well be asked: Is this really possible? Is not the confusion of the social sciences an inevitable reflection of what their practitioners are trying to study? My answer is that perhaps the variety is not as 'disorderly' as the mere listing of a small part of it makes it seem; perhaps not even as disorderly as it is often made to seem by the courses of study offered in colleges and universities. Order as well as disorder is relative to viewpoint: to come to an orderly understanding of men and societies requires a set of viewpoints that are simple enough to make understanding possible, yet comprehensive enough to permit us to include in our views the range and depth of the human variety. The struggle for such viewpoints is the first and continuing struggle of social science.

Any viewpoint, of course, rests upon a set of questions, and the over-all questions of the social sciences (which I suggested in chapter 1) come readily to the mind that has firm hold of the orienting conception of social science as the study of biography, of history, and of the problems of their intersection within social structure. To study these problems, to realize the human variety, requires that our work be continuously and closely related to the level of historical reality—and to the meanings of this reality for individual men and women. Our aim is to define this reality and to discern these meanings; it is in terms of them that the problems of classic social science are formulated, and thus the issues and troubles these problems incorporate are confronted. It requires that we seek a fully comparative understanding of the social structures that have appeared and do now exist in world history. It requires that smaller-scale milieux be selected and studied in terms of larger-scale historical structures. It requires that we avoid the arbitrary specialization of academic depart- ments, that we specialize our work variously according to topic and above all according to problem, and that in doing so we draw upon the perspectives and ideas, the materials and the methods, of any and all suitable studies of man as an historical actor.

Historically, social scientists have paid most attention to polit- ical and economic institutions, but military and kinship, religious and educational institutions have also been much studied. Such classification according to the objective functions institutions gen- erally serve is deceptively simple, but still it is handy. If we un- derstand how these institutional orders are related to one another, we understand the social structure of a society. For 'social struc- ture,' as the conception is most commonly used, refers to just that—to the combination of institutions classified according to the functions each performs. As such, it is the most inclusive working unit with which social scientists deal. Their broadest aim, accordingly, is to understand each of the varieties of social structure, in its components and in its totality. The term 'social structure' itself is quite variously defined, and other terms are used for the conception, but if the distinction between milieu and structure is kept in mind, along with the notion of institution, no one will fail to recognize the idea of social structure when he comes upon it.

2

In our period, social structures are usually organized under a political state. In terms of power, and in many other interesting terms as well, the most inclusive unit of social structure is the nation-state. The nation-state is now the dominating form in world history and, as such, a major fact in the life of every man. The nation-state has split up and organized, in varying degree and manner, the 'civilizations' and continents of the world. The extent of its spread and the stages of its development are major clues to modern and now to world history. Within the nation-state, the political and military, cultural and economic means of decision and power are now organized; all the institutions and specific milieux in which most men live their public and private lives are now organized into one or the other of the nation-states.

Social scientists of course do not always study only national social structures. The point is that the nation-state is the frame within which they most often feel the need to formulate the problems of smaller and of larger units. Other 'units' are most readily understood as 'pre-national,'—or as 'post-national.' For of course national units may 'belong' to one of the 'civilizations,' which usually means that their religious institutions are those of one or another of the 'world religions.' Such facts of 'civilization,' as well as many others, may suggest ways to compare the present-day variety of nation-states. But as used for example by writers like Arnold Toynbee, 'civilizations,' it seems to me, are much too sprawling and imprecise to be the prime units, the 'intelligible fields of study,' of the social sciences.

In choosing the national social structure as our generic working unit, we are adopting a suitable level of generality: one that enables us to avoid abandoning our problems and yet to include the structural forces obviously involved in many details and troubles of human conduct today. Moreover, the choice of national social structures enables us most readily to take up the major issues of public concern, for it is within and between the nation-states of the world that the effective means of power, and hence to a considerable extent of history-making, are now, for better or for worse, tightly organized.

It is of course true that not all nation-states are equal in their power to make history. Some are so small and dependent upon others that what happens within them can only be understood by studying The Great Power States. But that is merely another problem in the useful classification of our units—the nations—and in their necessarily comparative study. It is also true that all nation-states interact, and some clusters of them derive from similar contexts of tradition. But that is true of any sizable unit we might choose for social study. Moreover, especially since World War One, every nation-state capable of it has become increasingly self-sufficient.

Most economists and political scientists consider it obvious that their prime unit is the nation-state; even when they are concerned with 'the international economy' and 'international relations,' they must work closely in the terms of various and specific nation-states. The condition and the continuing practice of anthropologists are of course to study 'the whole' of a society or 'culture,' and in so far as they study modern societies they readily attempt, with varying success, to understand nations as wholes. But sociologists—or more exactly, research technicians—who do not have a very firm hold on the conception of social structure, often consider nations dubiously grand in scale. Apparently this is owing to a bias in favor of 'data collection' which can be less expensively indulged only in smaller-scale units. This means of course that their choice of units is not in accordance with what is needed for whatever problems they have chosen; instead both problem and unit are determined by their choice of method.

In a sense, this book as a whole is an argument against this bias. I think that when most social scientists come seriously to examine a significant problem, they find it most difficult to formulate in terms of any unit smaller than the nation-state. This is true for the study of stratification and of economic policy, of public opinion and the nature of political power, of work and leisure; even problems of municipal government cannot be adequately formulated without quite full reference to their national frame. The unit of the nation-state thus recommends itself by a good deal of empirical evidence available to anyone who is experienced in working on the problems of social science.

3

The idea of social structure, along with the contention that it is the generic unit of social science, is historically most closely associated with sociology, and sociologists have been its classical exponents. The traditional subject matter of both sociology and anthropology has been the total society; or, as it is called by anthropologists, 'the culture.' What is specifically 'sociological' in the study of any particular feature of a total society is the continual effort to relate that feature to others, in order to gain a conception of the whole. The sociological imagination, I have noted, is in considerable part a result of training in this kind of effort. But nowadays such a view and such practice is by no means confined to sociologists and anthropologists. What was once a promise in these disciplines has become at least a faltering practice, as well as an intention, in the social sciences generally.

Cultural anthropology, in its classic tradition and in its current developments, does not seem to me in any fundamental way distinguishable from sociological study. Once upon a time, when there were few or no surveys of contemporary societies, anthropologists had to collect materials about pre-literate peoples in out-of-the-way places. Other social sciences—notably history, demography and political science—have from their beginnings depended upon documentary materials accumulated in literate societies. And this fact tended to separate the disciplines. But now 'empirical surveys' of various sorts are used in all the social sciences, in fact the technique has been most fully developed by psychologists and sociologists in connection with historical societies. In recent years, too, anthropologists have of course studied advanced communities and even nation-states, often at a considerable distance; in turn, sociologists and economists have studied 'the undeveloped peoples.' There is neither a distinction in method nor a boundary of subject matter that truly distinguishes anthropology from economics and sociology today.

Most economics and political science has been concerned with special institutional areas of social structure. About the 'economy' and about 'the state,' political scientists to a lesser extent, and economists to a greater, have developed 'classic theories' that have persisted for generations of scholars. They have, in short, built models, although the political scientists (along with the sociologists) have traditionally been less aware of their model building than the economists have been. Classical theory, of course, consists of making up conceptions and assumptions, from which deductions and generalizations are drawn; these in turn are compared with a variety of empirical propositions. In these tasks, conceptions and procedures and even questions are at least implicitly codified.

This may be all very well. However, for economics certainly and for political science and sociology in due course, two developments tend to make less relevant formal models of state and economy having neat, which is to say formal—and largely mutually exclusive—boundaries: (1) the economic and political development of the so-called underdeveloped areas, and (2) trends of twentieth-century forms of 'the political economy'—both totalitarian and formally democratic. The aftermath of World War Two has been at once erosive and fructifying for alert economic theorists, in fact, for all social scientists worthy of the title.

A 'theory of prices' that is merely economic may be logically neat, but it cannot be empirically adequate. Such a theory demands consideration of the administration of business institutions and the role of decision-makers within and between them; it requires attention to the psychology of expectations about costs, in particular about wages; to the fixing of prices by small business cartels whose leaders must be understood, etc. In a similar way, to understand 'the rate of interest' often requires knowledge of the official and personal traffic between bankers and government officials as well as impersonal economic mechanics.

There is nothing for it, I think, but for each social scientist to join social science, and with it to go fully comparative—and that, I believe, is now a quite strong drift of interest. Comparative work, both theoretical and empirical, is the most promising line of development for social science today; and such work can best be done within a unified social science.

4

As each social science advances, its interaction with the others has been intensified. The subject matter of economics is again becoming what it was in the beginning—the 'political economy,' which is increasingly viewed within a total social structure. An economist such as John Galbraith is as much a political scientist as Robert Dahl or David Truman; in fact his work on the current structure of American capitalism is as much a sociological theory of a political economy as Schumpeter's view of capitalism and democracy or Earl Latham's of group politics. Harold D. Lasswell or David Riesman or Gabriel Almond is as much a sociologist as a psychologist and a political scientist. They are in and out of the social sciences, and so are they all; in so far as a man comes to master any of these 'fields' he is forced into the bailiwicks of the others, which is to say, into the sphere of all those belonging to the classic tradition. They may of course specialize in one institutional order, but in so far as they grasp what is essential to it, they will also come to understand its place within the total social structure, and hence its relations with other institutional domains. For in considerable part, it is becoming clear, its every reality consists of these relations.

Of course, it should not be supposed that, faced with the great variety of social life, social scientists have rationally divided up the work at hand. In the first place, each of the disciplines involved has grown up on its own and in response to quite specific demands and conditions; none has been developed as part of some over-all plan. In the second place, there are of course many disagreements concerning the relations of these several disciplines and there are disagreements also about the appropriate degree of specialization. But the overriding fact today is that these disagreements can now be seen more as facts of the academic life than as intellectual difficulties, and even academically, I believe, they often tend nowadays to resolve themselves, to be outgrown.

Intellectually, the central fact today is an increasing fluidity of boundary lines; conceptions move with increasing ease from one discipline to another. There are several notable cases of careers based rather exclusively on the mastery of the vocabulary of one field and its adroit use in the traditional area of another. Specialization there is and there will be, but it ought not to be in terms of the more or less accidentally built disciplines as we know them. It should occur along the lines of problems the solution of which requires intellectual equipment traditionally belonging to these several disciplines. Increasingly, similar conceptions and methods are used by all social scientists.

Every social science has been shaped by internal developments of an intellectual sort; each has also been decisively influenced by institutional 'accidents'—a fact clearly revealed by the differing ways each has been shaped in each of the major Western nations. The tolerance or the indifference of already established disciplines, including philosophy, history, and the humanities, has often conditioned the fields of sociology, economics, anthropology, political science, and psychology. In fact, in some institutions of higher learning such tolerance or its absence has determined the presence or absence of social sciences as academic departments. In Oxford and in Cambridge, for example, there are no 'sociology departments.'

The danger of taking the departmentalization of social science too seriously lies in the accompanying assumption that economic and political and other social institutions are each an autonomous system. Of course, as I have indicated, that assumption has been and is used to construct 'analytical models' which are often very useful indeed. Generalized, and frozen into the departments of a school, the classic models of 'the polity' and of 'the economy' do probably approximate the early nineteenth-century structure of England and especially of the United States. In fact, historically, economics and political science as specialities must, in some part, be interpreted in terms of the historical phase of the modern West during which each institutional order was claimed to be an autonomous realm. But it is clear that a model of society as composed of autonomous institutional orders is certainly not the only model in terms of which to work in social science. We cannot take that one type as the suitable basis for our whole division of intellectual labor. Realization of this is one of the impulses now at work unifying the social sciences. A very active fusion of the several disciplines of political science and economics, cultural anthropology and history, sociology and at least one major division of psychology has been going on in the planning of academic courses, as well as in the ideal design of studies.

The intellectual problems posed by the unity of the social sciences have mainly to do with the relations of institutional orders—the political and the economic, the military and the religious, the family and education—in given societies and periods; they are, as I have said, important problems. The many practical difficulties posed by the working relations of the several social sciences have to do with the design of curricula and of academic careers, with linguistic confusion and the established job-markets for graduates of each field. One great obstacle to unified work in social science is the one-discipline introductory textbook. It is more frequently in terms of textbooks than of any other intellectual productions that the integration and the boundary-making of 'fields' occur. It is difficult to imagine a less suitable locale. Yet the textbook wholesalers do have a very real vested interest in their productions, even if producers and consumers come out on the short end. Along with textbook integration, the attempt to integrate the social sciences proceeds in terms of conceptions and methods, rather than in terms of problems and subject matters. Accordingly, the idea of distinct 'fields' is based less on iron problem-areas than on tinfoil Concepts. These Concepts are, nevertheless, difficult to overcome, and I do not know whether they will be. But there is just a chance, I feel, that within the society of academic disciplines certain structural trends will in due course overcome those who—often entrenched and obstinate—are still trapped in their specialized milieux.

In the meantime, certainly many individual social scientists realize that in 'their own disciplines' they can best fulfill their aims by recognizing more explicitly the common orienting tasks of social science. It is now entirely possible for the individual practitioner to ignore the 'accidental' developments of departments, and to choose and shape his own specialty without much hindrance of a departmental sort. As he comes to have a genuine sense of significant problems and to be passionately concerned with solving them, he is often forced to master ideas and methods that happen to have arisen within one or another of these several disciplines. To him no social-science specialty will seem in any intellectually significant sense a closed world. He also comes to realize that he is in fact practicing social science, rather than any one of the social sciences, and that this is so no matter what particular area of social life he is most interested in studying.

Often it is asserted that no one can have an altogether encyclopedic mind without being dilettantish. I do not know that this is so, but if it is, still can we not at least gain something of an encyclopedic sense? It is quite impossible truly to master all the materials, conceptions, methods of every one of these disciplines. Moreover, attempts 'to integrate the social sciences' by 'conceptual translation' or detailed exposition of materials are usually mandarin rubbish; so is much of what goes on in many of the course sequences of 'general social science.' But such mastery, such translation, such exposition, such courses—are not what is meant by 'the unity of the social sciences.'

What is meant is this: To state and to solve any one of the significant problems of our period requires a selection of materials, conceptions, and methods from more than any one of these several disciplines. A social scientist need not 'master the field' in order to be familiar enough with its materials and perspectives to use them in clarifying the problems that concern him. It is in terms of such topical 'problems,' rather than in accordance with academic boundaries, that specialization ought to occur. This, it seems to me, is what is now happening.

8

Uses of History

SOCIAL SCIENCE deals with problems of biography, of history, and of their intersections within social structures. That these three—biography, history, society—are the co-ordinate points of the proper study of man has been a major platform on which I have stood when criticizing several current schools of sociology whose practitioners have abandoned this classic tradition. The problems of our time—which now include the problem of man's very nature—cannot be stated adequately without consistent practice of the view that history is the shank of social study, and recognition of the need to develop further a psychology of man that is sociologically grounded and historically relevant. Without use of history and without an historical sense of psychological matters, the social scientist cannot adequately state the kinds of problems that ought now to be the orienting points of his studies.

1

The weary debate over whether or not historical study is or should be considered a social science is neither important nor interesting. The conclusion depends so clearly upon what kinds of historians and what kinds of social scientists you are talking about. Some historians are clearly compilers of alleged fact, which they try to refrain from 'interpreting'; they are involved, often fruitfully, in some fragment of history and seem unwilling to locate it within any larger range of events. Some are beyond history, lost—often fruitfully so—in trans-historical visions of the coming doom or the coming glory. History as a discipline does invite grubbing for detail, but it also encourages a widening of one's view to embrace epochal pivotal events in the development of social structures.

Perhaps most historians are concerned with 'making sure of the facts' needed to understand the historical transformation of social institutions, and with interpreting such facts, usually by means of narratives. Many historians, moreover, do not hesitate to take up in their studies any and every area of social life. Their scope is thus that of social science, although like other social scientists, they may specialize in political history or economic history or the history of ideas. In so far as historians study types of institutions they tend to emphasize changes over some span of time and to work in a non-comparative way; whereas the work of many social scientists in studying types of institutions has been more comparative than historical. But surely this difference is merely one of emphasis and of specialization within a common task.

Many American historians, just now, are very much influenced by the conceptions, problems, and methods of the several social sciences. Barzun and Graff have recently suggested that perhaps 'social scientists keep urging historians to modernize their technique' because 'social scientists are too busy to read history' and 'they do not recognize their own materials when presented in a different pattern.' [1]

There are of course more problems of method in any work of history than many historians usually dream of. But nowadays some of them do dream, not so much of method as of epistemology —and in a manner that can only result in a curious retreat from historical reality. The influence upon some historians of certain kinds of 'social science' is often quite unfortunate, but it is an influence which is not, as yet, wide enough to require lengthy discussion here.

The master task of the historian is to keep the human record straight, but that is indeed a deceptively simple statement of aim. The historian represents the organized memory of mankind, and that memory, as written history, is enormously malleable. It changes, often quite drastically, from one generation of historians

[1] Jacques Barzun and Henry Graff, *The Modern Researcher*, New York, Harcourt, Brace, 1957, p. 221.

to another—and not merely because more detailed research later introduces new facts and documents into the record. It changes also because of changes in the points of interest and the current framework within which the record is built. These are the criteria of selection from the innumerable facts available, and at the same time the leading interpretations of their meaning. The historian cannot avoid making a selection of facts, although he may attempt to disclaim it by keeping his interpretations slim and circumspect. We did not need George Orwell's imaginative projection in order to know how easily history may be distorted in the process of its continual rewriting, although his *1984* made it dramatically emphatic, and, let us hope, properly frightened some of our historian colleagues.

All these perils of the historian's enterprise make it one of the most theoretical of the human disciplines, which makes the calm unawareness of many historians all the more impressive. Impressive, yes; but also rather unsettling. I suppose there have been periods in which perspectives were rigid and monolithic and in which historians could remain unaware of the themes taken for granted. But ours is not such a period; if historians have no 'theory,' they may provide materials for the writing of history, but they cannot themselves write it. They can entertain, but they cannot keep the record straight. That task now requires explicit attention to much more than 'the facts.'

The productions of historians may be thought of as a great file indispensable to all social science—I believe this a true and fruitful view. History as a discipline is also sometimes considered to contain all social science—but only by a few misguided 'humanists.' More fundamental than either view is the idea that every social science—or better, every well-considered social study—requires an historical scope of conception and a full use of historical materials. This simple notion is the major idea for which I am arguing.

At the beginning, perhaps we should confront one frequent objection to the use of historical materials by social scientists: It is held that such materials are not precise or even known fully enough to permit their use in comparisons with the better confirmed and more exact contemporary materials available. This objection does of course point to a very worrisome problem of social inquiry, but it has force only if one limits the kinds of information admitted. As I have already argued, the requirements of one's problem, rather than the limitations of any one rigid method, should be and have been the classic social analyst's paramount consideration. The objection, moreover, is relevant only for certain problems and may, in fact, frequently be turned around: For many problems we can obtain adequate information *only* about the past. The fact of official and unofficial secrecy, and the widespread use of public relations, are contemporary facts which surely must be taken into account as we judge the reliability of information about the past and about the present. This objection, in a word, is merely another version of the methodological inhibition, and often a feature of the 'know-nothing' ideology of the politically quiescent.

2

More important than the extent to which historians are social scientists, or how they should behave, is the still more controversial point that the social sciences are themselves historical disciplines. To fulfill their tasks, or even to state them well, social scientists must use the materials of history. Unless one assumes some transhistorical theory of the nature of history, or that man in society is a non-historical entity, no social science can be assumed to transcend history. All sociology worthy of the name is 'historical sociology.' It is, in Paul Sweezy's excellent phrase, an attempt to write 'the present as history.' There are several reasons for this intimate relation of history and sociology:

(1) In our very statement of what-is-to-be-explained, we need the fuller range that can be provided only by knowledge of the historical varieties of human society. That a given question—the relations of forms of nationalism with types of militarism, e.g.— must often be given a different answer when it is asked of different societies and periods means that the question itself often needs to be re-formulated. We need the variety provided by history in order even to ask sociological questions properly, much

less to answer them. The answers or explanations we would offer are often, if not usually, in terms of comparisons. Comparisons are required in order to understand what may be the essential conditions of whatever we are trying to understand, whether forms of slavery or specific meanings of crime, types of family or peasant communities or collective farms. We must observe whatever we are interested in under a variety of circumstances. Otherwise we are limited to flat description.

To go beyond that, we must study the available range of social structures, including the historical as well as the contemporary. If we do not take into account the range, which does not of course mean all existing cases, our statements cannot be empirically adequate. Such regularities or relations as may obtain among several features of society cannot be clearly discerned. Historical types, in short, are a very important part of what we are studying; they are also indispensable to our explanations of it. To eliminate such materials—the record of all that man has done and become—from our studies would be like pretending to study the process of birth but ignoring motherhood.

If we limit ourselves to one national unit of one contemporary (usually Western) society, we cannot possibly hope to catch many really fundamental differences among human types and social institutions. This general truth has one rather specific meaning for work in social science: In the cross-section moment of any one society there may often be so many common denominators of belief, value, institutional form, that no matter how detailed and precise our study, we will not find truly significant differences among the people and institutions at this one moment in this one society. In fact, the one-time-and-one-locale studies often assume or imply a homogeneity which, if true, very much needs *to be taken as a problem*. It cannot fruitfully be reduced, as it so often is in current research practice, to a problem of sampling procedure. It cannot be formulated as a problem within the terms of one moment and one locale.

Societies seem to differ with respect to the range of variation of specific phenomena within them as well as, in a more general way, with respect to their degree of social homogeneity. As Morris Ginsberg has remarked, if something we are studying 'exhibits sufficient individual variations within the same society, or at the same period of time, it may be possible to establish real connections without going outside that society or period.' [2] That is often true, but usually it is not so certain that it may simply be assumed; to know whether or not it is true, we must often design our studies as comparisons of social structures. To do that in an adequate way usually requires that we make use of the variety provided by history. The problem of social homogeneity—as in the modern mass society, or, in contrast, as in the traditional society—cannot even be properly stated, much less adequately solved, unless we consider in a comparative way the range of contemporary and historical societies.

The meaning, for example, of such key themes of political science as 'public' and 'public opinion' cannot be made clear without such work. If we do not take a fuller range into our study, we often condemn ourselves to shallow and misleading results. I do not suppose, for example, that anyone would argue with the statement that the fact of political indifference is one of the major facts of the contemporary political scene in Western societies. Yet in those studies of 'the political psychology of voters' which are non-comparative and non-historical, we do not find even a classification of 'voters'—or of 'political men'—that really takes into account such indifference. In fact, the historically specific idea of such political indifference, and much less its meaning, cannot be formulated in the usual terms of such voting studies.

To say of peasants of the pre-industrial world that they are 'politically indifferent' does not carry the same meaning as to say the same of man in modern mass society. For one thing, the importance of political institutions to ways of life and their conditions are quite different in the two types of society. For another thing, the formal opportunity to become politically engaged differs. And for another, the expectation of political involvement raised by the entire course of bourgeois democracy in the modern West has not always been raised in the pre-industrial world. To understand 'political indifference,' to explain it, to grasp its meaning for modern societies require that we consider the quite vari-

[2] Morris Ginsberg, *Essays in Sociology and Social Philosophy*, Vol. II, 39, London, Heinemann, 1956.

ous types and conditions of indifference, and to do that we must examine historical and comparative materials.

(2) A-historical studies usually tend to be static or very short-term studies of limited milieux. That is only to be expected, for we more readily become aware of larger structures when they are changing, and we are likely to become aware of such changes only when we broaden our view to include a suitable historical span. Our chance to understand how smaller milieux and larger structures interact, and our chance to understand the larger causes at work in these limited milieux thus require us to deal with historical materials. Awareness of structure, in all the meanings of this central term, as well as adequate statement of the troubles and problems of limited milieux, require that we recognize and that we practice the social sciences as historical disciplines.

Not only are our chances of becoming aware of structure increased by historical work; we cannot hope to understand any single society, even as a static affair, without the use of historical materials. The image of any society is an historically specific image. What Marx called the 'principle of historical specificity' refers, first, to a guide-line: any given society is to be understood in terms of the specific period in which it exists. However 'period' may be defined, the institutions, the ideologies, the types of men and women prevailing in any given period constitute something of a unique pattern. This does not mean that such an historical type cannot be compared with others, and certainly not that the pattern can be grasped only intuitively. But it does mean—and this is the second reference of the principle—that within this historical type various mechanisms of change come to some specific kind of intersection. These mechanisms, which Karl Mannheim—following John Stuart Mill—called *'principia media,'* are the very mechanisms that the social scientist, concerned with social structure, wishes to grasp.

Early social theorists tried to formulate invariant laws of society —laws that would hold of all societies, just as the abstracted procedures of physical science had led to laws that cut beneath the qualitative richness of 'nature.' There is, I believe, no 'law' stated by any social scientist that is trans-historical, that must not be understood as having to do with the specific structure of some period. Other 'laws' turn out to be empty abstractions or quite confused tautologies. The only meaning of 'social laws' or even of 'social regularities' is such *principia media* as we may discover, or if you wish, construct, for a social structure within an historically specific era. We do not know any universal principles of historical change; the mechanisms of change we do know vary with the social structure we are examining. For historical change *is* change of social structures, of the relations among their component parts. Just as there is a variety of social structures, there is a variety of principles of historical change.

(3) That knowledge of the history of a society is often indispensable to its understanding becomes quite clear to any economist or political scientist or sociologist once he leaves his advanced industrial nation to examine the institutions in some different social structure—in the Middle East, in Asia, in Africa. In the study of 'his own country' he has often smuggled in the history; knowledge of it is embodied in the very conceptions with which he works. When he takes up a fuller range, when he compares, he becomes more aware of the historical as intrinsic to what he wants to understand and not merely as 'general background.'

In our time problems of the Western societies are almost inevitably problems of the world. It is perhaps one defining characteristic of our period that it is one in which for the first time the varieties of social worlds it contains are in serious, rapid, and obvious interplay. The study of our period must be a comparative examination of these worlds and of their interactions. Perhaps that is why what was once the anthropologist's exotic preserve, has become the world's 'underdeveloped countries,' which economists no less than political scientists and sociologists regularly include among their objects of study. That is why some of the very best sociology being done today is work on world areas and regions.

Comparative study and historical study are very deeply involved with each other. You cannot understand the underdeveloped, the

Communist, the capitalist political economies as they exist in the world today by flat, timeless comparisons. You must expand the temporal reach of your analysis. To understand and to explain the comparative facts as they lie before you today, you must know the historical phases and the historical reasons for varying rates and varying directions of development and lack of development. You must know, for example, why the colonies founded by Westerners in North America and Australia in the sixteenth and seventeenth centuries became in due course industrially flourishing capitalist societies, but those in India, Latin America, and Africa remained impoverished, peasant, and underdeveloped right up into the twentieth century.

Thus the historical viewpoint leads to the comparative study of societies: you cannot understand or explain the major phases through which any modern Western nation has passed, or the shape that it assumes today, solely in terms of its own national history. I do not mean merely that in historical reality it has interacted with the development of other societies; I mean also that the mind cannot even formulate the historical and sociological problems of this one social structure without understanding them in contrast and in comparison with other societies.

(4) Even if our work is not explicitly comparative—even if we are concerned with some limited area of one national social structure—we need historical materials. Only by an act of abstraction that unnecessarily violates social reality can we try to freeze some knife-edge moment. We may of course construct such static glimpses or even panoramas, but we cannot conclude our work with such constructions. Knowing that what we are studying is subject to change, on the simplest of descriptive levels, we must ask: What are the salient trends? To answer that question we must make a statement of at least 'from what' and 'to what.'

Our statement of trend may be very short-term or of epochal length; that will of course depend upon our purpose. But usually, in work of any scale, we find a need for trends of considerable length. Longer-term trends are usually needed if only in order to overcome historical provincialism: the assumption that the present is a sort of autonomous creation.

If we want to understand the dynamic changes in a contemporary social structure, we must try to discern its longer-run developments, and in terms of them ask: What are the mechanics by which these trends have occurred, by which the structure of this society is changing? It is in questions such as these that our concern with trends comes to a climax. That climax has to do with the historical transition from one epoch to another and with what we may call the structure of an epoch.

The social scientist wishes to understand the nature of the present epoch, to outline its structure and to discern the major forces at work within it. Each epoch, when properly defined, is 'an intelligible field of study' that reveals mechanics of history-making peculiar to it. The role of power elites, for example, in the making of history, varies according to the extent to which the institutional means of decisions are centralized.

The notion of the structure and dynamics of 'the modern period,' and of such essential and unique features as it may have, is central, although often unacknowledged, to the social sciences. Political scientists study the modern state; economists, modern capitalism. Sociologists—especially in their dialectic with Marxism —pose many of their problems in terms of 'the characteristics of modern times,' and anthropologists use their sensibilities to the modern world in their examinations of pre-literate societies. Perhaps most classic problems of modern social science—of political science and economics no less than of sociology—have, in fact, had to do with one rather specific historical interpretation: the interpretation of the rise, the components, the shape, of the urban industrial societies of The Modern West—usually in contrast with The Feudal Era.

Many of the conceptions most commonly used in social science have to do with the historical transition from the rural community of feudal times to the urban society of the modern age: Maine's 'status' and 'contract,' Tönnies's 'community' and 'society,' Weber's 'status' and 'class,' St. Simon's 'three stages,' Spencer's 'military' and 'industrial,' Pareto's 'circulation of elites,' Cooley's 'primary and secondary groups,' Durkheim's 'mechanical' and 'organic,' Redfield's 'folk' and 'urban,' Becker's 'sacred' and 'secular,' Lasswell's 'bargaining society' and 'garrison state'—these, no matter how generalized in use, are all historically-rooted conceptions. Even those who believe they do not work historically, generally reveal by their use of such terms some notion of historical trends and even a sense of period.

It is in terms of this alertness to the shape and the dynamics of 'the modern period,' and to the nature of its crises, that the social scientist's standard concern with 'trends' ought to be understood. We study trends in an attempt to go behind events and to make orderly sense of them. In such studies we often try to focus on each trend just a little ahead of where it is now, and more importantly, to see all the trends at once, as moving parts of the total structure of the period. It is, of course, intellectually easier (and politically more advisable) to acknowledge one trend at a time, keeping them scattered, as it were, than to make the effort to see them all together. To the literary empiricist, writing balanced little essays, first on this and then on that, any attempt to 'see it whole' often seems an 'extremist exaggeration.'

There *are* of course many intellectual dangers in the attempt to 'see it whole.' For one thing, what one man sees as a whole, another sees as only a part, and sometimes, for lack of synoptic vision, the attempt becomes overwhelmed by the need for description. The attempt may of course be biased, but I do not think any more so than the selection of precisely examinable detail without reference to any idea of any whole, for such selection must be arbitrary. In historically oriented work, we are also liable to confuse 'prediction' with 'description.' These two, however, are not to be sharply separated, and they are not the only ways of looking at trends. We can examine trends in an effort to answer the question 'where are we going?'—and that is what social scientists are often trying to do. In doing so, we are trying to study history rather than to retreat into it, to pay attention to contemporary trends without being 'merely journalistic,' to gauge the future of these trends without being merely prophetic. All this is hard to do. We must remember that we *are* dealing with historical materials; that they do change very rapidly; that there are countertrends. And we have always to balance the immediacy of the knife-edge present with the generality needed to bring out the meaning of specific trends for the period as a whole. But above all, the social scientist is trying to see the several major trends together—structurally, rather than as happenings in a scatter of milieux, adding up to nothing new, in fact not adding up at all. This is the aim that lends to the study of trends its relevance to the understanding of a period, and which demands full and adroit use of the materials of history.

3

There is one 'use of history,' rather common in social science today, that is, in fact, more a ritual than a genuine use. I refer to the dull little padding known as 'sketching in the historical background,' with which studies of contemporary society are often prefaced, and to the *ad hoc* procedure known as 'giving an historical explanation.' Such explanations, resting upon the past of a single society, are seldom adequate. There are three points which should be made about them:

First, I think we must accept the point that we must often study history in order to get rid of it. By this I mean that what are often taken as historical explanations would better be taken as part of the statement of that which is to be explained. Rather than 'explain' something as 'a persistence from the past,' we ought to ask, 'why has it persisted?' Usually we will find that the answer varies according to the phases through which whatever we are studying has gone; for each of these phases we may then attempt to find out what role it has played, and how and why it has passed on to the next phase.

Second, in work on a contemporary society, I think it is very often a good rule first to attempt to explain its contemporary features in terms of their contemporary function. This means to locate them, to see them as parts of and even as due to other features of their contemporary setting. If only to define them, to delimit them clearly, to make their components more specific, it is best to begin with a more or less narrow—although still of course historical—span.

In their work on the adult problems of individuals, some neo-Freudians—most clearly perhaps Karen Horney—seem to have come to the use of a similar order of procedure. One works back to the genetic, biographical causes only after having exhausted the contemporary features and setting of the character. And of course, a classic debate on the whole matter has occurred between the functional and the historical schools of anthropology. One reason for it, I suppose, is that 'historical explanations' so often become conservative ideologies: institutions have taken a long time to evolve, and accordingly they are not to be tampered with hastily. Another is that historical consciousness so often becomes the root of one kind of radical ideology: institutions are after all transitory; accordingly these particular institutions are not eternal or 'natural' to man; they too will change. Both these views often rest upon a kind of historical determinism or even inevitability that may easily lead to a quiescent posture—and a mistaken conception of how history has been and how it can be made. I do not want to mute such historical sense as I have worked hard to acquire, but neither do I want to prop up my ways of explanation with conservative or radical uses of the notion of historical fate. I do not accept 'fate' as a universal historical category, as I shall explain later on.

My final point is even more controversial, but if it is true, it is of considerable importance: I believe that periods and societies differ in respect to whether or not understanding them requires direct references to 'historical factors.' The historical nature of a given society in a given period may be such that 'the historical past' is only indirectly relevant to its understanding.

It is, of course, quite clear that to understand a slow-moving society, trapped for centuries in a cycle of poverty and tradition and disease and ignorance, requires that we study the historical ground, and the persistent historical mechanisms of its terrible entrapment in its own history. Explanation of that cycle, and of the mechanics of each of its phases, require a very deep-going historical analysis. What is to be explained, first of all, is the mechanism of the full cycle.

But the United States, for example, or the north-western European nations, or Australia, in their present condition, are not trapped in any iron cycle of history. That kind of cycle—as in the desert world of Ibn Khaldoun [3]—does not grip them. All attempts to understand them in such terms, it seems to me, have failed, and tend in fact to become trans-historical nonsense.

The *relevance* of history, in short, is itself subject to the principle of historical specificity. 'Everything,' to be sure, may be said always to have 'come out of the past,' but the meaning of that phrase—'to come out of the past'—is what is at issue. Sometimes there are quite new things in the world, which is to say that 'history' does and 'history' does not 'repeat itself'; it depends upon the social structure and upon the period with whose history we are concerned.[4]

That this sociological principle may be applicable to the United States today, that ours may be a society in a period for which historical explanations are less relevant than for many other societies and periods, goes far, I believe, to help us to understand several important features of American social science: (1) why many social scientists, concerned only with contemporary Western societies or, even more narrowly, only with the United States, consider historical study irrelevant to their work; (2) why some historians talk now, rather wildly it seems to me, about Scientific

[3] See Muhsin Mahdi, *Ibn Khaldoun's Philosophy of History*, London, George Allen & Unwin, 1957; and *Historical Essays*, London, Macmillan, 1957, which contains H. R. Trevor-Roper's revealing comment on it.

[4] I note supportive reasoning in an excellent account of types of labor history, for example, by Walter Galenson: '. . . the marginal revenue from cultivating the older ground is apt to be small . . . in the absence of . . . important new material. . . . But this is not the only justification for concentrating upon more recent events. The contemporary labor movement differs not only quantitatively but qualitatively from that of thirty years ago. Prior to the 1930's it was sectarian in character; its decisions were not a major economic factor, and it was concerned more with narrow internal problems than with national policy.' (Walter Galenson, 'Reflections on the Writing of Labor History,' *Industrial and Labor Relations Review*, October, 1957.) In connection with anthropology, of course, the debate between 'functional' and 'historical' explanations has long been under way. More often than not anthropologists must be functional because they cannot find out anything about the history of the 'cultures' they examine. They really must try to explain the present by the present, seeking explanations in the meaningful interrelations of various contemporary features of a society. For a recent perceptive discussion, see Ernest Gellner, 'Time and Theory in Social Anthrolopogy,' *Mind*, April, 1958.

History and attempt in their work to use highly formalist, even explicitly a-historical, techniques; (3) why other historians so often give us the impression, especially in the Sunday supplements, that history is indeed bunk, that it is a myth-making about the past for current ideological uses, both liberal and conservative. The past of the United States is indeed a wonderful source for happy images; and—if I am correct about the contemporary irrelevance of much history—that very fact makes such ideological use of history all the easier.

The relevance of historical work to the tasks and to the promise of social science is not, of course, confined to 'historical explanations' of this one 'American type' of social structure. Moreover, this notion of the varying relevance of historical explanation is itself an historical idea, which must be debated and tested on historical grounds. Even for this one type of contemporary society, the irrelevance of history can easily be pushed too far. It is only by comparative studies that we can become aware of the *absence* of certain historical phases from a society, which is often quite essential to understanding its contemporary shape. The absence of a Feudal Era is an essential condition of many features of American society, among them the character of its elite and its extreme fluidity of status, which has so often been confused with lack of class structure and 'lack of class consciousness.' Social scientists may—in fact, many now do—attempt to retreat from history by means of undue formality of Concept and technique. But these attempts require them to make assumptions about the nature of history and of society that are neither fruitful nor true. Such a retreat from history makes it impossible— and I choose the word with care—to understand precisely the most contemporary features of this one society, which is an historical structure that we cannot hope to understand unless we are guided by the sociological principle of historical specificity.

4

The problems of social and historical psychology are in many ways the most intriguing that we can study today. It is in this area that the major intellectual traditions of our times, in fact of

Western civilization, now come to a most exciting confluence. It is in this area that 'the nature of human nature'—the generic image of man, inherited from the Enlightenment—has in our time been brought into question by the rise of totalitarian governments, by ethnographic relativism, by discovery of the great potential of irrationality in man, and by the very rapidity with which men and women can apparently be historically transformed.

We have come to see that the biographies of men and women, the kinds of individuals they variously become, cannot be understood without reference to the historical structures in which the milieux of their everyday life are organized. Historical transformations carry meanings not only for individual ways of life, but for the very character—the limits and possibilities of the human being. As the history-making unit, the dynamic nation-state is also the unit within which the variety of men and women are selected and formed, liberated and repressed—it is the man-making unit. That is one reason why struggles between nations and between blocs of nations are also struggles over the types of human beings that will eventually prevail in the Middle East, in India, in China, in the United States; that is why culture and politics are now so intimately related; and that is why there is such need and such demand for the sociological imagination. For we cannot adequately understand 'man' as an isolated biological creature, as a bundle of reflexes or a set of instincts, as an 'intelligible field' or a system in and of itself. Whatever else he may be, man is a social and an historical actor who must be understood, if at all, in close and intricate interplay with social and historical structures.

There is, of course, no end of arguments about the relations between 'psychology' and 'the social sciences.' Most of the arguments have been formal attempts to integrate a variety of ideas about 'the individual' and 'the group.' No doubt they are all useful, in some way, to somebody; fortunately, in our attempt to formulate here the scope of social science, they need not concern us. However psychologists may define their field of work, the economist, the sociologist, the political scientist, the anthropologist, and the historian, in their studies of human society, must make assumptions about 'human nature.' These assumptions now usually fall into the borderline discipline of 'social psychology.'

Interest in this area has increased because psychology, like history, is so fundamental to work in social sciences that in so far as psychologists have not turned to the problems involved, social scientists have become their own psychologists. Economists, long the most formalized of social scientists, have become aware that the old 'economic man,' hedonistic and calculating, can no longer be assumed as the psychological foundation of an adequate study of economic institutions. Within anthropology there has grown up a strong interest in 'personality and culture'; within sociology as well as psychology, 'social psychology' is now a busy field of study.

In reaction to these intellectual developments, some psychologists have taken up a variety of work in 'social psychology,' others have attempted, in a variety of ways, to re-define psychology so as to retain a field of study apart from obviously social factors, and some have confined their activities to work in human physiology. I do not wish to examine here the academic specialties within psychology—a field now greatly torn and split—much less to judge them.

There is one style of psychological reflection which has not usually been taken up explicitly by academic psychologists but which none the less has exerted influence upon them—as well as upon our entire intellectual life. In psychoanalysis, and especially in the work of Freud himself, the problem of the nature of human nature is stated in its broadest bearings. During the last generation, in brief, two steps forward have been taken by the less rigid of the psychoanalysts and those influenced by them:

First, the physiology of the individual organism was transcended, and there began the study of those little family circles in which such dreadful melodramas occur. Freud may be said to have discovered from an unexpected viewpoint—the medical—the analysis of the individual in his parental family. Of course, the 'influence' of the family upon man had been noticed; what was new was that as a social institution it became, in Freud's view, intrinsic to the inner character and life-fate of the individual.

Second, the social element in the lens of psychoanalysis was greatly broadened, especially by what must be called sociological work on the super-ego. In America, to the psychoanalytic tradition was joined one having quite different sources, which came to early flower in the social behaviorism of George H. Mead. But then a limitation or a hesitancy set in. The small-scale setting of 'interpersonal relations' is now clearly seen; the broader context in which these relations themselves, and hence the individual himself, are situated has not been. There are, of course, exceptions, notably Erich Fromm, who has related economic and religious institutions and traced out their meanings for types of individuals. One reason for the general hesitancy is the limited social role of the analyst: his work and his perspective are professionally tied to the individual patient; the problems of which he can readily become aware, under the specialized conditions of his practice, are limited. Unfortunately, psychoanalysis has not become a firm and integral part of academic research.[5]

The next step forward in psychoanalytic studies is to do fully for other institutional areas what Freud began to do so magnificently for kinship institutions of a selected type. What is needed is the idea of social structure as a composition of institutional orders, each of which we must study psychologically as Freud studied certain kinship institutions. In psychiatry—the actual therapy of 'interpersonal' relations—we have already begun to raise questions about a troublesome central point: the tendency to root values and norms in the supposed needs of the individuals *per se*. But if the individual's very nature cannot be understood without close reference to social reality, then we must analyze it

---

[5] Another major reason for the tendency to apotheosize 'interpersonal relations' is the sponge-like quality and limitations of the word 'culture,' in terms of which much of the social in man's depths has been recognized and asserted. In contrast with social structure, the concept 'culture' is one of the spongiest words in social science, although, perhaps for that reason, in the hands of an expert, enormously useful. In practice, the conception of 'culture' is more often a loose reference to social milieux plus 'tradition' than an adequate idea of social structure.

in such reference. Such analysis includes not only the locating of the individual, as a biographical entity, within various interpersonal milieux—but the locating of these milieux within the social structures which they form.

5

On the basis of developments in psychoanalysis, as well as in social psychology as a whole, it is now possible to state briefly the psychological concerns of the social sciences. I list here, in the barest of summary, only those propositions which I take as the most fruitful hunches, or, at the least, as legitimate assumptions on the part of the working social scientist.[6]

The life of an individual cannot be adequately understood without references to the institutions within which his biography is enacted. For this biography records the acquiring, dropping, modifying, and in a very intimate way, the moving from one role to another. One is a child in a certain kind of family, one is a playmate in a certain kind of child's group, a student, a workman, a foreman, a general, a mother. Much of human life consists of playing such roles within specific institutions. To understand the biography of an individual, we must understand the significance and meaning of the roles he has played and does play; to understand these roles we must understand the institutions of which they are a part.

But the view of man as a social creature enables us to go much deeper than merely the external biography as a sequence of social roles. Such a view requires us to understand the most internal and 'psychological' features of man: in particular, his self-image and his conscience and indeed the very growth of his mind. It may well be that the most radical discovery within recent psychology and social science is the discovery of how so many of the most intimate features of the person are socially patterned and even implanted. Within the broad limits of the glandular and nervous apparatus, the emotions of fear and hatred and love and

[6] For detailed discussion of the point of view expressed here, see Gerth and Mills, *Character and Social Structure*, New York, Harcourt, Brace, 1953.

rage, in all their varieties, must be understood in close and continual reference to the social biography and the social context in which they are experienced and expressed. Within the broad limits of the physiology of the sense organs, our very perception of the physical world, the colors we discriminate, the smells we become aware of, the noises we hear, are socially patterned and socially circumscribed. The motivations of men, and even the varying extents to which various types of men are typically aware of them, are to be understood in terms of the vocabularies of motive that prevail in a society and of social changes and confusions among such vocabularies.

The biography and the character of the individual cannot be understood merely in terms of milieux, and certainly not entirely in terms of the early environments—those of the infant and the child. Adequate understanding requires that we grasp the interplay of these intimate settings with their larger structural framework, and that we take into account the transformations of this framework, and the consequent effects upon milieux. When we understand social structures and structural changes as they bear upon more intimate scenes and experiences, we are able to understand the causes of individual conduct and feelings of which men in specific milieux are themselves unaware. The test of an adequate conception of any type of man cannot rest upon whether individuals of this type find it pleasantly in line with their own self-images. Since they live in restricted milieux, men do not and cannot be expected to know all the causes of their condition and the limits of their selfhood. Groups of men who have truly adequate views of themselves and of their own social positions are indeed rare. To assume the contrary, as is often done by virtue of the very methods used by some social scientists, is to assume a degree of rational self-consciousness and self-knowledge that not even eighteenth-century psychologists would allow. Max Weber's idea of 'The Puritan Man,' of his motives and of his function within religious and economic institutions, enables us to understand him better than he understood himself: Weber's use of the notion of structure enabled him to transcend 'the individual's' own awareness of himself and his milieux.

The relevance of earlier experience, 'the weight' of childhood in the psychology of adult character, is itself relative to the type of childhood and the type of social biography that prevail in various societies. It is, for example, now apparent that the role of 'the father' in the building of a personality must be stated within the limits of specific types of families, and in terms of the place such families occupy within the social structure of which these families are a part.

The idea of social structure cannot be built up only from ideas or facts about a specific series of individuals and their reactions to their milieux. Attempts to explain social and historical events on the basis of psychological theories about 'the individual' often rest upon the assumption that society is nothing but a great scatter of individuals and that, accordingly, if we know all about these 'atoms' we can in some way add up the information and thus know about society. It is not a fruitful assumption. In fact, we cannot even know what is most elemental about 'the individual' by any psychological study of him as a socially isolated creature. Except in the abstract building of models, which of course may be useful, the economist cannot assume The Economic Man; nor can the psychiatrist of family life (and practically all psychiatrists are, in fact, specialists of this one social area) assume the classical Oedipal Man. For just as the structural relations of economic and political roles are now often decisive for understanding the economic conduct of individuals, so are the great changes, since Victorian fatherhood, in the roles within the family and in the family's location as an institution within modern societies.

The principle of historical specificity holds for psychology as well as for the social sciences. Even quite intimate features of man's inner life are best formulated as problems within specific historical contexts. To realize that this is an entirely reasonable assumption, one has only to reflect for a moment upon the wide variety of men and women that is displayed in the course of human history. Psychologists, as well as social scientists, should indeed think well before finishing any sentences the subject of which is 'man.'

The human variety is such that no 'elemental' psychologies, no theory of 'instincts,' no principles of 'basic human nature' of which we know, enables us to account for the enormous human variety of types and individuals. Anything that can be asserted about man apart from what is inherent in the social-historical realities of human life will refer merely to the wide biological limits and potentialities of the human species. But within these limits and rising out of these potentialities, a panorama of human types confronts us. To attempt to explain it in terms of a theory of 'basic human nature' is to confine human history itself in some arid little cage of Concepts about 'human nature'—as often as not constructed from some precise and irrelevant trivialities about mice in a maze.

Barzun and Graff remark that 'The title of Dr. Kinsey's famous book *Sexual Behavior in the Human Male* is a striking instance of a hidden—and in this case false—assumption: the book is not about human males, but about men in the United States in the mid-twentieth century... The very idea of human nature is an assumption of social science and to say that it forms the subject of its reports is to beg the fundamental question. There may be nothing but "human culture," a highly mutable affair.' [7]

The idea of some 'human nature' common to man as man is a violation of the social and historical specificity that careful work in the human studies requires; at the very least, it is an abstraction that social students have not earned the right to make. Surely we ought occasionally to remember that in truth we do not know much about man, and that all the knowledge we do have does not entirely remove the element of mystery that surrounds his variety as it is revealed in history and biography. Sometimes we do want to wallow in that mystery, to feel that we are, after all, a part of it, and perhaps we should; but being men of the West, we will inevitably also study the human variety, which for us means removing the mystery from our view of it. In doing so, let us not forget what it is we are studying and how little we know of man, of history, of biography, and of the societies of which we are at once creatures and creators.

[7] Barzun and Graff, *The Modern Researcher*, New York, Harcourt, Brace, 1957, pp. 222-3.

9

On Reason and Freedom

THE CLIMAX of the social scientist's concern with history is the idea he comes to hold of the epoch in which he lives. The climax of his concern with biography is the idea he comes to hold of man's basic nature, and of the limits it may set to the transformation of man by the course of history.

All classic social scientists have been concerned with the salient characteristics of their time—and the problem of how history is being made within it; with 'the nature of human nature'—and the variety of individuals that come to prevail within their periods. Marx and Sombart and Weber, Comte and Spencer, Durkheim and Veblen, Mannheim, Schumpeter, and Michel—each in his own way has confronted these problems. In our immediate times, however, many social scientists have not. Yet it is precisely now, in the second half of the twentieth century, that these concerns become urgent as issues, persistent as troubles, and vital for the cultural orientation of our human studies.

1

Nowadays men everywhere seek to know where they stand, where they may be going, and what—if anything—they can do about the present as history and the future as responsibility. Such questions as these no one can answer once and for all. Every period provides its own answers. But just now, for us, there is a difficulty. We are now at the ending of an epoch, and we have got to work out our own answers.

We are at the ending of what is called The Modern Age. Just

as Antiquity was followed by several centuries of Oriental ascendancy, which Westerners provincially call The Dark Ages, so now The Modern Age is being succeeded by a post-modern period. Perhaps we may call it: The Fourth Epoch.

The ending of one epoch and the beginning of another is, to be sure, a matter of definition. But definitions, like everything social, are historically specific. And now our basic definitions of society and of self are being overtaken by new realities. I do not mean merely that never before within the limits of a single generation have men been so fully exposed at so fast a rate to such earthquakes of change. I do not mean merely that we feel we are in an epochal kind of transition, and that we struggle to grasp the outline of the new epoch we suppose ourselves to be entering. I mean that when we try to orient ourselves—if we do try—we find that too many of our old expectations and images are, after all, tied down historically: that too many of our standard categories of thought and of feeling as often disorient us as help to explain what is happening around us; that too many of our explanations are derived from the great historical transition from the Medieval to the Modern Age; and that when they are generalized for use today, they become unwieldy, irrelevant, not convincing. I also mean that our major orientations—liberalism and socialism—have virtually collapsed as adequate explanations of the world and of ourselves.

These two ideologies came out of The Enlightenment, and they have had in common many assumptions and values. In both, increased rationality is held to be the prime condition of increased freedom. The liberating notion of progress by reason, the faith in science as an unmixed good, the demand for popular education and the faith in its political meaning for democracy—all these ideals of The Enlightenment have rested upon the happy assumption of the inherent relation of reason and freedom. Those thinkers who have done the most to shape our ways of thinking have proceeded under this assumption. It lies under every movement and nuance of the work of Freud: To be free, the individual must become more rationally aware; therapy is an aid to giving reason its chance to work freely in the course of an individual's life. The same assumption underpins the main line of marxist work:

Men, caught in the irrational anarchy of production, must become rationally aware of their position in society; they must become 'class conscious'—the marxian meaning of which is as rationalistic as any term set forth by Bentham.

Liberalism has been concerned with freedom and reason as supreme facts about the individual; marxism, as supreme facts about man's role in the political making of history. The liberals and the radicals of The Modern Period have generally been men who believed in the rational making of history and of his own biography by the free individual.

But what has been happening in the world makes evident, I believe, why the ideas of freedom and of reason now so often seem so ambiguous in both the new capitalist and the communist societies of our time: why marxism has so often become a dreary rhetoric of bureaucratic defense and abuse; and liberalism, a trivial and irrelevant way of masking social reality. The major developments of our time, I believe, can be correctly understood neither in terms of the liberal nor the marxian interpretation of politics and culture. These ways of thought arose as guidelines to reflection about types of society which do not now exist. John Stuart Mill never examined the kinds of political economy now arising in the capitalist world. Karl Marx never analyzed the kinds of society now arising in the Communist bloc. And neither of them ever thought through the problems of the so-called underdeveloped countries in which seven out of ten men are trying to exist today. Now we confront new kinds of social structure which, in terms of 'modern' ideals, resist analysis in the liberal and in the socialist terms we have inherited.

The ideological mark of The Fourth Epoch—that which sets it off from The Modern Age—is that the ideas of freedom and of reason have become moot; that increased rationality may not be assumed to make for increased freedom.

2

The role of reason in human affairs and the idea of the free individual as the seat of reason are the most important themes inherited by twentieth-century social scientists from the philosophers of the Enlightenment. If they are to remain the key values in terms of which troubles are specified and issues focused, then the ideals of reason and of freedom must now be re-stated as problems in more precise and solvable ways than have been available to earlier thinkers and investigators. For in our time these two values, reason and freedom, are in obvious yet subtle peril.

The underlying trends are well known. Great and rational organizations—in brief, bureaucracies—have indeed increased, but the substantive reason of the individual at large has not. Caught in the limited milieux of their everyday lives, ordinary men often cannot reason about the great structures—rational and irrational —of which their milieux are subordinate parts. Accordingly, they often carry out series of apparently rational actions without any ideas of the ends they serve, and there is the increasing suspicion that those at the top as well—like Tolstoy's generals—only pretend they know. The growth of such organizations, within an increasing division of labor, sets up more and more spheres of life, work, and leisure, in which reasoning is difficult or impossible. The soldier, for example, 'carries out an entire series of functionally rational actions accurately without having any idea as to the ultimate end of this action' or the function of each act within the whole.[1] Even men of technically supreme intelligence may efficiently perform their assigned work and yet not know that it is to result in the first atom bomb.

Science, it turns out, is not a technological Second Coming. That its techniques and its rationality are given a central place in a society does not mean that men live reasonably and without myth, fraud, and superstition. Universal education may lead to technological idiocy and nationalist provinciality—rather than to the informed and independent intelligence. The mass distribution of historic culture may not lift the level of cultural sensibility, but rather, merely banalize it—and compete mightily with the chance for creative innovation. A high level of bureaucratic rationality and of technology does not mean a high level of either individual or social intelligence. From the first you cannot infer the second. For social, technological, or bureaucratic rationality is not merely

[1] Cf. Mannheim, *Man and Society*, New York, Harcourt, Brace, 1940, p. 54.

a grand summation of the individual will and capacity to reason. The very chance to acquire that will and that capacity seems in fact often to be decreased by it. Rationally organized social arrangements are not necessarily a means of increased freedom—for the individual or for the society. In fact, often they are a means of tyranny and manipulation, a means of expropriating the very chance to reason, the very capacity to act as a free man.

Only from a few commanding positions or—as the case may be—merely vantage points, in the rationalized structure is it readily possible to understand the structural forces at work in the whole which thus affect each limited part of which ordinary men are aware.

The forces that shape these milieux do not originate within them, nor are they controllable by those sunk in them. Moreover, these milieux are themselves increasingly rationalized. Families as well as factories, leisure as well as work, neighborhoods as well as states—they, too, tend to become parts of a functionally rational totality—or they are subject to uncontrolled and irrational forces.

The increasing rationalization of society, the contradiction between such rationality and reason, the collapse of the assumed coincidence of reason and freedom—these developments lie back of the rise into view of the man who is 'with' rationality but without reason, who is increasingly self-rationalized and also increasingly uneasy. It is in terms of this type of man that the contemporary problem of freedom is best stated. Yet such trends and suspicions are often not formulated as problems, and they are certainly not widely acknowledged as issues or felt as a set of troubles. Indeed, it is the fact of its unrecognized character, its lack of formulation, that is the most important feature of the contemporary problem of freedom and reason.

3

From the individual's standpoint, much that happens seems the result of manipulation, of management, of blind drift; authority is often not explicit; those with power often feel no need to make it explicit and to justify it. That is one reason why ordinary men, when they are in trouble or when they sense that they are up against issues, cannot get clear targets for thought and for action; they cannot determine what it is that imperils the values they vaguely discern as theirs.

Given these effects of the ascendant trend of rationalization, the individual 'does the best he can.' He gears his aspirations and his work to the situation he is in, and from which he can find no way out. In due course, he does not seek a way out: he adapts. That part of his life which is left over from work, he uses to play, to consume, 'to have fun.' Yet this sphere of consumption is also being rationalized. Alienated from production, from work, he is also alienated from consumption, from genuine leisure. This adaptation of the individual and its effects upon his milieux and self results not only in the loss of his chance, and in due course, of his capacity and will to reason; it also affects his chances and his capacity to act as a free man. Indeed, neither the value of freedom nor of reason, it would seem, are known to him.

Such adapted men are not necessarily unintelligent, even after they have lived and worked and played in such circumstances for quite some time. Karl Mannheim has made the point in a clear way by speaking of 'self rationalization,' which refers to the way in which an individual, caught in the limited segments of great, rational organizations, comes systematically to regulate his impulses and his aspirations, his manner of life and his ways of thought, in rather strict accordance with 'the rules and regulations of the organization.' The rational organization is thus an alienating organization: the guiding principles of conduct and reflection, and in due course of emotion as well, are not seated in the individual conscience of the Reformation man, or in the independent reason of the Cartesian man. The guiding principles, in fact, are alien to and in contradiction with all that has been historically understood as individuality. It is not too much to say that in the extreme development the chance to reason of most men is destroyed, as rationality increases and its locus, its control, is moved from the individual to the big-scale organization. There is then rationality without reason. Such rationality is not commensurate with freedom but the destroyer of it.

It is no wonder that the ideal of individuality has become moot: in our time, what is at issue is the very nature of man, the image we have of his limits and possibilities as man. History is not yet done with its exploration of the limits and meanings of 'human nature.' We do not know how profound man's psychological transformation from the Modern Age to the contemporary epoch may be. But we must now raise the question in an ultimate form: Among contemporary men will there come to prevail, or even to flourish, what may be called The Cheerful Robot?

We know of course that man can be turned into a robot, by chemical and psychiatric means, by steady coercion and by controlled environment; but also by random pressures and unplanned sequences of circumstances. But can he be made to want to become a cheerful and willing robot? Can he be happy in this condition, and what are the qualities and the meanings of such happiness? It will no longer do merely to assume, as a metaphysic of human nature, that down deep in man-as-man there is an urge for freedom and a will to reason. Now we must ask: What in man's nature, what in the human condition today, what in each of the varieties of social structure makes for the ascendancy of the cheerful robot? And what stands against it?

The advent of the alienated man and all the themes which lie behind his advent now affect the whole of our serious intellectual life and cause our immediate intellectual malaise. It is a major theme of the human condition in the contemporary epoch and of all studies worthy of the name. I know of no idea, no theme, no problem, that is so deep in the classic tradition—and so much involved in the possible default of contemporary social science.

It is what Karl Marx so brilliantly discerned in his earlier essays on 'alienation'; it is the chief concern of Georg Simmel in his justly famous essay on 'The Metropolis'; Graham Wallas was aware of it in his work on The Great Society. It lies behind Fromm's conception of the 'automaton.' The fear that such a type of man will become ascendant underlies many of the more recent uses of such classic sociological conceptions as 'status and contract,' 'community and society.' It is the hard meaning of such notions as Riesman's 'other-directed' and Whyte's 'social ethic.' And of course, most popularly, the triumph—if it may be called that—of such a man is the key meaning of George Orwell's *1984*.

On the positive side—a rather wistful side nowadays—the larger meanings of Freud's 'id,' Marx's 'Freiheit,' George Mead's 'I,' Karen Horney's 'spontaneity,' lie in the use of such conceptions against the triumph of the alienated man. They are trying to find some center in man-as-man which would enable them to believe that in the end he cannot be made into, that he cannot finally become, such an alien creature—alien to nature, to society, to self. The cry for 'community' is an attempt, a mistaken one I believe, to assert the conditions that would eliminate the probability of such a man, and it is because many humanist thinkers have come to believe that many psychiatrists by their practice produce such alienated and self-rationalized men that they reject these adaptive endeavors. Back of all this—and much more of traditional and current worrying and thinking among serious and sensible students of man—there lies the simple and decisive fact that the alienated man is the antithesis of the Western image of the free man. The society in which this man, this cheerful robot, flourishes is the antithesis of the free society—or in the literal and plain meaning of the word, of a democratic society. The advent of this man points to freedom as trouble, as issue, and—let us hope—as problem for social scientists. Put as a trouble of the individual—of the terms and values of which he is uneasily unaware—it is the trouble called 'alienation.' As an issue for publics—to the terms and values of which they are mainly indifferent—it is no less than the issue of democratic society, as fact and as aspiration.

It is just because this issue and thîs trouble are not now widely recognized, and so do not in fact exist as explicit troubles and issues, that the uneasiness and the indifference that betoken them are so deep and so wide in meaning and in effect. That is a major part of the problem of freedom today, seen in its political context, and it is a major part of the intellectual challenge which the formulation of the problem of freedom offers to contemporary social scientists.

It is not merely paradoxical to say that the values of freedom and reason are back of the absence of troubles, back of the uneasy feeling of malaise and alienation. In a similar manner, the issue to which modern threats to freedom and reason most typically lead is, above all, the absence of explicit issues—to apathy rather than to issues explicitly defined as such.

The issues and troubles have not been clarified because the chief capacities and qualities of man required to clarify them are the very freedom and reason that are threatened and dwindling. Neither the troubles nor the issues have been seriously formulated as the problems of the kinds of social science I have been criticizing in this book. The promise of classic social science, in considerable part, is that they will be.

4

The troubles and issues raised up by the crises of reason and freedom cannot of course be formulated as one grand problem, but neither can they be confronted, much less solved, by handling each of them microscopically as a series of small-scale issues, or of troubles confined to a scatter of milieux. They are structural problems, and to state them requires that we work in the classic terms of human biography and of ephocal history. Only in such terms can the connections of structure and milieux that effect these values today be traced and casual analysis be conducted. The crisis of individuality and the crisis of history-making; the role of reason in the free individual life and in the making of history—in the re-statement and clarification of these problems lies the promise of the social sciences.

The moral and the intellectual promise of social science is that freedom and reason will remain cherished values, that they will be used seriously and consistently and imaginatively in the formulation of problems. But this is also the political promise of what is loosely called Western culture. Within the social sciences, political crises and intellectual crises of our time coincide: serious work in either sphere is also work in the other. The political traditions of classic liberalism and of classic socialism together exhaust our major political traditions. The collapse of these traditions as ideologies has had to do with the decline of free individuality and the decline of reason in human affairs. Any contemporary political re-statement of liberal and socialist goals must include as central the idea of a society in which all men would become men of substantive reason, whose independent reasoning would have structural consequences for their societies, its history, and thus for their own life fates.

The interest of the social scientist in social structure is not due to any view that the future is structurally determined. We study the structural limits of human decision in an attempt to find points of effective intervention, in order to know what can and what must be structurally changed if the role of explicit decision in history-making is to be enlarged. Our interest in history is not owing to any view that the future is inevitable, that the future is bounded by the past. That men have lived in certain kinds of society in the past does not set exact or absolute limits to the kinds of society they may create in the future. We study history to discern the alternatives within which human reason and human freedom can now make history. We study historical social structures, in brief, in order to find within them the ways in which they are and can be controlled. For only in this way can we come to know the limits and the meaning of human freedom.

Freedom is not merely the chance to do as one pleases; neither is it merely the opportunity to choose between set alternatives. Freedom is, first of all, the chance to formulate the available choices, to argue over them—and then, the opportunity to choose. That is why freedom cannot exist without an enlarged role of human reason in human affairs. Within an individual's biography and within a society's history, the social task of reason is to formulate choices, to enlarge the scope of human decisions in the making of history. The future of human affairs is not merely some set of variables to be predicted. The future is what is to be decided—within the limits, to be sure, of historical possibility. But this possibility is not fixed; in our time the limits seem very broad indeed.

Beyond this, the problem of freedom is the problem of how decisions about the future of human affairs are to be made and who is to make them. Organizationally, it is the problem of a just machinery of decision. Morally, it is the problem of political responsibility. Intellectually, it is the problem of what are now the possible futures of human affairs. But the larger aspects of the problem of freedom today concern not only the nature of history and the structural chance for explicit decisions to make a difference in its course; they concern also the nature of man and the fact that the value of freedom cannot be based upon 'man's basic nature.' The ultimate problem of freedom is the problem of the cheerful robot, and it arises in this form today because today it has become evident to us that *all* men do *not* naturally *want* to be free; that all men are not willing or not able, as the case may be, to exert themselves to acquire the reason that freedom requires.

Under what conditions do men come to *want* to be free and capable of acting freely? Under what conditions are they willing and able to bear the burdens freedom does impose and to see these less as burdens than as gladly undertaken self-transformations? And on the negative side: Can men be made to want to become *cheerful* robots?

In our time, must we not face the possibility that the human mind as a social fact might be deteriorating in quality and cultural level, and yet not many would notice it because of the overwhelming accumulation of technological gadgets? Is not that one meaning of rationality without reason? Of human alienation? Of the absence of any free role for reason in human affairs? The accumulation of gadgets hides these meanings: Those who use these devices do not understand them; those who invent them do not understand much else. That is why we may *not*, without great ambiguity, use technological abundance as the index of human quality and cultural progress.

To formulate any problem requires that we state the values involved and the threat to those values. For it is the felt threat to cherished values—such as those of freedom and reason—that is the necessary moral substance of all significant problems of social inquiry, and as well of all public issues and private troubles.

The values involved in the cultural problem of individuality are conveniently embodied in all that is suggested by the ideal of The Renaissance Man. The threat to that ideal is the ascendancy among us of The Cheerful Robot.

The values involved in the political problem of history-making are embodied in the Promethean ideal of its human making. The threat to that ideal is twofold: On the one hand, history-making may well go by default, men may continue to abdicate its wilful making, and so merely drift. On the other hand, history may indeed be made—but by narrow elite circles without effective responsibility to those who must try to survive the consequences of their decisions and of their defaults.

I do not know the answer to the question of political irresponsibility in our time or to the cultural and political question of The Cheerful Robot. But is it not clear that no answers will be found unless these problems are at least confronted? Is it not obvious, that the ones to confront them, above all others, are the social scientists of the rich societies? That many of them do not now do so is surely the greatest human default being committed by privileged men in our times.

10

On Politics

THERE IS NO NECESSITY for working social scientists to allow the political meaning of their work to be shaped by the 'accidents' of its setting, or its use to be determined by the purposes of other men. It is quite within their powers to discuss its meanings and decide upon its uses as matters of their own policy. To a considerable, and largely untested, extent, they can influence or even determine these policies. Such determination requires that they make explicit judgments, as well as decisions upon theory, method, and fact. As matters of policy, these judgments are the proper concern of the individual scholar as well as of the fraternity. Yet is it not evident that implicit moral and political judgments have much more influence than explicit discussions of personal and professional policy? Only by making these influences matters of debated policy can men become fully aware of them, and so try to control their effects upon the work of social science and upon its political meaning.

There is no way in which any social scientist can avoid assuming choices of value and implying them in his work as a whole. Problems, like issues and troubles, concern threats to expected values, and cannot be clearly formulated without acknowledgment of those values. Increasingly, research is used, and social scientists are used, for bureaucratic and ideological purposes. This being so, as individuals and as professionals, students of man and society face such questions as: whether they are aware of the uses and values of their work, whether these may be subject to their own control, whether they want to seek to control them.

How they answer these questions, or fail to answer them, and how they use or fail to use the answers in their work and in their professional lives determine their answer to the final question: whether in their work as social scientists they are (a) morally autonomous, (b) subject to the morality of other men, or (c) morally adrift. The catchwords with which these problems have been carried along—often, I am certain, with good intentions— are no longer good enough. Social scientists must now really confront these quite fateful questions. In this chapter I am going to suggest some of the things it seems necessary to consider in any answer to them, and also to set forth the kind of answer I have come, in the last few years, to believe reasonable.

1

The social scientist at work is not suddenly confronted with the need to choose values. He is already working on the basis of certain values. The values that these disciplines now embody have been selected from the values created in Western society; elsewhere social science is an import. Of course some do talk as if the values they have selected 'transcend' Western or any other society; others speak of their standards as if they were 'immanent' within some existing society, as a sort of unrealized potential. But surely it will now be widely agreed that the values inherent in the traditions of social science are neither transcendent nor immanent. They are simply values proclaimed by many and within limits practiced in small circles. What a man calls moral judgment is merely his desire to generalize, and so make available for others, those values he has come to choose.

Three overriding political ideals seem to me inherent in the traditions of social science, and certainly involved in its intellectual promise. The first of these is simply the value of truth, of fact. The very enterprise of social science, as it determines fact, takes on political meaning. In a world of widely communicated nonsense, any statement of fact is of political and moral significance. All social scientists, by the fact of their existence, are involved in the struggle between enlightenment and obscurantism. In such a world as ours, to practice social science is, first of all, to practice the politics of truth.

But the politics of truth is not an adequate statement of the values that guide our enterprise. The truth of our findings, the accuracy of our investigations—when they are seen in their social setting—may or may not be relevant to human affairs. Whether they are, and how they are, is in itself the second value, which in brief, is the value of the role of reason in human affairs. Along with that goes a third value—human freedom, in all the ambiguity of its meaning. Both freedom and reason, I have already argued, are central to the civilization of the Western world; both are readily proclaimed as ideals. But in any given application, as criteria and as goals, they lead to much disagreement. That is why it is one of our intellectual tasks, as social scientists, to clarify the ideal of freedom and the ideal of reason.

If human reason is to play a larger and more explicit role in the making of history, social scientists must surely be among its major carriers. For in their work they represent the use of reason in the understanding of human affairs; that is what they are about. If they wish to work and thus to act in a consciously chosen way, they must first locate themselves within the intellectual life and the social-historical structure of their times. Within the social domains of intelligence, they must locate themselves; and they must relate these domains, in turn, to the structure of historical society. This is not the place to do such work. Here I want only briefly to distinguish three political roles in terms of which the social scientist as a man of reason may conceive of himself.

Much social science, perhaps especially sociology, contains the theme of the philosopher-king. From August Comte to Karl Mannheim, one finds the plea for and the attempted justification of greater power for 'the man of knowledge.' In a more specific statement the enthronement of reason means, of course, the enthronement of 'the man of reason.' This one idea of the role of reason in human affairs has done much to cause social scientists to keep very general indeed their acceptance of reason as a social value. They have wished to avoid the foolishness of such an idea when it is considered alongside the facts of power. The idea also goes against the grain of many versions of democracy, for it involves an aristocracy, even if an aristocracy of talent rather than of birth or wealth. But the rather foolish idea that he should become a philosopher-king is only one idea of the public role that the social scientist may attempt to enact.

The quality of politics depends very much upon the intellectual qualities of those who are engaged in it. Were the 'philosopher' king, I should be tempted to leave his kingdom; but when kings are without any 'philosophy,' are they not incapable of responsible rule?

The second, and now the most usual role, is to become an advisor to the king. The bureaucratic uses which I have described are a current embodiment of this. The individual social scientist tends to become involved in those many trends of modern society that make the individual a part of a functionally rational bureaucracy, and to sink into his specialized slot in such a way as not to be explicitly concerned with the structure of post-modern society. In this role, we have seen, social science itself often tends to become a functionally rational machine; the individual social scientist tends to lose his moral autonomy and his substantive rationality, and the role of reason in human affairs tends to become merely a refinement of techniques for administrative and manipulative uses.

But that is the role of advisor to kings in one of its worst forms; this role need not, I believe, assume the shape and meaning of the bureaucratic style. It is a difficult role to fulfill in such a way as to retain moral and intellectual integrity, and hence, freedom to work on the tasks of social science. It is easy for consultants to imagine themselves philosophers and their clients enlightened rulers. But even should they be philosophers, those they serve may not be enlightenable. That is one reason I am so impressed by the loyalty of some consultants to the unenlightened despots they serve. It is a loyalty that seems strained neither by despotic incompetence nor by dogmatic silliness.

I do not assert that the role of advisor cannot be performed well; in fact I know that it can, and that there are men who are doing it. Were there more such men the political and intellectual tasks of those social scientists who elect the third role would become much less burdensome, for it overlaps this one.

The third way in which the social scientist may attempt to realize the value of reason and its role in human affairs is also well known, and sometimes even practiced. It is to remain independent, to do one's own work, to select one's own problems, but to direct this work *at* kings as well as *to* 'publics.' Such a conception prompts us to imagine social science as a sort of public intelligence apparatus, concerned with public issues and private troubles and with the structural trends of our time underlying them both—and to imagine individual social scientists as rational members of a self-controlled association, which we call the social sciences.

In taking up such a role, which I shall explain more fully in a moment, we are trying to *act* upon the value of reason; in assuming that we may not be altogether ineffective, we are assuming a theory of history-making: we are assuming that 'man' is free and that by his rational endeavors he can influence the course of history. I am not now concerned to debate the *values* of freedom and reason, but only to discuss under what theory of history they may be realizable.

2

Men are free to make history, but some men are much freer than others. Such freedom requires access to the means of decisions and of power by which history may now be made. It is not always so made; in the following, I am speaking only of the contemporary period in which the means of history-making power have become so enlarged and so centralized. It is with reference to this period that I am contending that if men do not make history, they tend increasingly to become the utensils of history-makers and also the mere objects of history-making.

How large a role any explicit decisions do play in the making of history is itself an historical problem. It depends very much upon the means of power that are available at any given time in any given society. In some societies, the innumerable actions of innumerable men modify their milieux, and so gradually modify the structure itself. These modifications are the course of history; history is drift, although in total 'men make it.' Thus, innumerable entrepreneurs and innumerable consumers, by ten thousand decisions per minute, may shape and re-shape the free-market economy. Perhaps this was the chief kind of limitation Marx had in mind when he wrote, in *The 18th Brumaire:* 'Men make their own history, but they do not make it just as they please; they do not make it under circumstances chosen by themselves. . . .'

Fate, or 'inevitability,' has to do with events in history that are beyond the control of any circle or group of men having three characteristics: (1) compact enough to be identifiable, (2) powerful enough to decide with consequence, and (3) in a position to foresee these consequences and so to be held accountable for them. Events, according to this conception, are the summary and unintended results of innumerable decisions of innumerable men. Each of their decisions is minute in consequence and subject to cancellation or reinforcement by other such decisions. There is no link between any one man's intention and the summary result of the innumerable decisions. Events are beyond human decisions: History is made behind men's backs.

So conceived, fate is not a universal fact; it is not inherent in the nature of history or in the nature of man. Fate is a feature of an historically specific kind of social structure. In a society in which the ultimate weapon is the rifle; in which the typical economic unit is the family-farm and the small shop; in which the national-state does not yet exist or is merely a distant framework; in which communication is by word-of-mouth, handbill, pulpit—in *such* a society, history is indeed fate.

But consider now, the major clue to our condition: Is it not, in a word, the enormous enlargement and the decisive centralization of all the means of power and decision, which is to say—all the means of history-making? In modern industrial society, the facilities of economic production are developed and centralized—as peasants and artisans are replaced by private corporations and government industries. In the modern nation-state, the means of violence and of political administration undergo similar developments—as kings control nobles, and self-equipped knights are replaced by standing armies and now by fearful military machines. The *post-modern* climax of all three developments—in economics, in politics, and in violence—is now occurring most dramatically in the United States and the USSR. In our time, international as well as national means of history-making are being centralized. Is it not thus clear that the scope and the chance for conscious human agency in history-making is just now uniquely available? Elites of power in charge of these means do now make history—to be sure, 'under circumstances not of their own choosing'—but compared to other men and other epochs, these circumstances themselves certainly do not appear to be overwhelming.

Surely this is the paradox of our immediate situation: The facts about the newer means of history-making are a signal that men are not necessarily in the grip of fate, that men *can* now make history. But this fact is made ironic by the further fact that just now those ideologies which offer men the hope of making history have declined and are collapsing in the Western societies. That collapse is also the collapse of the expectations of The Enlightenment, that reason and freedom would come to prevail as paramount forces in human history. And behind it there is also the intellectual and political default of the intellectual community.

Where is the intelligentsia that is carrying on the big discourse of the Western world *and* whose work as intellectuals is influential among parties and publics and relevant to the great decisions of our time? Where are the mass media open to such men? Who among those who are in charge of the two-party state and its ferocious military machines are alert to what goes on in the world of knowledge and reason and sensibility? Why is the free intellect so divorced from decisions of power? Why does there now prevail among men of power such a higher and irresponsible ignorance?

In the United States today, intellectuals, artists, ministers, scholars, and scientists are fighting a cold war in which they echo and elaborate the confusions of officialdoms. They neither raise demands on the powerful for alternative policies, nor set forth such alternatives before publics. They do not try to put responsible content into the politics of the United States; they help to empty politics and to keep it empty. What must be called the Christian default of the clergy is as much a part of this sorry moral condition as is the capture of scientists by nationalist Science-Machines. The journalistic lie, become routine, is part of it too; and so is much of the pretentious triviality that passes for social science.

3

I do not expect (nor does my present argument as a whole require) that this view be accepted by all social scientists. What I want most to say here is that, having accepted the values of reason and freedom, it is a prime task of any social scientist to determine the limits of freedom and the limits of the role of reason in history.

In assuming the third role, the social scientist does not see himself as some autonomous being standing 'outside society.' In common with most other people, he *does* feel that he stands outside the major history-making decisions of this period; at the same time he knows that he is among those who take many of the consequences of these decisions. That is one major reason why to the extent that he is aware of what he is doing, he becomes an explicitly political man. No one is 'outside society'; the question is where each stands within it.

The social scientist usually lives in circumstances of middling class and status and power. By his activities in these milieux, he is often in no better position than the ordinary individual to solve structural problems, for their solution can never be merely intellectual or merely private. Their proper statement cannot be confined to the milieux open to the will of social scientists; neither can their solutions, which means, of course, that they are problems of social and political and economic power. But the social scientist is not only an 'ordinary man.' It is his very task intellectually to transcend the milieux in which he happens to live, and this he does when he considers the economic order of nineteenth-century England or the status hierarchy of twentieth-century America, the military institutions of Imperial Rome, or the political structure of the Soviet Union.

In so far as the values of freedom and reason concern him, one of his themes for study has to do with the objective chances available for given types of men within given types of social structure to become free and rational as individuals. Another of his themes has to do with what chances, if any, men of different positions in differing types of society have, first, by their reason and experience, to transcend their everyday milieux, and second, by virtue of their power, to act with consequence for the structure of their society and their periods. These are the problems of the role of reason in history.

In considering them, it is easy to see that in modern societies, some men have the power to act with much structural relevance and are quite aware of the consequences of their actions; others have such power but are not aware of its effective scope; and there are many who cannot transcend their everyday milieux by their awareness of structure or effect structural change by any means of action available to them.

Then, as social scientists, we locate ourselves. By the nature of our work, we are aware of social structure and somewhat aware of the historical mechanics of its movement. But clearly we do not have access to the major means of power which now exist and with which these mechanics can now be influenced. We do, however, have one often fragile 'means of power,' and it is this which provides a clue to our political role and to the political meaning of our work.

It is, I think, the political task of the social scientist who accepts the ideals of freedom and reason, to address his work to each of the other three types of men I have classified in terms of power and knowledge.

To those with power and with awareness of it, he imputes varying measures of responsibility for such structural consequences as he finds by his work to be decisively influenced by their decisions and their lack of decisions.

To those whose actions have such consequences, but who do not seem to be aware of them, he directs whatever he has found out about those consequences. He attempts to educate and then, again, he imputes responsibility.

To those who are regularly without such power and whose awareness is confined to their everyday milieux, he reveals by his work the meaning of structural trends and decisions for these milieux, the ways in which personal troubles are connected with public issues; in the course of these efforts, he states what he has found out concerning the actions of the more powerful. These are his major educational tasks, and they are his major public tasks when he speaks to any larger audience. Let us now examine some of the problems and tasks set by this third role.

4

Regardless of the scope of his awareness, the social scientist is usually a professor, and this occupational fact very much determines what he is able to do. As a professor, he addresses students, and on occasion, by speeches and by writings, publics of larger scale and more strategic position. In discussing what his public role may be, let us stick close to these simple facts of power, or if you like, to the facts of his powerlessness.

In so far as he is concerned with liberal, that is to say liberating, education, his public role has two goals: What he ought to do for the individual is to turn personal troubles and concerns into social issues and problems open to reason—his aim is to help the individual become a self-educating man, who only then would be reasonable and free. What he ought to do for the society is to combat all those forces which are destroying genuine publics and creating a mass society—or put as a positive goal, his aim is to help build and to strengthen self-cultivating publics. Only then might society be reasonable and free.

These are very large goals, and I must explain them in a slightly indirect way. We are concerned with skills and with values. Among 'skills,' however, some are more and some are less relevant to the tasks of liberation. I do not believe that skills and values can be so easily separated as in our search for 'neutral skills' we often assume. It is a matter of degree, with skills at one extreme and values at the other. But in the middle ranges of this scale, there are what I shall call sensibilities, and it is these which should interest us most. To train someone to operate a lathe or to read and write is in large part a training of skill; to help someone decide what he really wants out of his life, or to debate with him Stoic, Christian, and Humanist ways of living, is a cultivation or an education of values.

Alongside skill and value, we ought to put sensibility, which includes them both, and more besides: it includes a sort of therapy in the ancient sense of clarifying one's knowledge of self. It includes the cultivation of all those skills of controversy with one-self that we call thinking, and which, when engaged in with others, we call debate. An educator must begin with what interests the individual most deeply, even if it seems altogether trivial and cheap. He must proceed in such a way and with such materials as to enable the student to gain increasingly rational insight into these concerns, and into others he will acquire in the process of his education. And the educator must try to develop men and women who can and who will by themselves continue what he has begun: the end product of any liberating education is simply the self-educating, self-cultivating man and woman; in short, the free and rational individual.

A society in which such individuals are ascendant is, by one major meaning of the word, democratic. Such a society may also be defined as one in which genuine publics rather than masses prevail. By this, I mean the following:

Whether or not they are aware of them, men in a mass society are gripped by personal troubles which they are not able to turn into social issues. They do not understand the interplay of these personal troubles of their milieux with problems of social structure. The knowledgeable man in a genuine public, on the other hand, is able to do just that. He understands that what he thinks and feels to be personal troubles are very often also problems shared by others, and more importantly, not capable of solution by any one individual but only by modifications of the structure of the groups in which he lives and sometimes the structure of the entire society. Men in masses have troubles, but they are not usually aware of their true meaning and source; men in publics confront issues, and they usually come to be aware of their public terms.

It is the political task of the social scientist—as of any liberal educator—continually to translate personal troubles into public issues, and public issues into the terms of their human meaning for a variety of individuals. It is his task to display in his work—and, as an educator, in his life as well—this kind of sociological imagination. And it is his purpose to cultivate such habits of mind among the men and women who are publicly exposed to him. To secure these ends is to secure reason and individuality, and to make these the predominant values of a democratic society.

You may now be saying to yourself, 'Well, here it comes. He is going to set up an ideal so high that in terms of it everything must seem low.' That I might be thought to be doing so testifies to the lack of seriousness with which the word democracy is now taken, and to the indifference of many observers to the drift away from any plain meaning of the word. Democracy is, of course, a complicated idea about which there is much legitimate disagreement. But surely it is not so complicated or ambiguous that it may no longer be used by people who wish to reason together.

What I mean by democracy as an ideal I have already tried to indicate. In essence, democracy implies that those vitally affected by any decision men make have an effective voice in that decision. This, in turn, means that all power to make such decisions be publicly legitimated and that the makers of such decisions be held publicly accountable. None of these three points can prevail, it seems to me, unless there are dominant within a society the kinds of publics and the kinds of individuals I have described. Certain further conditions will presently become evident.

The social structure of the United States is not an altogether democratic one. Let us take that as a point of minimum agreement. I do not know of any society which is altogether democratic —that remains an ideal. The United States today I should say is generally democratic mainly in form and in the rhetoric of expectation. In substance and in practice it is very often non-democratic, and in many institutional areas it is quite clearly so. The corporate economy is run neither as a set of town meetings nor as a set of powers responsible to those whom their activities affect very seriously. The military machines and increasingly the political state are in the same condition. I do not wish to give the impression that I am optimistic about the chances that many social scientists can or will perform a democratic public role, or—even if many of them do so—about the chances that this would necessarily result in a rehabilitation of publics. I am merely outlining one role that seems to me to be open and is, in fact, practiced by some social scientists. It happens also to be a role that is in line with both liberal and socialist views of the role of reason in human affairs.[1]

My point is that the political role of social science—what that role may be, how it is enacted, and how effectively—this is relevant to the extent to which democracy prevails.

If we take up the third role of reason, the autonomous role, we are trying to act in a democratic manner in a society that is not altogether democratic. But we are acting as if we were in a fully democratic society, and by doing so, we are attempting to remove the 'as if.' We are trying to make the society more democratic. Such a role, I contend, is the only role by which we may as social scientists attempt to do this. At least I do not know of any other way by which we might try to help build a democratic polity. And because of this, the problem of the social sciences as a prime car-

---

[1] In passing, I should like to remind the reader that, quite apart from its present bureaucratic context and use, the style of abstracted empiricism (and the methodological inhibition it sustains) is not well suited for the democratic political role I am describing. Those who practice this style as their sole activity, who conceive of it as the 'real work of social science,' and who live in its ethos, cannot perform a liberating educational role. This role requires that individuals and publics be given confidence in their own capacities to reason, and by individual criticism, study, and practice, to enlarge its scope and improve its quality. It requires that they be encouraged, in George Orwell's phrase, to 'get outside the whale,' or in the wonderful American phrase, 'to become their own men.' To tell them that they can 'really' know social reality only by depending upon a necessarily bureaucratic kind of research is to place a taboo, in the name of Science, upon their efforts to become independent men and substantive thinkers. It is to undermine the confidence of the individual craftsman in his own ability to know reality. It is, in effect, to encourage men to fix their social beliefs by reference to the authority of an alien apparatus, and it is, of course, in line with, and is reinforced by, the whole bureaucratization of reason in our time. The industrialization of academic life and the fragmentation of the problems of social science cannot result in a liberating educational role for social scientists. For what these schools of thought take apart they tend to keep apart, in very tiny pieces about which they claim to be very certain. But all they could thus be certain of are abstracted fragments, and it is precisely the job of liberal education, *and* the political role of social science, *and* its intellectual promise, to enable men to transcend such fragmented and abstracted milieux: to become aware of historical structures and of their own place within them.

rier of reason in human affairs is in fact a major problem of democracy today.

5

What are the chances of success? Given the political structure within which we must now act, I do not believe it is very likely that social scientists will become effective carriers of reason. For men of knowledge to enact this strategic role, certain conditions must be present. Men make their own history, Marx said, but they do not make it under conditions of their own choice. Well then, what are the conditions *we* require to play this role effectively? What are required are parties and movements and publics having two characteristics: (1) within them ideas and alternatives of social life are truly debated, and (2) they have a chance really to influence decisions of structural consequence. Only if such organizations existed, could we become realistic and hopeful about the role of reason in human affairs which I have been trying to outline. Such a situation, by the way, I should consider one major requirement for any fully democratic society.

In such a polity social scientists in their political roles would probably 'speak for' and 'against' a variety of movements and strata and interests, rather than merely address an often vague, and— I fear—dwindling, public. Their ideas, in short, would compete, and this competition (as a process as well as in its result at any given time) would be politically relevant. If we take the idea of democracy seriously, if we take the democratic role of reason in human affairs seriously, our engagement in such a competition will in no way distress us. Surely we cannot suppose that all definitions of social reality, much less all statements of political ways and means, much less all suggestions of goals, would result in some undebatable, unified doctrine.[2]

In the absence of such parties and movements and publics, we live in a society that is democratic mainly in its legal forms and

---

[2] The idea of such a monopoly in the sphere of social ideas is one of the authoritarian notions which lie under the view of 'The Method' of the science-makers as administrators of reason, and which is so thinly disguised in the 'sacred values' of grand theorists. More obviously it is embodied in the technocratic slogans I have analyzed in chapter 5.

its formal expectations. We ought not to minimize the enormous value and the considerable opportunity these circumstances make available. We should learn their value from the fact of their absence in the Soviet world, and from the kind of struggle the intellectuals of that world are up against. We should also learn that whereas there many intellectuals are physically crushed, here many morally crush themselves. That democracy in the United States is so largely formal does not mean that we can dodge the conclusion that if reason is to play any free part in a democratic making of history, one of its chief carriers must surely be the social sciences. The absence of democratic parties and movements and publics does not mean that social scientists as educators ought not to try to make their educational institutions a framework within which such a liberating public of individuals might exist, at least in its beginnings, and one in which their discussions might be encouraged and sustained. Nor does it mean that they should not try to cultivate such publics in their less academic roles.

To do so of course, is to risk 'trouble'; or what is more serious, to face a quite deadly indifference. It requires that we deliberately present controversial theories and facts, and actively encourage controversy. In the absence of political debate that is wide and open and informed, people can get into touch neither with the effective realities of their world nor with the realities of themselves. Nowadays especially, it seems to me, the role I have been describing requires no less than the presentation of conflicting definitions of reality itself. What is usually termed 'propaganda,' especially of a nationalist sort, consists not only of opinions on a variety of topics and issues. It is the promulgation, as Paul Kecskemeti once noted, of official definitions of reality.

Our public life now often rests upon such official definitions, as well as upon myths and lies and crackbrained notions. When many policies—debated and undebated—are based on inadequate and misleading definitions of reality, then those who are out to define reality more adequately are bound to be upsetting influences. That is why publics of the sort I have described, as well as men of individuality, are, by their very existence in such a society, radical. Yet such is the role of mind, of study, of intellect, of reason, of ideas: to define reality adequately and in a publicly relevant way. The educational and the political role of social science in a democracy is to help cultivate and sustain publics and individuals that are able to develop, to live with, and to act upon adequate definitions of personal and social realities.

The role of reason I have been outlining neither means nor requires that one hit the pavement, take the next plane to the scene of the current crisis, run for Congress, buy a newspaper plant, go among the poor, set up a soap box. Such actions are often admirable, and I can readily imagine occasions when I should personally find it impossible not to want to do them myself. But for the social scientist to take them to be his normal activities is merely to abdicate his role, and to display by his action a disbelief in the promise of social science and in the role of reason in human affairs. This role requires only that the social scientist get on with the work of social science and that he avoid furthering the bureaucratization of reason and of discourse.

Not every social scientist accepts all the views I happen to hold on these issues, and it is not my wish that he should. My point is that one of his tasks is to determine his own views of the nature of historical change and the place, if any, of free and reasonable men within it. Only then can he come to know his own intellectual and political role within the societies he is studying, and in doing so find out just what he does think of the values of freedom and of reason which are so deeply a part of the tradition and the promise of social science.

If individual men and small groups of men are not free to act with historical consequence, and at the same time are not reasonable enough to see those consequences; if the structure of modern societies, or of any one of them, is now such that history is indeed blind drift and cannot be made otherwise with the means at hand and the knowledge that may be acquired—then the only autonomous role of social science is to chronicle and to understand; the idea of the responsibility of the powerful is foolish; and the values of freedom and of reason are realizable only in the exceptional milieux of certain favored private lives.

But that is a lot of 'ifs.' And although there is ample room for disagreement over degrees of freedom and scales of consequence,

I do not believe that there is sufficient evidence to necessitate abandoning the values of freedom and reason as they might now orient the work of social science.

Attempts to avoid such troublesome issues as I have been discussing are nowadays widely defended by the slogan that social science is 'not out to save the world.' Sometimes this is the disclaimer of a modest scholar; sometimes it is the cynical contempt of a specialist for all issues of larger concern; sometimes it is the disillusionment of youthful expectations; often it is the pose of men who seek to borrow the prestige of The Scientist, imagined as a pure and disembodied intellect. But sometimes it is based upon a considered judgment of the facts of power.

Because of such facts, I do not believe that social science will 'save the world' although I see nothing at all wrong with 'trying to save the world'—a phrase which I take here to mean the avoidance of war and the re-arrangement of human affairs in accordance with the ideals of human freedom and reason. Such knowledge as I have leads me to embrace rather pessimistic estimates of the chances. But even if that is where we now stand, still we must ask: If there *are* any ways out of the crises of our period by means of intellect, is it not up to the social scientist to state them? What we represent—although this is not always apparent— is man become aware of mankind. It is on the level of human awareness that virtually all solutions to the great problems must now lie.

To *appeal* to the powerful, on the basis of any knowledge we now have, is utopian in the foolish sense of that term. Our relations with them are more likely to be only such relations as they find useful, which is to say that we become technicians accepting their problems and aims, or ideologists promoting their prestige and authority. To be more than that, so far as our political role is concerned, we must first of all re-consider the nature of our collective endeavor as social scientists. It is not at all utopian for one social scientist to appeal to his colleagues to undertake such a re-consideration. Any social scientist who is aware of what he is about must confront the major moral dilemma I have implied in this chapter—the difference between what men are interested in and what is to men's interest.

If we take the simple democratic view that *what men are interested in* is all that concerns us, then we are accepting the values that have been inculcated, often accidentally and often deliberately by vested interests. These values are often the only ones men have had any chance to develop. They are unconsciously acquired habits rather than choices.

If we take the dogmatic view that *what is to men's interests*, whether they are interested in it or not, is all that need concern us morally, then we run the risk of violating democratic values. We may become manipulators or coercers, or both, rather than persuaders within a society in which men are trying to reason together and in which the value of reason is held in high esteem.

What I am suggesting is that by addressing ourselves to issues and to troubles, and formulating them as problems of social science, we stand the best chance, I believe the only chance, to make reason democratically relevant to human affairs in a free society, and so realize the classic values that underlie the promise of our studies.

On Intellectual Craftsmanship

To the individual social scientist who feels himself a part of the classic tradition, social science is the practice of a craft. A man at work on problems of substance, he is among those who are quickly made impatient and weary by elaborate discussions of method-and-theory-in-general; so much of it interrupts his proper studies. It is much better, he believes, to have one account by a working student of how he is going about his work than a dozen 'codifications of procedure' by specialists who as often as not have never done much work of consequence. Only by conversations in which experienced thinkers exchange information about their actual ways of working can a useful sense of method and theory be imparted to the beginning student. I feel it useful, therefore, to report in some detail how I go about my craft. This is necessarily a personal statement, but it is written with the hope that others, especially those beginning independent work, will make it less personal by the facts of their own experience.

1

It is best to begin, I think, by reminding you, the beginning student, that the most admirable thinkers within the scholarly community you have chosen to join do not split their work from their lives. They seem to take both too seriously to allow such dissociation, and they want to use each for the enrichment of the other. Of course, such a split is the prevailing convention among men in general, deriving, I suppose, from the hollowness of the work which men in general now do. But you will have recognized that as a scholar you have the exceptional opportunity of designing a way of living which will encourage the habits of good workmanship. Scholarship is a choice of how to live as well as a choice of career; whether he knows it or not, the intellectual workman forms his own self as he works toward the perfection of his craft; to realize his own potentialities, and any opportunities that come his way, he constructs a character which has as its core the qualities of the good workman.

What this means is that you must learn to use your life experience in your intellectual work: continually to examine and interpret it. In this sense craftsmanship is the center of yourself and you are personally involved in every intellectual product upon which you may work. To say that you can 'have experience,' means, for one thing, that your past plays into and affects your present, and that it defines your capacity for future experience. As a social scientist, you have to control this rather elaborate interplay, to capture what you experience and sort it out; only in this way can you hope to use it to guide and test your reflection, and in the process shape yourself as an intellectual craftsman. But how can you do this? One answer is: you must set up a file, which is, I suppose, a sociologist's way of saying: keep a journal. Many creative writers keep journals; the sociologist's need for systematic reflection demands it.

In such a file as I am going to describe, there is joined personal experience and professional activities, studies under way and studies planned. In this file, you, as an intellectual craftsman, will try to get together what you are doing intellectually and what you are experiencing as a person. Here you will not be afraid to use your experience and relate it directly to various work in progress. By serving as a check on repititious work, your file also enables you to conserve your energy. It also encourages you to capture 'fringe-thoughts': various ideas which may be by-products of everyday life, snatches of conversation overheard on the street, or, for that matter, dreams. Once noted, these may lead to more systematic thinking, as well as lend intellectual relevance to more directed experience.

You will have often noticed how carefully accomplished thinkers treat their own minds, how closely they observe their development and organize their experience. The reason they treasure their smallest experiences is that, in the course of a lifetime, modern man has so very little personal experience and yet experience is so important as a source of original intellectual work. To be able to trust yet to be skeptical of your own experience, I have come to believe, is one mark of the mature workman. This ambiguous confidence is indispensable to originality in any intellectual pursuit, and the file is one way by which you can develop and justify such confidence.

By keeping an adequate file and thus developing self-reflective habits, you learn how to keep your inner world awake. Whenever you feel strongly about events or ideas you must try not to let them pass from your mind, but instead to formulate them for your files and in so doing draw out their implications, show yourself either how foolish these feelings or ideas are, or how they might be articulated into productive shape. The file also helps you build up the habit of writing. You cannot 'keep your hand in' if you do not write something at least every week. In developing the file, you can experiment as a writer and thus, as they say, develop your powers of expression. To maintain a file is to engage in the controlled experience.

One of the very worst things that happens to social scientists is that they feel the need to write of their 'plans' on only one occasion: when they are going to ask for money for a specific piece of research or 'a project.' It is as a request for funds that most 'planning' is done, or at least carefully written about. However standard the practice, I think this very bad: It is bound in some degree to be salesmanship, and, given prevailing expectations, very likely to result in painstaking pretensions; the project is likely to be 'presented,' rounded out in some arbitrary manner long before it ought to be; it is often a contrived thing, aimed at getting the money for ulterior purposes, however valuable, as well as for the research presented. A practicing social scientist ought periodically to review 'the state of my problems and plans.' A young man, just at the beginning of his independent work, ought to reflect on this, but he cannot be expected—and shouldn't expect himself—to get very far with it, and certainly he ought not to become rigidly committed to any one plan. About all he can do is line up his thesis, which unfortunately is often his first supposedly independent piece of work of any length. It is when you are about half-way through the time you have for work, or about one-third through, that such reviewing is most likely to be fruitful —and perhaps even of interest to others.

Any working social scientist who is well on his way ought at all times to have so many plans, which is to say ideas, that the question is always, which of them am I, ought I, to work on next? And he should keep a special little file for his master agenda, which he writes and rewrites just for himself and perhaps for discussion with friends. From time to time he ought to review this very carefully and purposefully, and sometimes too, when he is relaxed.

Some such procedure is one of the indispensable means by which your intellectual enterprise is kept oriented and under control. A widespread, informal interchange of such reviews of 'the state of my problems' among working social scientists is, I suggest, the only basis for an adequate statement of 'the leading problems of social science.' It is unlikely that in any free intellectual community there would be and certainly there ought not to be any 'monolithic' array of problems. In such a community, were it flourishing in a vigorous way, there would be interludes of discussion among individuals about future work. Three kinds of interludes—on problems, methods, theory—ought to come out of the work of social scientists, and lead into it again; they should be shaped by work-in-progress and to some extent guide that work. It is for such interludes that a professional association finds its intellectual reason for being. And for them too your own file is needed.

Under various topics in your file there are ideas, personal notes, excerpts from books, bibliographical items and outlines of projects. It is, I suppose, a matter of arbitrary habit, but I think you will find it well to sort all these items into a master file of 'projects,' with many subdivisions. The topics, of course, change, sometimes quite frequently. For instance, as a student working toward the preliminary examination, writing a thesis, and, at the same time, doing term papers, your files will be arranged in those three areas of endeavor. But after a year or so of graduate work, you will begin to re-organize the whole file in relation to the main project of your thesis. Then as you pursue your work you will notice that no one project ever dominates it, or sets the master categories in which it is arranged. In fact, the use of the file encourages expansion of the categories which you use in your thinking. And the way in which these categories change, some being dropped and others being added—is an index of your intellectual progress and breadth. Eventually, the files will come to be arranged according to several large projects, having many sub-projects that change from year to year.

All this involves the taking of notes. You will have to acquire the habit of taking a large volume of notes from any worth-while book you read—although, I have to say, you may get better work out of yourself when you read really bad books. The first step in translating experience, either of other men's writing, or of your own life, into the intellectual sphere, is to give it form. Merely to name an item of experience often invites you to explain it; the mere taking of a note from a book is often a prod to reflection. At the same time, of course, the taking of a note is a great aid in comprehending what you are reading.

Your notes may turn out, as mine do, to be of two sorts: in reading certain very important books you try to grasp the structure of the writer's argument, and take notes accordingly; but more frequently, and after a few years of independent work, rather than read entire books, you will very often read parts of many books from the point of view of some particular theme or topic in which you are interested and concerning which you have plans in your file. Therefore, you will take notes which do not fairly represent the books you read. You are *using* this particular idea, this particular fact, for the realization of your own projects.

2

But how is this file—which so far must seem to you more like a curious sort of 'literary' journal—used in intellectual production? The maintenance of such a file *is* intellectual production.

It is a continually growing store of facts and ideas, from the most vague to the most finished. For example, the first thing I did upon deciding on a study of the elite was to make a crude outline based on a listing of the types of people that I wished to understand.

Just how and why I decided to do such a study may suggest one way in which one's life experiences feed one's intellectual work. I forget just when I became technically concerned with 'stratification,' but I think it must have been on first reading Veblen. He had always seemed to me very loose, even vague, about his 'business' and 'industrial' employments, which are a kind of translation of Marx for the academic American public. At any rate, I wrote a book on labor organizations and labor leaders—a politically motivated task; then a book on the middle classes—a task primarily motivated by the desire to articulate my own experience in New York City since 1945. It was thereupon suggested by friends that I ought to round out a trilogy by writing a book on the upper classes. I think the possibility had been in my mind; I had read Balzac off and on especially during the 'forties, and had been much taken with his self-appointed task of 'covering' all the major classes and types in the society of the era he wished to make his own. I had also written a paper on 'The Business Elite,' and had collected and arranged statistics about the careers of the topmost men in American politics since the Constitution. These two tasks were primarily inspired by seminar work in American history.

In doing these several articles and books and in preparing courses in stratification, there was of course a residue of ideas and facts about the upper classes. Especially in the study of social stratification is it difficult to avoid going beyond one's immediate subject, because 'the reality' of any one stratum is in large part its relations to the rest. Accordingly, I began to think of a book on the elite.

And yet that is not 'really' how 'the project' arose; what really happened is (1) that the idea and the plan came out of my files, for all projects with me begin and end with them, and books are simply organized releases from the continuous work that goes into them; (2) that after a while, the whole set of problems involved came to dominate me.

After making my crude outline I examined my entire file, not only those parts of it that obviously bore on my topic, but also those which seemed to have no relevance whatsoever. Imagination is often successfully invited by putting together hitherto isolated items, by finding unsuspected connections. I made new units in the file for this particular range of problems, which of course, led to new arrangements of other parts of the file.

As you re-arrange a filing system, you often find that you are, as it were, loosening your imagination. Apparently this occurs by means of your attempt to combine various ideas and notes on different topics. It is a sort of logic of combination, and 'chance' sometimes plays a curiously large part in it. In a relaxed way, you try to engage your intellectual resources, as exemplified in the file, with the new themes.

In the present case, I also began to use my observations and daily experiences. I thought first of experiences I had had which bore upon elite problems, and then I went and talked with those who, I thought, might have experienced or considered the issues. As a matter of fact, I now began to alter the character of my routine so as to include in it (1) people who *were* among those whom I wanted to study, (2) people in close contact with them, and (3) people interested in them usually in some professional way.

I do not know the full social conditions of the best intellectual workmanship, but certainly surrounding oneself by a circle of people who will listen and talk—and at times they have to be imaginary characters—is one of them. At any rate I try to surround myself with all the relevant environment—social and intellectual—that I think might lead me into thinking well along the lines of my work. That is one meaning of my remarks above about the fusion of personal and intellectual life.

Good work in social science today is not, and usually cannot be, made up of one clear-cut empirical 'research.' It is, rather, composed of a good many studies which at key points anchor general statements about the shape and the trend of the subject. So the decision—what are these anchor points?—cannot be made until existing materials are re-worked and general hypothetical statements constructed.

Now, among 'existing materials,' I found in the files three types relevant to my study of the elite: several theories having to do with the topic; materials already worked up by others as evidence for *those* theories; and materials already gathered and in various stages of accessible centralization, but not yet made theoretically relevant. Only after completing a first draft of a theory with the aid of such existing materials as these can I efficiently locate my own pivotal assertions and hunches and design researches to test them—and maybe I will not have to, although of course I know I will later have to shuttle back and forth between existing materials and my own research. Any final statement must not only 'cover the data' so far as the data are available and known to me, but must also in some way, positively or negatively, take into account the available theories. Sometimes this 'taking into account' of an idea is easily done by a simple confrontation of the idea with overturning or supporting fact; sometimes a detailed analysis or qualification is needed. Sometimes I can arrange the available theories systematically as a range of choices, and so allow their range to organize the problem itself.[1] But sometimes I allow such theories to come up only in my own arrangement, in quite various contexts. At any rate, in the book on the elite I had to take into account the work of such men as Mosca, Schumpeter, Veblen, Marx, Lasswell, Michel, Weber, and Pareto.

In looking over some of the notes on these writers, I find that they offer three types of statement: (*a*) from some, you learn directly by restating systematically what the man says on given points or as a whole; (*b*) some you accept or refute, giving reasons and arguments; (*c*) others you use as a source of suggestions for your own elaborations and projects. This involves grasping a

[1] See, for example, Mills, *White Collar*, New York, Oxford University Press, 1951, chapter 13. I did the same kind of thing, in my notes, with Lederer and Gasset *vs* 'elite theorists' as two reactions to eighteenth- and nineteenth-century democratic doctrine.

point and then asking: How can I put this into testable shape, and how can I test it? How can I use this as a center from which to elaborate—as a perspective from which descriptive details emerge as relevant? It is in this handling of existing ideas, of course, that you feel yourself in continuity with previous work. Here are two excerpts from preliminary notes on Mosca, which may illustrate what I have been trying to describe:

In addition to his historical anecdotes, Mosca backs up his thesis with this assertion: It's the power of organization that enables the minority always to rule. There are organized minorities and they run things and men. There are unorganized majorities and they are run.[2] But: why not also consider (1) the organized minority, (2) the organized majority, (3) the unorganized minority, (4) the unorganized majority. This is worth full-scale exploration. The first thing that has to be straightened out: just what is the meaning of 'organized'? I think Mosca means: capable of more or less continuous and co-ordinated policies and actions. If so, his thesis is right by definition. He would also say, I believe, that an 'organized majority' is impossible because all it would amount to is that new leaders, new elites, would be on top of these majority organizations, and he is quite ready to pick up these leaders in his 'The Ruling Class.' He calls them 'directing minorities,' all of which is pretty flimsy stuff alongside his big statement.

One thing that occurs to me (I think it is the core of the problems of definition that Mosca presents to us) is this: from the nineteenth to the twentieth century, we have witnessed a shift from a society organized as 1 and 4 to a society established *more* in terms of 3 and 2. We have moved from an elite state to an organization state, in which the elite is no longer so organized nor so unilaterally powerful, and the mass is more organized and more powerful. Some power has been made in the streets, and around it the whole social structures and their 'elites' have pivoted. And what section of the ruling class is more organized than the farm bloc? That's not a rhetorical question: I can answer it either way at this time; it's a matter of degree. All I want now is to get it out in the open.

Mosca makes one point that seems to me excellent and worth elaborating further: There is often in 'the ruling class,' according to him, a top clique and there is this second and larger stratum, with which (a) the top is in continuous and immediate contact, and with which

---

[2] There are also statements in Mosca about psychological laws supposed to support his view. Watch his use of the word 'natural.' But this isn't central, and in addition, it's not worth considering.

(b) it shares ideas and sentiments and hence, he believes, policies. (page 430) Check and see if anywhere else in the book, he makes other points of connection. Is the clique recruited largely from the second level? Is the top, in some way, responsible for, or at least sensitive to, this second stratum?

Now forget Mosca: in another vocabulary, we have, (a) the elite, by which we here mean that top clique, (b) those who count, and (c) all the others. Membership in the second and third, in this scheme, is defined by the first, and the second may be quite varied in its size and composition and relations with the first and the third. (What, by the way, is the range of variations of the relations of (b) to (a) and to (c)? Examine Mosca for hints and further extend this by considering it systematically.)

This scheme may enable me more neatly to take into account the different elites, which are elites according to the several dimensions of stratification. Also, of course, to pick up in a neat and meaningful way the Paretian distinction of governing and non-governing elites, in a way less formal than Pareto. Certainly many top-status people would at least be in the second. So would the big rich. The Clique or The Elite would refer to power, or to authority, as the case may be. The elite in this vocabulary would always mean the power elite. The other top people would be the upper classes or the upper circles.

So in a way, maybe, we can use this in connection with two major problems: the structure of the elite; and the conceptual—later perhaps, the substantive—relations of stratification and elite theories. (Work this out.)

From the standpoint of power, it is easier to pick out those who count than those who rule. When we try to do the first we select the top levels as a sort of loose aggregate and we are guided by position. But when we attempt the second, we must indicate in clear detail how they wield power and just how they are related to the social instrumentalities through which power is exercised. Also we deal more with persons than positions, or at least have to take persons into account.

Now power in the United States involves more than one elite. How can we judge the relative positions of these several elites? Depends upon the issue and decisions being made. One elite sees another as among those who count. There is this mutual recognition among the elite, that other elites count; in one way or another they are important people to one another. Project: select 3 or 4 key decisions of last decade—to drop the atom, to cut or raise steel production, the G.M. strike of '45—and trace in detail the personnel involved in each of them. Might use 'decisions' and decision-making as interview pegs when you go out for intensives.

3

There comes a time in the course of your work when you are through with other books. Whatever you want from them is down in your notes and abstracts; and on the margins of these notes, as well as in a separate file, are ideas for empirical studies.

Now I do not like to do empirical work if I can possibly avoid it. If one has no staff it is a great deal of trouble; if one does employ a staff, then the staff is often even more trouble.

In the intellectual condition of the social sciences today, there is so much to do by way of initial 'structuring' (let the word stand for the kind of work I am describing) that much 'empirical research' is bound to be thin and uninteresting. Much of it, in fact, is a formal exercise for beginning students, and sometimes a useful pursuit for those who are not able to handle the more difficult substantive problems of social science. There is no more virtue in empirical inquiry as such than in reading as such. The purpose of empirical inquiry is to settle disagreements and doubts about facts, and thus to make arguments more fruitful by basing all sides more substantively. Facts discipline reason; but reason is the advance guard in any field of learning.

Although you will never be able to get the money with which to do many of the empirical studies you design, it is necessary that you continue designing them. For once you lay out an empirical study, even if you do not follow it through, it leads you to a new search for data, which often turn out to have unsuspected relevance to your problems. Just as it is foolish to design a field study if the answer can be found in a library, it is foolish to think you have exhausted the books before you have translated them into appropriate empirical studies, which merely means into questions of fact.

Empirical projects necessary to my kind of work must promise, first, to have relevance for the first draft, of which I wrote above; they have to confirm it in its original form or they have to cause its modification. Or to put it more pretentiously, they must have implications for theoretical constructions. Second, the projects must be efficient and neat and, if possible, ingenious. By this I mean that they must promise to yield a great deal of material in proportion to the time and effort they involve.

But how is this to be done? The most economical way to state a problem is in such a way as to solve as much of it as possible by reasoning alone. By reasoning we try (*a*) to isolate each question of fact that remains; (*b*) to ask these questions of fact in such ways that the answers promise to help us solve further problems by further reasoning.[3]

To take hold of problems in this way, you have to pay attention to four stages; but it is usually best to go through all four many times rather than to get stuck in any one of them too long. The steps are: (1) the elements and definitions that, from your general awareness of the topic, issue, or area of concern, you think you are going to have to take into account; (2) the logical relations between these definitions and elements; building these little preliminary models, by the way, affords the best chance for the play of the sociological imagination; (3) the elimination of false views due to omissions of needed elements, improper or unclear definitions of terms, or undue emphasis on some part of the range and its logical extensions; (4) statement and re-statement of the questions of fact that remain.

The third step, by the way, is a very necessary but often neglected part of any adequate statement of a problem. The popular awareness of the problem—the problem as an issue and as a trouble—must be carefully taken into account: that is part of the problem. Scholarly statements, of course, must be carefully ex-

---

[3] Perhaps I ought to say the same things in a more pretentious language, in order to make evident to those who do not know, how important all this may be, to wit:

Problematic situations have to be formulated with due attention to their theoretical and conceptual implications, and also to appropriate paradigms of empirical research and suitable models of verification. These paradigms and models in turn, must be so constructed that they permit further theoretical and conceptual implications to be drawn from their employment. The theoretical and conceptual implications of problematic situations should first be fully explored. To do this requires the social scientist to specify each such implication and consider it in relation to every other one, but also in such a way that it fits the paradigms of empirical research and the models of verification.

amined and either used up in the re-statement being made, or thrown out.

Before deciding upon the empirical studies necessary for the job at hand, I began to sketch a larger design within which various small-scale studies began to arise. Again, I excerpt from the files:

I am not yet in a position to study the upper circles as a whole in a systematic and empirical way. So what I do is set forth some definitions and procedures that form a sort of ideal design for such a study. I can then attempt, *first,* to gather existing materials that approximate this design; *second,* to think of convenient ways of gathering materials, given the existing indices, that satisfy it at crucial points; and third, as I proceed, to make more specific the full-scale, empirical researches that would in the end be necessary.

The upper circles must, of course, be defined systematically in terms of specific variables. Formally—and this is more or less Pareto's way— they are the people who 'have' the most of whatever is available of any given value or set of values. So I have to make two decisions: What variables shall I take as the criteria, and what do I mean by 'the most'? After I've decided on my variables, I must construct the best indices I can, if possible quantifiable indices, in order to distribute the population in terms of them; only then can I begin to decide what I mean by 'the most.' For this should, in part, be left for determination by empirical inspection of the various distributions, and their overlaps.

My key variables should, at first, be general enough to give me some latitude in the choice of indices, yet specific enough to invite the search for empirical indices. As I go along, I'll have to shuttle between conceptions and indices, guided by the desire not to lose intended meanings and yet to be quite specific about them. Here are the four Weberian variables with which I will begin:

1. Class refers to sources and amounts of income. So I'll need property distributions and income distributions. The ideal material here (which is very scarce, and unfortunately dated) is a cross-tabulation of source and amount of annual income. Thus, we know that X per cent of the population received during 1936 Y millions or over, and that Z per cent of all this money was from property, W per cent from entrepreneurial withdrawal, Q per cent from wages and salaries. Along this class dimension, I can define the upper circles—those who have the most—either as those who receive given amounts of income during a given time—or, as those who make up the upper two per cent of the income pyramid. Look into treasury records and lists of big taxpayers. See if TNEC tables on source and amount of income can be brought up to date.

II. Status refers to the amounts of deference received. For this, there are no simple or quantifiable indices. Existing indices require personal interviews for their application, are limited so far to local community studies, and are mostly no good anyway. There is the further problem that, unlike class, status involves social relations: at least one to receive and one to bestow the deference.

It is easy to confuse publicity with deference—or rather, we do not yet know whether or not volume of publicity should be used as an index to status position, although it is the most easily available (For example: On one or two successive days in mid-March 1952, the following categories of people were mentioned by name in the *New York Times*—or on selected pages—work this out).

III. Power refers to the realization of one's will even if others resist. Like status, this has not been well indexed. I don't think I can keep it a single dimension, but will have to talk (*a*) of formal authority— defined by rights and powers of positions in various institutions, especially military, political, and economic. And (*b*) powers known informally to be exercised but not formally instituted—pressure group leaders, propagandists with extensive media at their disposal, and so on.

IV. Occupation refers to activities that are paid for. Here, again, I must choose just which feature of occupation I should seize upon. (*a*) If I use the average incomes of various occupations, to rank them, I am of course using occupation as an index, and as the basis of, class. In like manner (*b*) if I use the status or the power typically attached to different occupations, then I am using occupations as indices, and bases, of power and skill or talent. But this is by no means an easy way to classify people. Skill—no more than status—is not a homogeneous something of which there is more or less. Attempts to treat it as such have usually been put in terms of the length of time required to acquire various skills, and maybe that will have to do, although I hope I can think of something better.

Those are the types of problems I will have to solve in order to define analytically and empirically the upper circles, in terms of these four key variables. For purposes of design, assume I have solved them to my satisfaction, and that I have distributed the population in terms of each of them. I would then have four sets of people: those at the top in class, status, power, and skill. Suppose further, that I had singled out the top two per cent of each distribution, as an upper circle. I then confront this empirically answerable question: How much, if any, overlap is there among each of these four distributions? One range of possibilities can be located within this simple chart: (+ = top two per cent; − = lower 98 per cent).

			CLASS			
			+ STATUS		− STATUS	
			+	−	+	−
Power	+ Skill	+	1	2	3	4
		−	5	6	7	8
	− Skill	+	9	10	11	12
		−	13	14	15	16

This diagram, if I had the materials to fill it, would contain major data and many important problems for a study of the upper circles. It would provide keys to many definitional and substantive questions.

I don't have the data, and I shan't be able to get it—which makes it all the more important that I speculate about it, for in the course of such reflection, if it is guided by the desire to approximate the empirical requirements of an ideal design, I'll come upon important areas, on which I might be able to get materials that are relevant as anchor points and guides to further reflection.

There are two additional points which I must add to this general model in order to make it formally complete. Full conceptions of upper strata require attention to duration and mobility. The task here is to determine positions (1-16) between which there is typical movement of individuals and groups—within the present generation, and among the last two or three generations.

This introduces the temporal dimension of biography (or career-lines) and of history into the scheme. These are not merely further empirical questions; they are also definitionally relevant. For (a) we want to leave open whether or not in classifying people in terms of any of our key variables, we should define our categories in terms of how long they, or their families, have occupied the position in question. For example, I might want to decide that the upper two per cent of status—or at least one important type of status rank—consists of those up there for at least two generations. Also (b) I want to leave open the question of whether or not I should construct 'a stratum' not only in terms of an intersection of several variables, but also, in line with Weber's neglected definition of 'social class,' as composed of those positions between which there is 'typical and easy mobility.' Thus, the lower white-collar occupations and middle and upper wage-worker jobs in certain industries seem to be forming, in this sense, a stratum.

In the course of the reading and analyzing of others' theories, designing ideal research, and perusing the files, you will begin to draw up a list of specific studies. Some of them are too big to handle, and will in time be regretfully given up; some will end as materials for a paragraph, a section, a sentence, a chapter; some will become pervading themes to be woven into an entire book. Here again are initial notes for several such projects:

(1) A time-budget analysis of a typical working day of ten top executives of large corporations, and the same for ten federal administrators. These observations will be combined with detailed 'life history' interviews. The aim here is to describe the major routines and decisions, partly at least in terms of time devoted to them, and to gain an insight into the factors relevant to the decisions made. The procedure will naturally vary with the degree of co-operation secured, but ideally will involve first, an interview in which the life history and present situation of the man is made clear; second, observations of the day, actually sitting in a corner of the man's office, and following him around; third, a longish interview that evening or the next day in which we go over the whole day and probe the subjective processes involved in the external behavior we've observed.

(2) An analysis of upper-class week ends, in which the routines are closely observed and followed by probing interviews with the man and other members of the family on the Monday following.

For both these tasks I've fairly good contacts and of course good contacts, if handled properly, lead to better ones. [added 1957: this turned out to be an illusion.]

(3) A study of the expense account and other privileges which, along with salaries and other incomes, form the standard and the style of living of the top levels. The idea here is to get something concrete on 'the bureaucratization of consumption,' the transfer of private expenses to business accounts.

(4) Bring up to date the type of information contained in such books as Lundberg's *America's Sixty Families*, which is dated as of the tax returns for 1923.

(5) Gather and systematize, from treasury records and other government sources, the distribution of various types of private property by amounts held.

(6) A career-line study of the Presidents, all cabinet members, and all members of the Supreme Court. This I already have on IBM cards from the Constitutional period through Truman's second term, but I want to expand the items used and analyze it afresh.

There are other—some 35—'projects' of this sort (for example, comparison of the amounts of money spent in the presidential elections of 1896 and 1952, detailed comparison of Morgan of 1910 and Kaiser of 1950, and something concrete on the careers of 'Admirals and Generals'). But, as one goes along, one must of course adjust his aim to what is accessible.

After these designs were written down, I began to read historical works on top groups, taking random (and unfiled) notes and interpreting the reading. You do not really have to *study* a topic you are working on; for as I have said, once you are into it, it is everywhere. You are sensible to its themes; you see and hear them everywhere in your experience, especially, it always seems to me, in apparently unrelated areas. Even the mass media, especially bad movies and cheap novels and picture magazines and night radio, are disclosed in fresh importance to you.

4

But, you may ask, how do ideas come? How is the imagination spurred to put all the images and facts together, to make images relevant and lend meaning to facts? I do not think I can really answer that; all I can do is talk about the general conditions and a few simple techniques which have seemed to increase my chances to come out with something.

The sociological imagination, I remind you, in considerable part consists of the capacity to shift from one perspective to another, and in the process to build up an adequate view of a total society and of its components. It is this imagination, of course, that sets off the social scientist from the mere technician. Adequate technicians can be trained in a few years. The sociological imagination can also be cultivated; certainly it seldom occurs without a great deal of often routine work.[4] Yet there is an unexpected quality about it, perhaps because its essence is the combination of ideas that no one expected were combinable— say, a mess of ideas from German philosophy and British economics. There is a playfulness of mind back of such combining as well as a truly fierce drive to make sense of the world, which the technician as such usually lacks. Perhaps he is too

[4] See the excellent articles on 'insight' and 'creative endeavor' by Hutchinson in *Study of Interpersonal Relations,* edited by Patrick Mullahy, New York, Nelson, 1949.

well trained, too precisely trained. Since one can be *trained* only in what is already known, training sometimes incapacitates one from learning new ways; it makes one rebel against what is bound to be at first loose and even sloppy. But you must cling to such vague images and notions, if they are yours, and you must work them out. For it is in such forms that original ideas, if any, almost always first appear.

There are definite ways, I believe, of stimulating the sociological imagination:

(1) On the most concrete level, the re-arranging of the file, as I have already said, is one way to invite imagination. You simply dump out heretofore disconnected folders, mixing up their contents, and then re-sort them. You try to do it in a more or less relaxed way. How often and how extensively you re-arrange the files will of course vary with different problems and with how well they are developing. But the mechanics of it are as simple as that. Of course, you will have in mind the several problems on which you are actively working, but you will also try to be passively receptive to unforeseen and unplanned linkages.

(2) An attitude of playfulness toward the phrases and words with which various issues are defined often loosens up the imagination. Look up synonyms for each of your key terms in dictionaries as well as in technical books, in order to know the full range of their connotations. This simple habit will prod you to elaborate the terms of the problem and hence to define them less wordily and more precisely. For only if you know the several meanings which might be given to terms or phrases can you select the exact ones with which you want to work. But such an interest in words goes further than that. In all work, but especially in examining theoretical statements, you will try to keep close watch on the level of generality of every key term, and you will often find it useful to break down a high-level statement into more concrete meanings. When that is done, the statement often falls into two or three components, each lying along different dimensions. You will also try to move up the level of generality: remove the specific qualifiers and examine the re-formed statement or inference more abstractly, to see if you can stretch it or elaborate

it. So from above and from below, you will try to probe, in search of clarified meaning, into every aspect and implication of the idea.

(3) Many of the general notions you come upon, as you think about them, will be cast into types. A new classification is the usual beginning of fruitful developments. The skill to make up types and then to search for the conditions and consequences of each type will, in short, become an automatic procedure with you. Rather than rest content with existing classifications, in particular, common-sense ones, you will search for their common denominators and for differentiating factors within and between them. Good types require that the criteria of classification be explicit and systematic. To make them so you must develop the habit of cross-classification.

The technique of cross-classifying is not of course limited to quantitative materials; as a matter of fact, it is the best way to imagine and to get hold of *new* types as well as to criticize and clarify old ones. Charts, tables, and diagrams of a qualitative sort are not only ways to display work already done; they are very often genuine tools of production. They clarify the 'dimensions' of the types, which they also help you to imagine and build. As a matter of fact, in the past fifteen years, I do not believe I have written more than a dozen pages first-draft without some little cross-classification—although, of course, I do not always or even usually display such diagrams. Most of them flop, in which case you have still learned something. When they work, they help you to think more clearly and to write more explicitly. They enable you to discover the range and the full relationships of the very terms with which you are thinking and of the facts with which you are dealing.

For a working sociologist, cross-classification is what diagramming a sentence is for a diligent grammarian. In many ways, cross-classification is the very grammar of the sociological imagination. Like all grammar, it must be controlled and not allowed to run away from its purposes.

(4) Often you get the best insights by considering extremes —by thinking of the opposite of that with which you are directly concerned. If you think about despair, then also think about

elation; if you study the miser, then also the spendthrift. The hardest thing in the world is to study one object; when you try to contrast objects, you get a better grip on the materials and you can then sort out the dimensions in terms of which the comparisons are made. You will find that shuttling between attention to these dimensions and to the concrete types is very illuminating. This technique is also logically sound, for without a sample, you can only guess about statistical frequencies anyway: what you can do is to give the range and the major types of some phenomenon, and for that it is more economical to begin by constructing 'polar types,' opposites along various dimensions. This does not mean, of course, that you will not strive to gain and to maintain a sense of proportion—to look for some lead to the frequencies of given types. One continually tries, in fact, to combine this quest with the search for indices for which one might find or collect statistics.

The idea is to use a variety of viewpoints: you will, for instance, ask yourself how would a political scientist whom you have recently read approach this, and how would that experimental psychologist, or this historian? You try to think in terms of a variety of viewpoints and in this way to let your mind become a moving prism catching light from as many angles as possible. In this connection, the writing of dialogues is often very useful.

You will quite often find yourself thinking against something, and in trying to understand a new intellectual field, one of the first things you might well do is to lay out the major arguments. One of the things meant by 'being soaked in the literature' is being able to locate the opponents and the friends of every available viewpoint. By the way, it is not well to be too 'soaked in the literature'; you may drown in it, like Mortimer Adler. Perhaps the point is to know when you ought to read, and when you ought not to.

(5) The fact that, for the sake of simplicity, in cross-classification, you first work in terms of yes-or-no, encourages you to think of extreme opposites. That is generally good, for qualitative analysis cannot of course provide you with frequencies or magnitudes. Its technique and its end is to give you the range of types. For many purposes you need no more than that, although for

some, of course, you do need to get a more precise idea of the proportions involved.

The release of imagination can sometimes be achieved by deliberately inverting your sense of proportion.[5] If something seems very minute, imagine it to be simply enormous, and ask yourself: What difference might that make? And vice versa, for gigantic phenomena. What would pre-literate villages look like with populations of 30 millions? Nowadays at least, I should never think of actually counting or measuring anything, before I had played with each of its elements and conditions and consequences in an imagined world in which I control the scale of everything. This is one thing statisticians ought to mean, but never seem to, by that horrible little phrase about 'knowing the universe before you sample it.'

(6) Whatever the problem with which you are concerned, you will find it helpful to try to get a *comparative* grip on the materials. The search for comparable cases, either in one civilization and historical period or in several, gives you leads. You would never think of describing an institution in twentieth-century America without trying to bear in mind similar institutions in other types of structures and periods. That is so even if you do not make explicit comparisons. In time you will come almost automatically to orient your reflection historically. One reason for doing so is that often what you are examining is limited in number: to get a comparative grip on it, you have to place it inside an historical frame. To put it another way, the contrasting-type approach often requires the examination of historical materials. This sometimes results in points useful for a trend analysis, or it leads to a typology of phases. You will use historical materials, then, because of the desire for a fuller range, or for a more convenient range of some phenomenon—by which I mean a range that includes the variations along some known set of dimensions. Some knowledge of world history is indispensable to the sociologist; without such knowledge, no matter what else he knows, he is simply crippled.

[5] By the way, some of this is what Kenneth Burke, in discussing Nietzsche, has called 'perspective by incongruity.' See, by all means, Burke, *Permanence and Change*, New York, New Republic Books, 1936.

(7) There is, finally, a point which has more to do with the craft of putting a book together than with the release of the imagination. Yet these two are often one: how you go about arranging materials for presentation always affects the content of your work. The idea I have in mind I learned from a great editor, Lambert Davis, who, I suppose, after seeing what I have done with it, would not want to acknowledge it as his child. It is the distinction between theme and topic.

A topic is a subject, like 'the careers of corporation executives' or 'the increased power of military officials' or 'the decline of society matrons.' Usually most of what you have to say about a topic can readily be put into one chapter or a section of a chapter. But the order in which all your topics are arranged often brings you into the realm of themes.

A theme is an idea, usually of some signal trend, some master conception, or a key distinction, like rationality and reason, for example. In working out the construction of a book, when you come to realize the two or three, or, as the case may be, the six or seven themes, then you will know that you are on top of the job. You will recognize these themes because they keep insisting upon being dragged into all sorts of topics and perhaps you will feel that they are mere repetitions. And sometimes that is all they are! Certainly very often they will be found in the more clotted and confused, the more badly written, sections of your manuscript.

What you must do is sort them out and state them in a general way as clearly and briefly as you can. Then, quite systematically, you must cross-classify them with the full range of your topics. This means that you will ask of each topic: Just how is it affected by each of these themes? And again: Just what is the meaning, if any, for each of these themes of each of the topics?

Sometimes a theme requires a chapter or a section for itself, perhaps when it is first introduced or perhaps in a summary statement toward the end. In general, I think most writers—as well as most systematic thinkers—would agree that at some point all the themes ought to appear together, in relation to one another. Often, although not always, it is possible to do this at the beginning of a book. Usually, in any well-constructed book, it must be done near the end. And, of course, all the way through you ought at least to try to relate the themes to each topic. It is easier to write about this than to do it, for it is usually not so mechanical a matter as it might appear. But sometimes it is—at least if the themes are properly sorted out and clarified. But that, of course, is the rub. For what I have here, in the context of literary craftsmanship, called themes, in the context of intellectual work are called ideas.

Sometimes, by the way, you may find that a book does not really have any themes. It is just a string of topics, surrounded, of course, by methodological introductions to methodology, and theoretical introductions to theory. These are indeed quite indispensable to the writing of books by men without ideas. And so is lack of intelligibility.

5

I know you will agree that you should present your work in as clear and simple language as your subject and your thought about it permit. But as you may have noticed, a turgid and polysyllabic prose does seem to prevail in the social sciences. I suppose those who use it believe they are imitating 'physical science,' and are not aware that much of *that* prose is not altogether necessary. It has in fact been said with authority that there is 'a serious crisis in literacy'—a crisis in which social scientists are very much involved.[6] Is this peculiar language due to the fact that profound and subtle issues, concepts, methods, are being discussed? If not, then what are the reasons for what Malcolm Cowley aptly calls 'socspeak'?[7] Is it really necessary to your proper work? If it is, there is nothing you can do about it; if it is not, then how can you avoid it?

[6] By Edmund Wilson, widely regarded as 'the best critic in the English-speaking world,' who writes: 'As for my experience with articles by experts in anthropology and sociology, it has led me to conclude that the requirement, in my ideal university, of having the papers in every department passed by a professor of English might result in revolutionizing these subjects—if indeed the second of them survived at all.' *A Piece of My Mind*, New York, Farrar, Straus and Cudahy, 1956, p. 164.

[7] Malcolm Cowley, 'Sociological Habit Patterns in Linguistic Transmogrification,' *The Reporter*, 20 September 1956, pp. 41 ff.

Such lack of ready intelligibility, I believe, usually has little or nothing to do with the complexity of subject matter, and nothing at all with profundity of thought. It has to do almost entirely with certain confusions of the academic writer about his own status.

In many academic circles today anyone who tries to write in a widely intelligible way is liable to be condemned as a 'mere literary man' or, worse still, 'a mere journalist.' Perhaps you have already learned that these phrases, as commonly used, only indicate the spurious inference: superficial because readable. The academic man in America is trying to carry on a serious intellectual life in a social context that often seems quite set against it. His prestige must make up for many of the dominant values he has sacrificed by choosing an academic career. His claims for prestige readily become tied to his self-image as a 'scientist.' To be called a 'mere journalist' makes him feel undignified and shallow. It is this situation, I think, that is often at the bottom of the elaborate vocabulary and involved manner of speaking and writing. It is less difficult to learn this manner than not. It has become a convention—those who do not use it are subject to moral disapproval. It may be that it is the result of an academic closing of the ranks on the part of the mediocre, who understandably wish to exclude those who win the attention of intelligent people, academic and otherwise.

To write is to raise a claim for the attention of readers. That is part of *any* style. To write is also to claim for oneself at least status enough to be read. The young academic man is very much involved in both claims, and because he feels his lack of public position, he often puts the claim for his own status before his claim for the attention of the reader to what he is saying. In fact, in America, even the most accomplished men of knowledge do not have much status among wide circles and publics. In this respect, the case of sociology has been an extreme one: in large part sociological habits of ·tyle stem from the time when sociologists had little status even with other academic men. Desire for status is one reason why academic men slip so readily into unintelligibility. And that, in turn, is one reason why they do not have the status they desire. A truly vicious circle—but one out of which any scholar can easily break.

To overcome the academic *prose* you have first to overcome the academic *pose*. It is much less important to study grammar and Anglo-Saxon roots than to clarify your own answers to these three questions: (1) How difficult and complex after all is my subject? (2) When I write, what status am I claiming for myself? (3) For whom am I trying to write?

(1) The usual answer to the first question is: Not so difficult and complex as the way in which you are writing about it. Proof of that is everywhere available: it is revealed by the ease with which 95 per cent of the books of social science can be translated into English.[8]

But, you may ask, do we not sometimes need technical terms?[9] Of course we do, but 'technical' does not necessarily mean difficult, and certainly it does not mean jargon. If such technical terms are really necessary and also clear and precise, it is not difficult to use them in a context of plain English and thus introduce them meaningfully to the reader.

Perhaps you may object that the ordinary words of common usage are often 'loaded' with feelings and values, and that ac-

---

[8] For some examples of such translation see above: chapter 2. By the way, on writing, the best book I know is Robert Graves and Alan Hodge, *The Reader Over Your Shoulder*, New York, Macmillan, 1944. See also the excellent discussions by Barzun and Graff, *The Modern Researcher*, op. cit., G. E. Montague, *A Writer's Notes on His Trade*, London, Pelican Books, 1930-1949, and Bonamy Dobrée, *Modern Prose Style*, Oxford, The Clarendon Press, 1934-50.

[9] Those who understand mathematical language far better than I tell me that it is precise, economical, clear. That is why I am so suspicious of many social scientists who claim a central place for mathematics among the methods of social study but who write prose imprecisely, uneconomically, and unclearly. They should take a lesson from Paul Lazarsfeld, who believes in mathematics, very much indeed, *and* whose prose always reveals, even in first draft, the mathematical qualities indicated. When I cannot understand his mathematics, I know that it is because I am too ignorant; when I disagree with what he writes in non-mathematical language, I know it is because he is mistaken, for one always knows just what he is saying and hence just where he has gone wrong.

cordingly it might be well to avoid them in favor of new words or technical terms. Here is my answer: it is true that ordinary words are often so loaded. But many technical terms in common use in social science are also loaded. To write clearly is to control these loads, to say exactly what you mean in such a way that this meaning and only this will be understood by others. Assume that your intended meaning is circumscribed by a six-foot circle, in which you are standing; assume that the meaning understood by your reader is another such circle, in which he is standing. The circles, let us hope, do overlap. The extent of that overlap is the extent of your communication. In the reader's circle the part that does not overlap—that is one area of uncontrolled meaning: he has made it up. In your circle the part that does not overlap—that is another token of your failure: you have not got it across. The skill of writing is to get the reader's circle of meaning to coincide exactly with yours, to write in such a way that both of you stand in the same circle of controlled meaning.

My first point, then, is that most 'socspeak' is unrelated to any complexity of subject matter or thought. It is used—I think almost entirely—to establish academic claims for one's self; to write in this way is to say to the reader (often I am sure without knowing it): 'I know something that is so difficult you can understand it only if you first learn my difficult language. In the meantime, you are merely a journalist, a layman, or some other sort of underdeveloped type.'

(2) To answer the second question, we must distinguish two ways of presenting the work of social science according to the idea the writer has of himself, and the voice with which he speaks. One way results from the idea that he is a man who may shout, whisper, or chuckle—but who is always there. It is also clear what sort of man he is: whether confident or neurotic, direct or involuted, he *is* a center of experience and reasoning; now he has found out something, and he is telling us about it, and how he found it out. This is the voice behind the best expositions available in the English language.

The other way of presenting work does not use any voice of

any man. Such writing is not a 'voice' at all. It is an autonomous sound. It is a prose manufactured by a machine. That it is full of jargon is not as noteworthy as that it is strongly mannered: it is not only impersonal; it is pretentiously impersonal. Government bulletins are sometimes written in this way. Business letters also. And a great deal of social science. Any writing—perhaps apart from that of certain truly great stylists—that is not imaginable as human speech is bad writing.

(3) But finally there is the question of those who are to hear the voice—thinking about that also leads to characteristics of style. It is very important for any writer to have in mind just what kinds of people he is trying to speak to—and also what he really thinks of them. These are not easy questions: to answer them well requires decisions about oneself as well as knowledge of reading publics. To write is to raise a claim to be read, but by whom?

One answer has been suggested by my colleague,' Lionel Trilling, who has given me permission to pass it on. You are to assume that you have been asked to give a lecture on some subject you know well, before an audience of teachers and students from all departments of a leading university, as well as an assortment of interested people from a near-by city. Assume that such an audience is before you and that they have a right to know; assume that you want to let them know. Now write.

There are some four broad possibilities available to the social scientist as a writer. If he recognizes himself as a voice and assumes that he is speaking to some such public as I have indicated, he will try to write readable prose. If he assumes he is a voice but is not altogether aware of any public, he may easily fall into unintelligible ravings. Such a man had better be careful. If he considers himself less a voice than an agent of some impersonal sound, then—should he find a public—it will most likely be a cult. If, without knowing his own voice, he should not find any public, but speaks solely for some record kept by no one, then I suppose we have to admit that he is a true manufacturer of the standardized prose: an autonomous sound in a great empty hall. It is all rather frightening, as in a Kafka novel, and it ought to be: we have been talking about the edge of reason.

The line between profundity and verbiage is often delicate, even perilous. No one should deny the curious charm of those who—as in Whitman's little poem—beginning their studies, are so pleased and awed by the first step that they hardly wish to go farther. Of itself, language does form a wonderful world, but, entangled in that world, we must not mistake the confusion of beginnings with the profundity of finished results. As a member of the academic community you should think of yourself as a representative of a truly great language, and you should expect and demand of yourself that when you speak or write you try to carry on the discourse of civilized man.

There is one last point, which has to do with the interplay of writing and thinking. If you write solely with reference to what Hans Reichenbach has called the 'context of discovery' you will be understood by very few people; moreover you will tend to be quite subjective in statement. To make whatever you think more objective, you must work in the context of presentation. At first, you 'present' your thought to yourself, which is often called 'thinking clearly.' Then when you feel that you have it straight, you present it to others—and often find that you have not made it clear. Now you are in the 'context of presentation.' Sometimes you will notice that as you try to present your thinking, you will modify it—not only in its form of statement but often in its content as well. You will get new ideas as you work in the context of presentation. In short, it will become a new context of discovery, different from the original one, on a higher level I think, because more socially objective. Here again, you cannot divorce how you think from how you write. You have to move back and forth between these two contexts, and whenever you move it is well to know where you might be going.

6

From what I have said, you will understand that in practice you never 'start working on a project'; you are already 'working,' either in a personal vein, in the files, in taking notes after browsing, or in guided endeavors. Following this way of living and working, you will always have many topics that you want to work out further. After you decide on some 'release,' you will try to use your entire file, your browsing in libraries, your conversation, your selections of people—all for this topic or theme. You are trying to build a little world containing all the key elements which enter into the work at hand, to put each in its place in a systematic way, continually to readjust this framework around developments in each part of it. Merely to live in such a constructed world is to know what is needed: ideas, facts, ideas, figures, ideas.

So you will discover and describe, setting up types for the ordering of what you have found out, focusing and organizing experience by distinguishing items by name. This search for order will cause you to seek patterns and trends, to find relations that may be typical and causal. You will search, in short, for the meanings of what you come upon, for what may be interpreted as a visible token of something else that is not visible. You will make an inventory of everything that seems involved in whatever you are trying to understand; you will pare it down to essentials; then carefully and systematically you will relate these items to one another in order to form a sort of working model. And then you will relate this model to whatever it is you are trying to explain. Sometimes it is that easy; often it just will not come.

But always, among all the details, you will be searching for indicators that might point to the main drift, to the underlying forms and tendencies of the range of society in the middle of the twentieth century. For, in the end, it is this—the human variety— that you are always writing about.

Thinking is a struggle for order and at the same time for comprehensiveness. You must not stop thinking too soon—or you will fail to know all that you should; you cannot leave it to go on forever, or you yourself will burst. It is this dilemma, I suppose, that makes reflection, on those rare occasions when it is more or less successful, the most passionate endeavor of which the human being is capable.

Perhaps I can best summarize what I have been trying to say in the form of a few precepts and cautions:

(1) Be a good craftsman: Avoid any rigid set of procedures. Above all, seek to develop and to use the sociological imagination. Avoid the fetishism of method and technique. Urge the rehabilitation of the unpretentious intellectual craftsman, and try to become such a craftsman yourself. Let every man be his own methodologist; let every man be his own theorist; let theory and method again become part of the practice of a craft. Stand for the primacy of the individual scholar; stand opposed to the ascendancy of research teams of technicians. Be one mind that is on its own confronting the problems of man and society.

(2) Avoid the Byzantine oddity of associated and disassociated Concepts, the mannerism of verbiage. Urge upon yourself and upon others the simplicity of clear statement. Use more elaborated terms only when you believe firmly that their use enlarges the scope of your sensibilities, the precision of your references, the depth of your reasoning. Avoid using unintelligibility as a means of evading the making of judgments upon society—and as a means of escaping your readers' judgments upon your own work.

(3) Make any trans-historical constructions you think your work requires; also delve into sub-historical minutiae. Make up quite formal theory and build models as well as you can. Examine in detail little facts and their relations, and big unique events as well. But do not be fanatic: relate all such work, continuously and closely, to the level of historical reality. Do not assume that somebody else will do this for you, sometime, somewhere. Take as your task the defining of this reality; formulate your problems in its terms; on its level try to solve these problems and thus resolve the issues and the troubles they incorporate. And never write more than three pages without at least having in mind a solid example.

(4) Do not study merely one small milieu after another; study the social structures in which milieux are organized. In terms of these studies of larger structures, select the milieux you need to study in detail, and study them in such a way as to understand the interplay of milieux with structure. Proceed in a smiliar way in so far as the span of time is concerned. Do not be merely a journalist, however precise a one. Know that journalism can be a great intellectual endeavor, but know also that yours is greater! So do not merely report minute researches into static knife-edge moments,

or very short-term runs of time. Take as your time-span the course of human history, and locate within it the weeks, years, epochs you examine.

(5) Realize that your aim is a fully comparative understanding of the social structures that have appeared and that do now exist in world history. Realize that to carry it out you must avoid the arbitrary specialization of prevailing academic departments. Specialize your work variously, according to topic, and above all according to significant problem. In formulating and in trying to solve these problems, do not hesitate, indeed seek, continually and imaginatively, to draw upon the perspectives and materials, the ideas and methods, of any and all sensible studies of man and society. They are *your* studies; they are part of what you are a part of; do not let them be taken from you by those who would close them off by weird jargon and pretensions of *expertise*.

(6) Always keep your eyes open to the image of man—the generic notion of his human nature—which by your work you are assuming and implying; and also to the image of history—your notion of how history is being made. In a word, continually work out and revise your views of the problems of history, the problems of biography, and the problems of social structure in which biography and history intersect. Keep your eyes open to the varieties of individuality, and to the modes of epochal change. Use what you see and what you imagine, as the clues to your study of the human variety.

(7) Know that you inherit and are carrying on the tradition of classic social analysis; so try to understand man not as an isolated fragment, not as an intelligible field or system in and of itself. Try to understand men and women as historical and social actors, and the ways in which the variety of men and women are intricately selected and intricately formed by the variety of human societies. Before you are through with any piece of work, no matter how indirectly on occasion, orient it to the central and continuing task of understanding the structure and the drift, the shaping and the meanings, of your own period, the terrible and magnificent world of human society in the second half of the twentieth century.

(8) Do not allow public issues as they are officially formulated, or troubles as they are privately felt, to determine the problems that you take up for study. Above all, do not give up your moral and political autonomy by accepting in somebody else's terms the illiberal practicality of the bureaucratic ethos or the liberal practicality of the moral scatter. Know that many personal troubles cannot be solved merely as troubles, but must be understood in terms of public issues—and in terms of the problems of history-making. Know that the human meaning of public issues must be revealed by relating them to personal troubles—and to the problems of the individual life. Know that the problems of social science, when adequately formulated, must include both troubles and issues, both biography and history, and the range of their intricate relations. Within that range the life of the individual and the making of societies occur; and within that range the sociological imagination has its chance to make a difference in the quality of human life in our time.

Acknowledgments

Earlier versions of this book were presented to a seminar in social science during the spring of 1957 arranged in Copenhagen by Henning Friis, Konsultant to the Socialministrat. I am very grateful to him and to the following members of this seminar for their penetrating criticisms and kind suggestions: Kirsten Rudfeld, Bent Andersen, P. H. Kühl, Poul Vidriksen, Knud Erik Svensen, Torben Agersnap, B. V. Elberling.

Chapter 1: 'The Promise,' along with other short sections of this book, was presented in abridged form to the American Political Science Association in September 1958 at St. Louis. In Chapter 6, I have drawn upon an essay, 'Two Styles of Research in Current Social Study,' published in *Philosophy of Science*, Volume XX, Number 4, October 1953. An earlier draft of the first five sections of the Appendix has appeared in *Symposium on Sociological Theory*, ed. by L. Gross, Evanston, Peterson, 1959. Sections 5 and 6 of Chapter 8 were printed in *Monthly Review*, October 1958. In a general way, I have also used remarks first published in *The Saturday Review* of 1 May 1954. Passages from chapters 9 and 10 were used in public lectures delivered at the London School of Economics and the Polish Academy of Sciences in Warsaw during January, and broadcast by the BBC on its Third Programme in February, 1959.

Later drafts of the manuscript were criticized, in whole or part, by the following colleagues, to whom I am beholden for much of any merit the book may have. I only wish there were some more adequate way to acknowledge their generous aid:

Harold Barger, Robert Bierstadt, Norman Birnbaum, Herbert Blumer, Tom Bottomore, Lyman Bryson, Lewis Coser, Arthur K. Davis, Robert Dubin, Si Goode, Marjorie Fiske, Peter Gay, Llewellyn Gross, Richard Hofstadter, Irving Howe, H. Stuart Hughes, Floyd Hunter, Sylvia Jarrico, David Kettler, Walter Klink, Charles E. Lindblom, Ernst Manheim, Reece McGee, Ralph Miliband, Barrington Moore Jr., David Riesman, Meyer Schapiro, George Rawick, Arnold Rogow, Paul Sweezy.

I am very grateful to my friends, William Miller and Harvey Swados, for their continued efforts to help me write clearly.

C.W.M.

Index

A Selected List of Black Cat Books

A Selected List of Evergreen Books